EXPANDING YOUR HORIZONS

Collegiate Football's Greatest Team

DONALD STEINBERG, M.D.

DORRANCE PUBLISHING CO., INC.
643 SMITHFIELD STREET • PITTSBURGH, PENNSYLVANIA 15222

This book is dedicated to Paul Brown and The Ohio State University. Paul Brown's concepts and values have left an indelible impact on the lives of thousands of young men. The responsibility to offer higher education to any person who prepares himself falls to The Ohio State University and to other state universities. These universities can be justly proud for they provide the foundations toward future successful opportunities. They enable the citizens of America to bring to reality the hopes and aspirations of our forefathers.

TABLE OF CONTENTS

ERNIE GODFREY
Mr. Ohio State Football

Captain George Lynn, Les Horvath, Coach Paul Brown, Tommy James and Gene Fekete.

PREFACE

T
he decade of the 1940's was a very exciting time in America. Movies, stories, and a whole host of material has been written about this period of our history. In spite of our desire for nations to live in peace with one another, World War II was being fought around the world. Once more the United States would need to come to the aid of our Allies. We joined in this world struggle to thwart the evil ambitions of dictators who were determined to dehumanize peaceful countries.

This book is a remembrance of those days. To the men who still have fond memories of the sports heroes of the 1940's, this book is a renewal of those exciting days. To the Alumni of The Ohio State University, this is the dream team that has never been forgotten in the annals of Ohio State football. Within each chapter or biography, the reader will gain a clearer conception of the details involved in developing football teams and the responsibilities of the players in each position on the team. To those people who are interested in the values of America and the values to be gained by higher education, this is a study of the lives of 40 young men who became "Movers and Doers" in our American society. Each player of Ohio State's 1942 football team was either dedicated to the educational development of hundreds or even thousands of young men who would follow them as their students, or each player would make significant contributions to society through his profession. Before coming to the university, there were no indications that they were different from other high school graduates. Except for being football players, their high school academic records were similar to other high school students. The foundations for the future successes of each of these players were laid in the classrooms of The Ohio State University and on the practice fields just South of the Ohio State stadium.

If a young man wishes to look for a role model for his future, one of these young men of the 1942 Ohio State football team would bear a close resemblance to any of the circumstances of his life before going off to college. If one is so poor that a higher education may seem impossible to obtain, almost everyone of these players was in a similar situation. If a young man feels that discrimination prevents him from fulfilling his goals in life, as well as obtaining a college education, I would suggest he read the biography of Bill Willis. If your physical development falls short of your dreams of athletic fame, Les Horvath's story of the trials and tribulations in reaching the pinnacle of success in being awarded the Heisman Trophy is for you. If you are a person who has become disheartened by unexpected interruptions in achieving his personal goals, there was a war to be fought, and after the war, an education to be completed and careers to be pursued for almost every one of these players.

Much has been assumed about the value of intercollegiate football. This book is a lifelong study of moral values that held fast to the separation of teenaged and adult responsibilities. It also reveals the motivations that coaches use as they are in constant association with their players. They correctly promised a life of success and happiness as the just rewards for each player's efforts in obtaining a college education and participating in intercollegiate sports. It is a combination that almost guarantees wonderful memories, a wonderful future and lifelong friendships.

In many respects, this book has been a "team effort". The original seed for this project was planted at one of our reunions when we gathered together to celebrate our being named the National Championship Football Team for 1942. I volunteered to collate all of the information necessary to convince one another of our "outstanding attributes". Robin Priday, Jim Rees, and a number of other players ably assisted in the various approaches we would need to complete our task. I became the team ambassador who visited or communicated with each of the players or their wives, if they had passed away. In Jim Rees, we have an outstanding team philosopher who wrote lengthy letters describing his attitudes and recommendations. In Robin Priday, we have an outstanding scholar devoted to syntax and context, as well as, being an able cheerleader to urge me on. In many of the biographies, there are people and events that each player has felt were important in his life. Other biographies are misleadingly quite short mostly due to the reluctance to boast or a natural shyness that has persisted since childhood. Each player offers valuable insights into living successfully and happily.

Arranged throughout the book are some of the biographies of the players that personalize the contents of each chapter. All of the biographies are written in a first person style. However, the players characteristically had very multifaceted lives that go well beyond the purposes of emphasis. For example, Dante Lavelli was a great student of football and his biography follows the chapter titled "The Psychology of Winning—A Player Views His Coach". Dante was also a valiant soldier in the 28th Infantry Division that fought its way across Europe in World War II. The same can be said about most of the other players. Chuck Csuri was awarded one of our highest military honors, The Bronze Medal for Bravery in Action, and his biography follows the chapter titled, "After Football, After Military Service, Afterwards" for his achievements in art and scholarship are singularly impressive. Within the biographies of Hal Dean, Don Steinberg, and several other players are descriptions of the primary responsibilities of their positions on the football team, Hal as a Guard and myself as an End. These descriptions should clarify the play of the game that may confuse a spectator. In his biography, Robin Priday brings Paul Brown's coaching and his relationship with his team into clear perspective.

The common denominator for becoming a good student or a good athlete is repetition. Repetition is absolutely necessary for long-term detailed learning. Through repetition on the practice field an athlete refines and maintains his athletic skills. It is a proven axiom that you will play like you practice.

LEARNING BEGETS LEARNING

For many years there has been a vigorous debate over the dichotomy between the intercollegiate athlete's perception of his years spent in college and the university's primary goals to educate its students. Whether it is true or not, the newspapers and books are filled with conclusions that today's scholar-athlete may be wasting these valuable years dreaming of a career in professional sports, or the scholar-athlete is not prepared educationally to enter a university. Perhaps these conclusions are not true when one surveys the lives of these athletes after they have left the university. The universities have noble purposes and intercollegiate sports must fit the aims of the university. No president of a university, no athletic director, nor any coach has ever deceived himself that there is any other purpose for the university than being the place where learning, in all its aspects, is the only goal and purpose for going to college.

Few people have chosen to narrate the lives of a group of men who stood out as great athletes and were then molded into a singularly outstanding football team. Through Paul Brown's coaching and attitudes toward Morality, to which he used the term, "Honesty", we were joined into a filial relationship that has persisted through these many years. We came from different cities, and towns or farms with equally diverse backgrounds to play football for The Ohio State University in 1942. During the War, this National Championship team became the Ft. Bragg "Bombardiers". After the War, they became the nucleus for the Cleveland Brown Professional football team for the first ten years of the team's existence. What cannot be disregarded, however, is the fact that through our educations that we obtained primarily at Ohio State, we represented most of the professional colleges at the university. With our 39 out of 40 undergraduate degrees, our 14 Master's degrees and our 5 Doctorate degrees, there were numerous significant contributions to the progress of each of these professions, or significant contributions in the education of young men and women. If there were ever a reason to look back with pride upon its graduates, The Ohio State University can look back with pride on this group of men. It would be difficult to identify another group of young men from any university who could match the achievements of these men. Our lives, which have now settled into retirement, may be catalysts for future generations of young people who wish to find the keys to success and happiness.

This "Labor of Love" has also evoked a number of thoughts that may be of interest to educators. Along with the furor created by the lack of money available to educate our children, there are conflicts between funds for classroom teaching and funds for extracurricular activities. This has created a lessening of the educations of our young people to the extent that functional illiteracy is rampant in America and total illiteracy is common. A return to our traditional educational expectations could well be enhanced by the introduction of the motivations used by coaches into the classrooms. It has often been suggested that parents take more interest in the educations of their children. This pathway may be unavailable for many reasons, the least of which, is that every parent feels his child is "a most perfect" child and any problems that arise are the fault of the educational system. In addition, these problems may already be two generations old so that the parent may not be able to recognize the need for higher or even a high school education. On the other hand, if a Motivator can capture the heart and respect of the student at any level, it would make the teacher's job immeasurably easier. Far more progress can be made by "opening the clam shell" than can be obtained by measuring achievement merely by intelligence. Secondly, the introduction of "team" responsibility into each classroom would introduce the concept that better students are responsible for the performance of poorer students. There is no better way to learn than to teach. These are the methods used by coaches to improve the performance of the second, third and fourth string players. The first string player teaches the third string player and the second string player teaches the fourth string player. This concept of player teaching player was related by Paul Selby at his retirement banquet as Dean of the Law School at West Virginia University. He said, in effect, that one of the most significant lessons that he remembered in his education was his "one on one" drill with Tommy James, the great Ohio State halfback, and, later, the Cleveland Brown's cornerback. Paul was much larger than Tommy and during the tackling drill, Paul tackled Tommy rather gently. When it was Tommy's turn to tackle Paul, he hit him so hard that Paul never forgot the occasion for the rest of his life.

Tommy said to Paul, "Never do that again for on this team, we go "all out, all of the time." To make his best effort all of the time was not taught in the classrooms but on the football field by his fellow player.

The Motivator, in this case, the coach, spends years in continual contact with each player. His presence is felt by the student-athlete both physically and emotionally. The emotional relationship exists throughout the year even off season and during vacations. This is a far different association when compared to a teacher who has only a few hours contact with the student each week, and then possibly only for several months. These two suggestions of student to student responsibility and a person who is a motivator brings the valuable assets of "team " and "coach" into the classrooms.

At the college level, from the conclusions I have drawn from studying the lives of these men, I believe that every scholarship given for financial need, be one that insists on some type of team participation at the intercollegiate level. Whether it be the football team or the debating team, the values of "team participation" are aspects of the education of our youth that cannot be disregarded or discounted.

One may question the relevance of the era of intercollegiate sports of the 40's to the problems that confront intercollegiate sports today. Although the accomplishments of this team can only be admired, the frame of reference of student bodies and university faculty of those yesteryears was similar to the situation today. The football player, in particular, was looked upon as a "dumb ox" who could only stay eligible by being a Physical Ed. major. There are only two differences between the 40's and the present era that I feel merit discussion. Today's entering Freshmen into universities, as a group, are poorly prepared for college courses compared to the 40's. My high school, Toledo Scott, had a tradition of academic excellence at that time and it is far different from the environment today. Scott students of the 40's were the children of poor families, but their parents appreciated the necessity of education. This appreciation was further emphasized by insistence. Today, the children at Toledo Scott are largely from families under public assistance. Education may not be a major concern when mere survival is an everyday necessity. These high school students may be a child of a one parent family, or the family is supported almost totally through public assistance. Even worse, the neighborhoods where the student lives may be ridden by crime or drugs. The other erroneous impression, similar to the "dumb ox" of the 40's is that with the marked increase in size and weight of the individual student-athletes, their brains have become proportionately smaller. These opinions then, as now, are largely false. In the 1920's and 1930's, American citizens often had a jaundiced opinion of destitute immigrants and their children who were seeking a new life in America. The pathway out of poverty for individual people was often sports. So it is today, with poor White and Black athletes whose dreams may be professional football or basketball. People may question their ability to learn in their years in high school and college. The classroom takes a decided second place to athletic excellence. However, most of the time, these dreams will never come true. The high schools and universities must accept the responsibility to actively influence these young people so they will not spend their years in high school and college foolishly. There are great dangers in professional sports. The careers are short and may even be shorter through injury. Sometime in the near future each professional athlete must return to everyday living with an everyday salary. There is left little more than a memory of fleeting renown about which our coach, Ernie Godfrey, often remarked, "You better study because you can't eat footballs."

In the 1940's there was a similar harangue like that of today's football scholarships. It was made about the scholarships Harvard offered the Navaho Indians. It was popularly concluded that after a full scholarship and four years at Harvard, the Navaho indian returned to his Reservation and resumed his pre-Harvard lifestyle and never made any use of his education. Education is often compared to religion. No matter the sinning of the congregation, the minister must never give up. Paying college athletes accomplishes absolutely nothing. Introducing mental calisthenics, student to student teaching, and continual contact with a Motivator will produce long term values and are the answers to our educational problems.

In more general terms, when we look back in history and judge man's efforts to create societies of enduring value, we are prone to praise the powerful and successful political or military leaders. We are also prone to be awed by the elitism of long established aristocracies. This is also true of the Renaissance of ideas when Western man emerged from the Middle Ages. A better judgement of any era would be the evaluation of the lives of a country's ordinary citizens and the advancements made by their sons and daughters. The "Glory that was Greece" or the "Power that was Rome" say little about the economies of slavery, the subjugation of peoples, or even the lives of their "free men" in these periods of history. The same could be said about the Renaissance and the Feudal periods. The average man lived in utter poverty, despair, and hopelessness for his children. Education was only available to the aristocracy or men of religious orders. Sadly, this state of affairs persisted unabated until only the last few generations when both basic and higher education have been offered to the general population. In our time, if we were to judge all of America by the standards of Harvard, Yale and other prestigious universities, without regard for the well being of the general population, we would never serve a proper historical perspective to the generations that will follow.

In this book we will see the effects and results of offering any person the advantages of unrestricted outlets for his goals and ambitions. It is a study, in depth, of a group of young men who were offered a university education. A university education can be compared to rowing upstream against the current of a great river with many tributaries. As each student rower enters one of these tributaries, this current becomes increasingly swifter. Surprisingly, the achievements of the members of the 1942 squad, not only in sports, but throughout their lives, were truly remarkable. Except for their athletic capabilities, they were no different from any group of young teenaged boys. These men are a testament to the greatness of America. In America, our laws prohibit the denial of our pursuits toward happiness for any reasons. In addition, we have successfully confronted the ethnic isolations so common in European countries. These self defeating, illogical isolations of people of different religions and ethnic backgrounds often "bury" the efforts of its citizens. This freedom to allow anyone with the will to fulfill his potential, this freedom to allow people of different ethnic and religious backgrounds to live next door to one another, and this freedom to rule by law are the basic ingredients that have powered the greatest society ever known in the history of man, here in America, and in our time.

THE YEAR OF THE BUCKEYE

Whether you live in New York or just visit, Fifth Avenue in Manhattan has a fascination all of its own. It is, perhaps, the most famous shopping street in the world. There are airline offices where tickets may be purchased to take you anywhere in the world. For people of culture or sophistication, there are art galleries and antique shops to satisfy almost any taste. World renown department stores offer the latest styles and fashions. To the unwary tourist, there are shops that offer deep discounts on all kinds of objects of questionable value. One afternoon, I was strolling along Fifth Avenue while I enjoyed the beautiful weather. I stopped in front of the Steuben Glass display at 56th St. admiring the beautiful glass objects of art and then entered the building. The display cases were filled with magnificent glass carvings. One prism-like cut of glass caught my eye. It repeated the engraving on one of its facets over and over again as one viewed the prism from various angles. I purchased the crystal prism with the number 42 to be engraved on one of its faces. I had finally found a suitable gift for my former football coach, Paul Brown, to express my thanks to him for being the one person most responsible for making my life so successful and happy. Little did I realize at the time that similar feelings were shared by all of my teammates. Of course each player had different expressions of thanks and gratitude, but it was felt by all of us as we have had many years to recall our days with Paul Brown.

There have been innumerable stories and books written about famous sports events and famous athletes. Ring Lardner, the New York sportswriter, captured the imagination of the men of the entire country for two generations by lauding the Four Horsemen of Notre Dame, the most famous backfield of its time early in the history of football. There were the Seven Pillars of Granite, the famous line of Fordham University. Books by and about individual athletes and their accomplishments have been in vogue for the past decades. These books, as a rule, seem to isolate these star athletes by devoting these stories to the years of their athletic fame and accomplishments. But, as we all know, there is always a tomorrow which may be even more significant or more important to the world than the years of sports fame. Paul

Brown was in his second year of collegiate coaching the year Ohio State University's football team was proclaimed the National Champions. One can make a convincing claim that this team was the most outstanding football team to ever play collegiate football. As famous as they were as a team, they were also stellar athletes who would become the nucleus of the Cleveland Brown Professional Football team after the War. After their sports careers were over, there followed a repeating pattern of notable contribution to our American way of life that may be unequalled in any other group of young men. The excellence, which was repeated over and over again by the players on this team, is illustrated in the life of Bill Willis. Bill spent many years in collegiate and professional football where he was honored by being awarded a place in The Intercollegiate Hall of Fame and also in the National Football League Hall of Fame. One has only to visit the Hall of Fame in Kings Island, Ohio or the Hall of Fame in Canton, Ohio to better appreciate the accomplishments of Bill Willis. While his football career spanned over fifteen years, his university training in Education and Sociology was central to his appointment as the Director of the Ohio Youth Commission. Nearby Columbus, Ohio, is the William Willis High School named in his honor for his many years of outstanding service to the youth of Ohio. Among the many players who were members of this squad of 43 players, but who infrequently played in the games of the 42 season, there were similar accomplishments. Paul Selby, one of our reserve quarterbacks, would become the Dean of The West Virginia University Law School. His work as a Chief United States Arbitrator in settling disputes between the coal miners and coal companies has set the framework for all types of arbitration of disputes between large labor groups and national corporations. These patterns of success were started in the classrooms of The Ohio State University and on the football field under the guidance of Paul Brown.

One might speculate about the reasons why this particular group of young men would reach these heights of success, not only in football, but in their chosen professions and businesses. Their years in service during the Second World War were also very noteworthy. The majority of the players were the children of the Great Depression of the thirties. Perhaps the drive to conquer poverty was the primary reason for their success, as in the goals of Lin Houston, but a number of the players did not fit this model. Most of the players were the children of immigrants from almost every country of Central Europe who had come to America to find a better life that powered their potential, but not all of them. The majority of the players had strong family ties to urge them to fulfill their ambitions, but still there were several players whose Fathers had passed away while they were infants or young children. Paul Sarringhaus, Bill Willis, and Tom Antonucci were among the players who had lost their Fathers early in their lives. However, there were a number of inferences that seemed to run through the lives of each of the players. Paul Brown was convinced that a player's intelligence was a necessity to be able to work as a team in achieving success. And intelligent we were. As a group, we had the highest academic average of any group of students in the university aside from the various honor societies. Even today, when a player is evaluated by Paul Brown to play for the Cincinnati Bengals, his intelligence evaluation is a primary factor in his acceptance to this team. Another thread of continuity was an intensely positive self-image that oftentimes began in early childhood and persisted throughout their lives. Lastly, we all admired our coach who used football to interject values that would result in a solid foundation for our futures.

Almost fifty years has passed since 1942. It may seem a long time ago, but it is like yesterday to us. There is one aspect of athletic competition that is infrequently mentioned. These past experiences formed wonderful memories or our former and formative years. Many men do not have such a storehouse of happy memories. Of the 43 players, there are 33 of us still living to relate our stories of this period of American history when we stood so proud and tall.

COMING TO AMERICA

My Uncle Sam, a fellow worker and my father, Julius Steinberg

COMING TO AMERICA

Only a few of the players' parents or grandparents had been born in America. They had come from every country of central Europe hoping for a better life to free themselves from the unending poverty that had beaten these people into hopeless resignation. Bob Jabbusch's ancestors had come from Eastern Germany. He has no knowledge of any of the members of his family who lived in Europe. These were generations of faceless people who lived their lives, had children, and died, without any discernable social or economic enhancement. One generation was merely a mirror image of the previous generation. There were other families whose sons found national conscription into military service to be intolerable. This is the reason that Gene Fekete's father migrated from Hungary to America. My mother's family left Russia when she was only four years old just prior to a massive pogrom that wiped out the lives of 100,000 people in one night. In these villages of central Europe, there was, at best a rudimentary education for the children. Letters were received from friends or relatives in America that there were jobs for anyone who wished to work and the children would be educated. For these men who had no knowledge of industrial skills, no familiarity with English, and no commercial experience, the path of freedom in America brought them to Northeastern Ohio, Western Pennsylvania, and West Virginia. The first turns in these pathways of freedom were predominately the coal mines, steel mills, and railroads. Here in America, they raised their children while working these back breaking jobs. They soon realized that this was no life for their children to follow. Their continuing poverty, in spite of a job that demanded hours and hours of laborious work, was not like the poverty in Europe where there was no hope. America was different. Here was a future, for nearby, was a school for their children.

Nevertheless, whatever good fortune that any of these families achieved through their work was wiped out by the Great Depression. Many of the families wandered from place to place seeking a better means to raise their families. Lin Houston's family were sharecroppers in Southern Illinois and John White's eked out a meager existence on a farm in Georgia. Almost all of the families who were farmers had lost their farms. By this time the children had grown and were high school students. By the end of the decade of the 30's, they were graduating from high school and ready for college. Oftentimes, they were the first of their families to go on to higher education. To quote Shakespeare, "Sweet are the virtues of adversity, Which like a toad, Ugly and venomous, Wears yet a precious jewel in its head." The groundwork had been laid for the greatest decade in American history.

There are two periods in American history that stand out above all others. The first built the foundation for the second. There was the Revolutionary Period when we produced an amazing number of outstanding political leaders. The second was the decade of the 40's that demonstrated to the rest of the world the quality of its citizens who upheld the almost Biblical tenets of our Democracy.

As one peruses the development of our Constitution and Bill of Rights, the quality of our political leadership joined each colony together to insure political and religious freedom. The political freedom differed markedly from the European countries that strived for Democracy. Unlike Europe, where each country was inhabited by a predominately single ethnic group, the people of America came from all of these ethnic groups. The Lavelli's, the Naples', and the Antonucci's were from Italy. The Fekete's, the Horvath's, and the Csuri's were from Hungary. The Matus's and Lipaj's were from Czechoslovakia. Bill Sedor's family came from Poland and Durtschi's from Switzerland. Sarringhaus's family and Jabbusch's were from Germany, and my mother from Russia. These players were only part of the families who had migrated from this cauldron called Europe. Our constitution responded by insuring that no ethnic group of people would ever have special advantages over another. Recognizing that everyone had dislikes or intolerances, none of these could ever be expressed in our laws.

Democracies or Monarchies of Europe that were still extant, rarely recognized the hazards in giving political advantages to its major religion. Little did they realize that the religion accepting these political advantages would spawn the wars or bring on the terrors to the people of less favored religions than the "State Religion". Our Constitution assiduously avoided these problems for all future generations.

The other outstanding period in our history was the decade of the 1940's. Where the Revolutionary Period was filled with outstanding leadership, the 1940's were outstanding by the actions and convictions of its citizens. They were, for the most part, the children of immigrants who had come from Europe bringing with them their languages, their cultures, and their religions. However, now they were living side by side in religious and political freedom. Their sons and daughters were offered opportunities and educations that they could never have dreamed of in Europe. These sons and daughters powered the development of our resources and were able to express their ingenuity that would create a standard of living for its average citizens that has always been admired by the people of the rest of the world. After conquering the Axis nations, they supplied the means to rebuild these ravished countries be they friend or foe. This pent up potential that was forever suppressed in Europe was now able to be expressed in America.

We were a typical but, still, a very special group of young citizens in the decade of the 40's. We were typical in that we were not distinguishable from any other high school graduates. There were a few young men who had excellent high school scholastic records, but there were many more who were only average in their academic achievements. Several others would need tutorial assistance to stay eligible for intercollegiate athletics. On the other hand, we were very special in that we excelled in football from high schools largely in the upper and eastern areas of Ohio. Athletically, we were "hand picked" although there were several players who made the squad as "walk ons". We had several special advantages which were not available to young men who did not participate in extramural or intercollegiate programs. For years we had been almost constantly motivated toward achievement—toward winning. This motivation was made possible by our willingness to train no matter the pain or near physical exhaustion. Even the possibility that our efforts might be in vain did not matter. There was always the sense of pride of just being on the team even if one did not become a member of the playing team. This sense of pride was always with Loren Staker who even as a Senior rarely played in a game. Other advantages were our motivators, our coaches, who gave inspiration to our efforts. They were constantly with us throughout the year. There was the personal contact during the Spring and the Fall seasons, but even off season they made their presence felt. Lastly, we could easily discern the worthy purposes of working together as a unit, as a team, in succeeding. These special advantages made "new individuals" of each of us. Our coaches were almost always correct when they predicted outstanding accomplishments as the true reward for each of us in later years.

The educations of most of the team were interrupted by the Second World War. No matter their fame on the football field where almost all of the players on the first, second, and most of the third team would achieve national recognition for their play as college football players or professional football players, they became the infantry, the seamen, and the airmen who fought their way across the world. Not the Generals, nor Politicians, they fought side by side their fellow Americans through the jungles and islands of the South Pacific, through the invasions of Africa and Europe and into the Battle of the Bulge and beyond to preserve our American Democracy.

After the war, they returned to Ohio State or other universities to complete their educations and marry their high school sweethearts. Almost every player received his undergraduate degree and more than half of the players of the 42 team would achieve Master's or Doctorate Degrees. Frequently, their athletic careers continued as collegiate or professional players, or both. Often, they became coaches on the high school, college or professional level. When their athletic days were over, if athletic coaching and teaching were not to be their lifelong careers, the other players made remarkable contributions to their professions and business careers, perhaps, unequalled in any other group of men.

CY LIPAJ

Football:	Ohio State, 1942
Education:	B.A. in Industrial Arts Masters in Education
Career:	Secondary Education and High School Coaching
Married:	Colleen Sue – 46 years Four children & nine grandchildren
Service:	Air Force Bomber Pilot

CY LIPAJ

In the spring of 1941, Paul Brown came to our home in Lakewood, just west of Cleveland. It is difficult to really describe my feelings of awe and excitement. The Paul Brown was coming to see me and my parents. In this part of Ohio, Paul was already a football legend and now he was the Head Coach of Ohio State University's football team. There are many high schools in Ohio with hundreds of football players, but there was only one Paul Brown, and he had come just to see me and talk with my parents. My father and mother greeted him when he entered our home, but I don't think they could understand my excitement. He spoke quietly to me and my parents about the importance of a college education, and the wonderful opportunities I would have if I enrolled at Ohio State. My father spoke very little English, but he listened intently to Coach Brown. However, I was very surprised by the attitude of my mother who for years had an anathema about football.

My mother's dislike for football had started many years ago. Mom and Dad had come to America from Czechoslovakia. Our native language was the only one spoken in our home. In fact, my education in public school was delayed for over a year as I had not yet learned to speak English. Before coming to Lakewood, they had settled in western Pennsylvania where my father worked in the coal mines for over ten years. Mining coal in the midst of the Great Depression was perhaps the most dangerous, back breaking, and lowest paying work a man could do. One afternoon the miners organized several football teams to play against one another. In one of the scrimmages, my dad was injured, breaking his collar bone. It was difficult enough trying to raise a family by mining coal, and now that her husband could not work, it was next to impossible. And all because of football. Nevertheless, as I progressed through grade school and high school, I was crazy about football. I spent most of these years thinking that I had succeeded in playing without my mother's knowledge. Perhaps, my high school coach, Mr. Ness, had something to do with both my mother and father listening so intently to Paul Brown while he spoke with them although I am not sure how much they understood as they conversed with each other in Slovak as Paul talked to them.

I started playing football in the eighth grade. After each game I would leave my uniform at my friend's home so my mother would not know was playing. However, playing football in junior high school presented another problem. Your parents had to sign a consent card to allow you to play football. I wasn't really a bad kid, and I loved playing football. The only solution I had was to sign my own card. This worked out well until high school. Things were getting a lot more serious as Lakewood High School's football team was an athletic powerhouse with players rapidly reaching their maturities in size and weight. Now the consent card had to be signed by your parents and no fooling around any longer. My mother continued to be adamant about my playing football. Every Saturday morning before our next game, Coach Ness would arrive at our home for breakfast. He must have really impressed my mother about her cooking, for each week, she would sign another consent form that allowed me to play that particular week. I am sure Coach Tom Ness had paved the way for Paul Brown who had come to Lakewood to recruit me to play for Ohio State.

My first year in high school was also unusual. Both the lightweight team coach and the varsity coach were impressed by my ability as a Fullback, and each wanted me to play on his team. They reached a compromise like King Solomon. I played one half a game with the lightweight team and the other half with the varsity. By my Senior year at Lakewood High, we were the conference champions, and I was honored as All Scholastic and first team All Conference. The newspapers had nicknamed me, "Cyclone Cy". I received many athletic scholarship offers from universities across the country, but Paul Brown and Ohio State fulfilled my ambitions. When Paul Brown had completed his presentation to my parents, my father asked a few questions and then spoke to my mother in his guttural English, "This is good for Cy, he should go to college with Mr. Brown."

Trevor Rees had been chosen by Paul to be the Freshman football coach at Ohio State. He was well known in the Cleveland area and very well liked as the head coach of Cleveland Shaw High School. Trevor being my Freshman coach made coming to Ohio State even more inviting. Both Trevor and Paul stressed the importance of education and contributing to your state and community. These beliefs and objectives would be my philosophy to young men when I, too, became a coach.

My football career at Ohio State was rather short. My sophomore year I was the second string Fullback behind Gene Fekete on the 1942 Championship team. These two fall seasons of 1941 as a Freshman and 1942 as a Sophomore left lifelong impressions on me. We were always aware of Paul's strict discipline. I firmly believe that properly directed discipline is essential to the development of young boys. Discipline restricts the choices each boy will make so that they will be less apt to get into trouble. Secondly, we were always aware of Paul's dominate leadership. This was not only true in his relationships with his players, but, also, with his assistant coaches and any other people who were closely involved with the team. During the 42 season, the best player always played each starting position and there was no cause for envy or "counting noses". Everyone on the squad worked as earnestly as possible to make the team as effective as possible. In every game, when it became apparent that victory was assured, the second and third string players would enter the game. In the Pittsburgh game, for example, Gene played only the first quarter and Dick Palmer and I played the remainder of the game. If a player were injured, his substitute would play equally as well. On both offense and defense, the second and third strings continued the pattern and intensity of play set by the first string. Any opposing team had no respite and, I am sure, accounts for so many of the players on the squad rising to the heights of national recognition during the years they played football in college or with the professional teams.

I remember one incident illustrating Paul's high moral standards. The Philip Morris Cigarette Co. had a midget dressed in a Bellhop's uniform making the rounds of the colleges and universities to promote the use of Philip Morris cigarettes. At that time, it was the most popular advertising the students were exposed to. The advertising manager and the midget came to seek Paul's endorsement as he was the most popular person on the campus. We were standing outside of the athletic offices listening to the ad-man's presentation, and to our dismay, Paul told him that he could not endorse a product that he did not admire and did not approve of. It still amazes me of how correct and perceptive Paul Brown was toward proper physical and mental health.

I enlisted in the Air Force in 1943 and became a B-24 Bomber pilot. I was badly injured in a plane crash and spent over a year in Walter Reed General Hospital with a fractured knee and pelvis. When

I had sufficiently recovered, I was given a Medical Discharge. My service and my promising athletic careers were now over. I returned to Ohio State to finish my degree in Industrial Arts, and would make my future the education of young people at the high school level.

It was at Ohio State that I began my courtship of Colleen Sue. I was the ex-football hero and she was an ex-cheerleader from Lakewood High. I persuaded her to marry me just before I was to leave for my first teaching and coaching job in Salem, Ohio. I taught industrial arts and was the assistant football coach. After two years, we returned to our home surroundings at Bay Village, another western suburb of Cleveland. Along with my teaching positions, I continued my education at Western Reserve University where I received my Master's degree in Physical Education. I continued my teaching and coaching careers at Bay Village High School and became the Athletic Director until my retirement in 1983. I have always taken great pride in organizing a safety program for pre-school children that has been often used as a model for similar programs in other areas of the country.

Colleen and I have four children and nine grandchildren. Each of our children has one or more college degrees. As a post-script to my athletic days at Lakewood High, I was recently inducted into their Hall of Fame where I share this honor with other famous athletes from Lakewood High School.

My appreciation for Paul Brown is more intense when I look back to my mother and father who could never have dreamed of improving their circumstances through education. This appreciation has extended to my experiences and to those of my children. In Europe, it was expected that a son should follow his father's way of life. This is not true in America where every path of the future is open to anyone who strives and studies. Football provided the means for me to obtain a college education and to be exposed to men like Paul Brown.

FOOTBALL AND AMERICA

To the uneducated eye, football may appear to be uncivilized violence between two teams of eleven men. But, in reality, football is a very detailed and complicated game, more so, than any other sport played at the collegiate level or even the high school level. What may appear to be mayhem to some spectators is oftentimes used as a framework for our daily activities.

Nothing so accurately exemplifies life than the football itself. Early in the history of the game, the football started out as an almost spherical ball. As the years past, it assumed a more and more elliptical shape. In its present configuration, when it falls to the ground, there is no way to determine the direction it will take. Dropping the football, like missing one of life's opportunities, can have strange consequences. It may bounce back into your arms, or it may roll to the right or left, or backwards or forwards or any unpredictable direction. So, like life, the fewer times you drop the ball, the more control you will have over your destiny.

Businessmen, as well as other people who are in charge of organizations, like to use football teams to illustrate group interrelationships. There are many interesting similarities. First, it requires a group of people (11) working together to accomplish a goal. Every businessman in the world strives to organize his employees into a system that he has conceived as the best way to reach a profitable goal. Secondly, it requires the recognition of each individual's capabilities in this team. Each employee must have the education, training and feeling of responsibility to be an effective force. And, lastly, there must be a "field of play" which will allow success. Thus, in addition to the enjoyment that one receives when his football team wins, football makes a very important contribution to American life.

For about sixty years before 1942, the game of football had started out with one group of eleven men struggling to push another group of eleven men back and forth until one group successfully reached the other team's goal line. The most popular play of the game was known as the Wedge. The oval football was kicked to the opposing team and a human wedge was formed to attempt to free the man carrying the ball through the line of the opposing team.

As the years passed, the rules of the game became increasingly refined. The football gradually assumed its present elliptical shape and pointed on its ends. This change in shape allowed the football to be passed with accuracy and also allowed the player carrying the ball to perform some very deceptive moves to distract or confuse the opposition. The pass made Knute Rockne and Gus Dorais legends in the early days of football. The deception allowed the coaches to devise systems of offense and defense other that the time worn Wedge. There were men like Alonzo Stagg, Pop Warner, Clark Shaughnessy, and Dana X. Bible who perfected their novel strategies with various formations that could spell success and winning in this increasingly sophisticated game. There was the T Formation, the Single Wing, the Double Wing, the Short Punt Formation, and the Deep Punt Formation. These formations were further complicated by a man in motion, a spread of the offensive line, or even a player far removed from the other players on his team. On defense, the strategies were changed from a seven or six man line or, in our time, to a five, four or three man front line to change with the positions of the teams on the field, the comparative strengths of individual players, and the time remaining to be played in each half of the game. In a sense it led to an endless variety of plays executed by the teams of players on both offense or defense

This maturation of the game is also seen in business. Oftentimes a decision must be made whether to be passive or aggressive. Should one person or a group of people make an individual or joint decision? Should the concept be open or kept as a secret? How shall our personnel be arranged to be most effective? All of these questions have a comparable situation on each football team and in every football game.

From the very onset in the history of football, various colleges and universities grouped together into conferences usually denoting the area of the United States where the colleges were geographically located. The oldest, of course, is the Ivy League in the east. Due to the nature of the game, football was particularly well suited to the rough and tumble societies of the early 1900's. What baseball was to the spring and summer, football was to the fall in the lives of the men of America. The rough and tumble area of America in the early 1900's stretched from Buffalo to Toledo and then Southward to Columbus, then Easterly to Pittsburgh and finally Northward again to Buffalo. Here, the average man worked in steel mills, coal mines, railroads and factories. For one reason or another they were the immigrants from the farms, towns, and cities of Europe hoping for a better future. In the last analysis, they labored through any job they could get and then struggled through the Great Depression. But the children of these families would not follow the continual labored futures of their fathers. They were sent to school.

Each of the towns and cities in this part of the United States had high schools whose number one sport was football. No other sport could even approach the importance of football. Each high school developed a football tradition. Some of these high schools would travel across the country, much as our universities do today, to play for a mythical championship. In the early twenties, my high school, Toledo Scott, traveled by train to Everett, Washington to play against their high school. High schools with great football traditions would often schedule one another to create fierce rivalries, not only between the students of the high school, but also between the men of the cities and towns as well. Scott vs. Waite in Toledo and Massillon vs. Canton McKinley were only two of the many well-known rivalries that filled this area of America each season. Each season always reached its zenith at the last game of the year when these traditional rivals would face each other on the football field filled with as many as 20,000 spectators in the stadium.

These high schools were the nurseries to provide the majority of the outstanding football players and coaches to the Northeastern universities and frequently to universities across the nation. In 1942, the sons of this diverse ethnic pool of families provided the coaches and players for the first National Championship team for The Ohio State University and perhaps the greatest aggregation of outstanding players ever assembled on one team in the history of collegiate football. After they returned from service they provided the core of the Cleveland Brown Professional team that dominated the All American Football League for five years and then, after the merger with the National Football League this domination continued for five more years. During these years almost a quarter of the entire Cleveland team was composed of players from the 1942 team or from the Freshman team at Ohio State in 1942.

Bo McMillan, who coached Indiana in one of their few losses in 1942, was so impressed by the talents and thorough football knowledge of the players from this Ohio State team that when he became the Head

Coach of the Detroit Lions, he actively recruited as many of these players as he could sign to professional contracts for the Lions. He was able to sign six of the 1942 and 1944 players. From the 1942 team he signed Paul Sarringhaus, Tommy James, and Cy Souders. From the 1944 team McMillan signed Ollie Cline, Russ Thomas and Dick Flanagan to play for the Lions. Russ Thomas would become an All-Pro tackle and stay on for many years as the General Manager of the Detroit Lions. Within a few years, Detroit developed into one of the finest teams in the National Football League when Bobby Layne quarterbacked the team.

During the years the Los Angeles Rams were champions of the National Football League, Bob Shaw, Les Horvath and Hal Dean were members of their squad along with Elroy Hirsch of Wisconsin and Michigan and Bob Waterfield, their famous quarterback. On the roster of present day professional teams, it is rare to find more than two players from the same college let alone those who had played on the same squad.

In the Athletic Department of Ohio State, as well as in most dominant football universities, are files of the most promising high school Senior athletes. Newspaper clippings would be collated throughout their last year of high school football. Friends and previous Ohio State graduates who were now high school coaches would alert the coaching staff at Ohio State of these prospective athletes. At the end of the season, the recruiting process would begin. All of the coaching staff is involved, making coaching a twelve month a year job. The most desired Seniors would be personally recruited by the Head Coach. Frequently the best players would be sought after by twenty or more universities. Paul Sarringhaus was recruited by over 40 universities as were many of our players. Each university would have its own inducements to influence the player or his family. All in all, this recruiting process would continue at a feverish pace for many months.

During the years when intercollegiate rules allowed only three years of varsity participation, these incoming Freshmen, as well as boys who had not been recruited but still wished to "go out" for football, formed the Freshmen team. While the year was primarily spent to acclimate the young men to college life away from home and earnest studying habits, the freshman squad was taught the essentials of each position a boy might play. They were gradually groomed to the Head

Coach's system of play on offense and defense. Each player was carefully evaluated as to strength, speed, size, agility, and, above all, heart. Without courage, all other capabilities are wasted. On offense, the centers must pass the ball to the quarterbacks unerringly and exactly at the signal of the quarterback so the action of the offensive line and the backfield will start at the same instant called the "Snap Count". The guards must be fast, agile, and physically very strong as they are the success or failure of every play. The tackles are usually the largest and strongest players who open the holes in the defensive line so the star halfback can become the beloved of the sportswriters in the newspapers. The Ends, usually with the assistance of the halfback, are required to move the opposing tackle inward or outward depending on whether the play is to be run inside or outside of the defensive tackle. This play is the "bread and butter" play of every offense. He must also be able to catch passes along with the backfield men. In the rules of football, these players, the Ends and the Backs, are the only eligible receivers on passing plays. The other offensive linemen are not allowed to move ahead of the line of scrimmage. The Quarterback and the other backs are trained to receive the ball and run into the line to block or carry the ball at precisely the exact moment. This cooperation forms a major part of the practice sessions so that the efforts of the offensive linemen will not go in vain. The opening or "hole" in the defensive line made by the blocking of the offensive line may last only an instant. It is during the freshman year that players are selected to join the Varsity for practice in the spring of the year. From the proven qualities, determined during the freshman year, in the spring, the football team is progressively reduced in numbers for the final effort in the fall.

GORDON APPLEBY

1944 O.S.U. Captain

Football: Ohio State, 1942, 1943, 1944

Education: A.B. in Education
Industrial Arts

Career: District Manager
Lincoln Electric Corp.

Married: Helen – 46 years
Three children & four grandchildren

Service: Medical Disability

GORDON APPLEBY

Every university has football traditions that are hallmarks of excellence to be renewed each year. There was one that Francis Schmidt often used to inspire his teams to win over a highly touted Michigan team that was predicted to win easily over Ohio State. Before the beginning of one such game, he "bellowed" softly that Michigan players put their pants on one leg at a time just as do all Ohio State football players. To commemorate this remark, if Ohio State beats Michigan, at the annual post season banquet, a medal of solid gold football pants engraved with his initials is given to each player. The medal usually ends up as part of every wife's charm bracelet. Another tradition at Ohio State is the Captain's Breakfast. The breakfast is usually held the morning of the annual Homecoming game. It was first started by Mr. J.F. Lincoln who had been Captain of the 1906 Ohio State football team.

Mr. Lincoln was the founder of the Lincoln Electric Corporation in Cleveland, Ohio. Through the years, many of Ohio State's outstanding athletes have been highly ranked executives with this vast corporation. Lincoln Electric remains even today as the conduit into corporation type businesses for Ohio State athletes. Al Patnick, the great Ohio State diving champion, is the Executive Vice President, Mickey Buchnick is President of Lincoln Electric Canada, and Frank Boucher was the Director of the Detroit offices of the company. The corporation's main business is welding equipment and electric motors. It was in the Ohio State-Notre Dame game of 1935, that Tom Antonnuci's brother, Frank, lateraled his intercepted pass to Frank Boucher who ran the football in for a touchdown. This put Ohio State ahead by two touchdowns and an apparent win until Notre Dame rallied to scored two touchdowns in the closing minutes of the fourth quarter to win another miraculous Notre Dame victory.

In 1944, I was the Captain of the Ohio State team and attended the Captain's Breakfast. I was approached by Mr. Lincoln who offered me a position with the corporation after I graduated in June. Here I would be spend my career as an executive with the Lincoln Electric Corporation. I recall shortly after my conversation with Mr. Lincoln that Dr. Duffey, our team physician at Ohio State, came up to me and said, " Gordon, I don't know what Mr. Lincoln said to you, but, whatever it was, take the job if he offered you one!"

I was born in Massillon, Ohio, of a family of Welsh-German ancestry. My grandfather had been a coal miner in Wales and was a coal miner in America after he immigrated. My father worked in the Republic Steel mill in Massillon. During my years on the football team at Massillon High School, we were undefeated. Like Lin Houston, Tommy James, and George Slusser, I had only known one football coach, Paul Brown, until 1944. In my Senior year in high school, I was named the All Ohio Center. As a Center, it is of primary importance to the entire offensive play to pass the ball to the backfield man with absolute accuracy and at the instant of the "snap count". Paul had a decidedly convincing method to correct any deficiency by the Center in these areas. If a Center made a bad pass, such as hitting Paul in the face when he was demonstrating a pass play, the Center would be placed in the Quarterback's position for the next play. The only difference from a normal play was the instruction to the offensive linemen. They were instructed to make no attempt to block the defensive line men from charging into the backfield to tackle the passer who, in this case, was the errant Center. It was a quick and convincing cure for a miscue.

After my high school graduation, I followed Paul to Ohio State along with many of my teammates. The freshman year in college filters out many of the students who have a poor concept of college life. Most of the boys from Massillon left Ohio State before the end of the year for many reasons, but the most important was not understanding what was expected of them. I enrolled in the College of Industrial Arts with the intention of teaching Industrial Arts and coaching. Industrial Arts was closely allied to my father's job at Republic Steel. In 1942, my sophomore year, I played second string to Bill Vickroy at Center. My recollections of Paul Brown remain steadfast in my mind. It is a rare privilege to have been coached by such a fair man. His demands for perfection and his advise to his players "to play the string out to the end" equates to Yogi Berra's famous quote, "It ain't over 'til it's over". This has been a proven axiom in all my life's experiences. Another example of his fairness gave no special advantage to me or any other player who had come to Ohio State from Massillon. The best player in each position played on the first string. This concept was of singular importance in bringing Ohio State its first National Championship in football.

With only three Seniors graduating from the 1942 team and with a 1942 Freshman team that was loaded with talented football players, no one was assured of a starting position in this growing dynasty. But this was not to be with World War II leading to the enlistment or drafting of almost the entire team. Instead of a dynasty, the 1943 Ohio State Buckeyes became know as the "Baby Bucks". There were no service programs at Ohio State that allowed intercollegiate participation as they were all Army programs. Ohio State faced a schedule filled with teams composed of previous college graduates or current players as well as professional players who were in service programs at these universities. With great fear for the safety of his inexperienced and young players, Paul faced the upcoming schedule with only five players with any intercollegiate experience. Bill Willis, with severe varicose veins, was the only 1942 starter. The other players were Jack Dugger with severe asthma, myself with a longstanding infected perforated eardrum since childhood, Bill Hackett and Cecil Souders. All of the other players were students who showed a desire to play football with only limited high school experience. It was amazing that we went through the year with no severe or permanent injuries which was Paul's major concern. We had a wonderful coach and through the season, we became increasingly competitive. We won only three games. When Paul left Ohio State for the service at the Great Lakes Training Center, he left Carol Widdows, the interim 1944 coach, with a maturing and well trained line.

The 1944 season was marked by two additions to round out this thoroughly trained and talented line. Three outstanding Freshmen backfield players had enrolled at Ohio State. The other addition was Les Horvath. Les, in Dental School, had been discharged from service but allowed to remain at Ohio State to finish his graduate courses. Les Horvath's stellar play and leadership throughout the season won him All American honors as well as the Heisman Trophy. He was voted the most outstanding football player in the country. Bill Willis, Bill Hackett and Jack Dugger were also recognized on All American teams. This team that had grown from the "Baby Bucks" in 1943 were well represented at the 1944 College All Star Game against the Chicago Bears even before the season began. Jack Duggar, Bill Willis and myself joined Lin Houston, Don McCafferty, Bob Jabbusch, Paul Sarringhaus and Gene Fekete. We were all from the 1942 team of the 43 players selected to face the Chicago Bears. The Chicago Tribune had chosen me as the awardee of the most outstanding Ohio State player in 1943. Our 1944 team went through the season undefeated. I have always been very proud to have been their team Captain. After my graduation, I was the second draft choice of the New York Giants Professional Football team. I felt I was too small to play professional football and I ended my football career after the 1944 season.

After I graduated with my B.S. degree in Education, I joined the Lincoln Electric Corporation. Helen, my high school sweetheart, and I were married the same year. We moved to Detroit where I joined the Lincoln Electric's auto division selling welding equipment and related supplies to the automobile manufacturers. I succeeded Frank Boucher as the District Manager after his retirement. The fierce competition we had learned in football served me well in business as the competition for selling is so intense. One satisfying experience had to do with saving General Motors millions of dollars each year by advising them to change a welding technique. It saved them two dollars for every car and truck they manufactured.

I have now retired but, as I think back, I had one coach and was employed by one company. Helen and I are about to celebrate our 46th wedding anniversary. We have three children and four grandchildren. My recent retirement has allowed us the freedom to do many things or just sit around remembering the many happy years in athletics, Paul Brown and the players on three Ohio State teams.

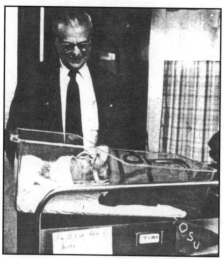

PASSING THE HERITAGE OF FOOTBALL IN OHIO TO THE NEXT GENERATION

Woody Hayes "recruiting" my eldest grandson Jimmy, age two days.

Grandsons Sammy and Benji horsing around.

Grandson Jonathan, future Nose Guard for OSU.

OHIO, FOOTBALL'S
HALLOWED GROUND

Football is played throughout the country in high schools, small colleges, and giant universities as a seemingly unending "Rite of Autumn". The geographic center of this enduring sport is the state of Ohio and those areas of the surrounding states that border on Ohio. For the young men in high schools throughout Ohio, the sport where one would gain recognition and fame was football. There are probably hundreds of high schools throughout the state varying in size from several thousands students to those with only a few hundred students. Invariably, regardless of their size, they would have football teams. A good example of this striving toward football, is seen in the Jim Rees's high school in Greenville, a tiny farm community north of Dayton. Their entire varsity squad consisted of twelve players, and this was the year in which they finally were able to win four games instead of being the winless "Green Wave" for the previous three years. Woody Hayes, the great and revered Ohio State coach, was raised in a tiny town of Newscomberstown. Newscomberstown would be an unlikely high school where the seed of football and football coaching would be planted unless one can appreciate the importance placed on football. The number of renowned coaches that began or established their careers at Miami University in Oxford, Ohio, is more than coincidental. There are dozens of coaches who have gained national prominence for their outstanding coaching who played and/or coached at Miami, including our coach, Paul Brown.

The newspapers throughout Ohio added emphasis to this aura of football fame. Each week throughout the fall, the sports pages were filled with the names of outstanding players in each high school in their areas. Each "star" player, each unexpected upset in a game where desire overcame the talents of the favored team, and each crucial and successful play, either on offense or defense, was long remembered. In my family, Thanksgiving day dinner during my childhood was almost the equal to many of our religious holidays in its importance to our family activities. The annual Scott-Waite game was played every year on Thanksgiving morning and the Thanksgiving day dinner had to wait for our return from the game.

The high schools in Ohio and in the areas of the surrounding states that border on Ohio supplied the game players and coaches for numerous universities in the first half of the century. This pattern continues even today. One has only to peruse the game programs of each major university to see the frequency of the first string players who had attended Ohio high schools. The rosters of the University of Michigan and Purdue are often filled with Ohio high school players who were successfully recruited to attend these and other out-of-state universities. Easterly from the Ohio River valley into Pennsylvania are numerous mill towns that have spawned some of the greatest names in football and other sports. Arnold Palmer in golf and Johnny Unitas and George Blanda in football are only a few of the sports giants that were born here and attended high schools in this area. It seems only fitting that Cedar Point on the shores of Lake Erie near Sandusky, Ohio, would be the place where Knute Rockne and Gus Dorais perfected the newly allowed forward pass, early in the history of football.

Our Ohio State 1942 team had another facet to emphasize the depth of commitment to football by players from Ohio. In addition to being the geographic center of the football world, many of the players were the sons of "football families". Older brothers who attained prominence for their football accomplishments would often be the role models for their younger brothers. Not only was their fame an incentive for a younger brother, but oftentimes they would instill the needed skills and emotional fortitude into their younger brothers. Jim Rees describes his ordeals in learning football skills from his older brother. When learning techniques did not go as well as his brother, John, expected from him the "hammer would fall". In the same vein, my brother, Mutt, used the term "cake eater" when he felt that I was not performing up to his expectations. My older brother, Mutt, (his real name was Morton) taught me the skills necessary for offensive and defense line play as well as the unbending courage needed for contact football. He did this while he was playing football for the University of Toledo when I was only 11 or 12 years old. These were the qualities that I would carry through my college career. There were no others. My high school and university coaches would further refine my brother's teachings and his exacting attitude on the football field, but brother, Mutt, laid the foundation for my football future.

With equal aplomb, an older brother would point with pride at the accomplishments of his younger brothers on the football field. I think they were as equally happy and impressed by their young brothers as they would have been if they were playing themselves.

As all philosophers do, Jim Rees made a detailed study of the players on the Ohio State 1942 team from each quarter of the state. He divided the state of Ohio into three parts, the Northern two quarters, the Southeastern quarter and the Southwestern quarter to analyze the recruiting efforts by the coaching staff for the players who composed the 1942 team. Taken from the segment of his biography which he titled "Out of Greenville", he wrote, "A segment of Ohio defined, arbitrarily, by a line extending from Toledo south to Kenton (forming the Western boundary) and from Kenton eastward to East Liverpool to the Pennsylvania border (the Southern boundary) includes 25 of the total 88 counties in Ohio. Of the 41 'home grown' members of the 42 team, 30 hailed from the cities and towns in this heavily industrialized area. Just 11 players came from the remaining 63 counties. The entire Southwestern quarter of the state contributed a mere two players. One of these lads from Hamilton county, Paul Sarringhaus, was one of the most outstanding power halfbacks in the country. My home was in Greenville in Drake County which was known as Fort Greenville in Revolutionary times. Here was the site of the peace treaty that would bring the Northwest Territory into the nation and establish those states whose universities would be joined together into the Western Conference, better known as The Big Ten.

This simple demographic breakdown suggests that the Ohio State recruiters used three types of optical instruments in their quest to find prospective players able to compete with the other powerhouse football teams in the Big Ten in 1942. They used microscopes in the Northern half of the state, simple magnifying glasses in the Southeastern quarter, and were looking through the wrong end of telescopes in the Southwestern quarter. This is a provocative study in itself as the abundant natural resources of the state brought hundreds of thousands of people into the Northern half of state for the manufacturing of basic materials, such as steel. In contrast, the Southwestern quarter of Ohio has some of the most fertile soil in the country and is less densely populated by farm families."

It is not unusual for more than one son to achieve athletic distinction, but twelve of the players on the 1942 team had brothers who also excelled in athletics and football, in particular. Brothers in the same family often became role models for their younger brothers. One of the most memorable games in the history of football was the Ohio State-Notre Dame game in 1935. The outcome of the game seemed assured for Ohio State when Tom Antonnuci's brother, Frank, intercepted a Notre Dame pass and then lateraled the ball to another Ohio State back who ran the ball in for a touchdown. In the closing minutes of the fourth quarter, Notre Dame came back to score twice. The last score being a pass from Bill Shakespeare to Wayne Milner to seal another amazing Notre Dame victory.

From early childhood Bob Jabbusch admired his Uncle Frank who lived with his family. He was a singularly important person who aroused Bob's interest in football. He was a star player called "Foxy Fabian" for Lorain High School and then played semi-pro football for the Cleveland Panthers. Gene Fekete's older brother, John, attended Ohio University in Athens, Ohio. His football career was so outstanding that he was named to the Little All American team whose selections were made from all of the small colleges and universities in the country. Les Horvath has an older brother, Charles, who Les admired both as a student and an athlete. As a student, he graduated from Northwestern and then went on to obtain his Doctor of Medicine degree. In athletics, Charles was one of the fastest sprinters in the country. He dominated three sprint events in track and at one time held the world record for the high hurdles. Ken Coleman whose early sports interest was baseball before changing to football, had an older brother who was a star Fullback for Syracuse University.

Tommy James's younger brother, Don, was the Quarterback for Miami and is now the Head Coach at the University of Washington. My brother, Morton, played football for the University of Toledo and also Arizona State. He was a member of the first Arizona State team when they initiated their football program. Martin Amling's younger brother, Warren, was an All American guard at Ohio State and is now in the Intercollegiate Hall of Fame. Jack Dugger, a third string tackle in 1942 became an All American in 1944 and later a professional football player. His younger brother, Dean, would follow him at Ohio State ten years later and also become an All American. Bill Willis had an older brother everyone called "Deacon", a nickname that Bill was also frequently called. His brother must have been an outstanding high school star as his talents were remembered for years by the fans of Columbus East High School. John White's younger brother, Paul, was a star Halfback for Michigan in 1942 and played against John in our Ohio State–Michigan game that year. Paul went on to play for the Pittsburgh Steelers. Jim Rees had an older brother who initiated Jim in the "art" of football blocking and tackling.

The class of all football families, probably unequaled in the history of football, are the families of Lin Houston and Archie Griffin. Besides Lin, there are three brothers who also excelled in football and became college stars and professional players. His brothers Jack and Walt played for Purdue University and Walt also played professional football for the Washington Redskins. Jim Houston was also an All American under Woody Hayes at Ohio State and played professional football for the Cleveland Browns for thirteen years and was the team captain of the Browns.

Football has been a major sport in America for an entire century, but nowhere has the game been so intensely followed and played than in Ohio. No matter what the size of the high school, there were lightweight and varsity football teams. The small colleges and large universities throughout Ohio and the areas of the states that border Ohio always have football teams. Year in and year out, Ohio reigns as the King of Football and Michigan and Notre Dame reign as the Princes of Football.

JIM REES

Football: Ohio State, 1942
              Bunker Hill Naval Air Station, 1943
              Great Lakes Naval Training Center
              North Carolina State, 1946, 1947

Education: B.S. in Agronomy – Soil Analysis
              Masters in Education

Career: Soil Analysis and Land Reclamation

Married: Patty
              Four children & two grandchildren

Service: Naval Air Cadet
              Aerographer's Mate

JIM REES

Putting My Shoulder Pads on Backwards at Ohio State University:
A Small Town Boy in the Land of the Football Giants

Preparing to Tackle Backwards

At the exact moment that I was slipping into the shoulder pads just handed me by the equipment manager (a kind of shoulder pad that I had never seen before), Coach Paul Brown strode through the door. Almost instantly he spotted my struggling, walked up to me and said, "You've got your pads on backwards!" With that remark, he turned on his heel and departed while nodding to several of the other players who I assumed were from Massillon. Try, friends, to imagine my embarrassment at that instant. This was my first "person to person" meeting with the man whom I had been reading and hearing so much about back in Greenville. Here, in the flesh, was the renown "Wizard of Washington High, the Merlin of Massillon". While the Greenville "Green Wave" football program was suffering the humiliation of three straight totally winless years, here was the coach who had developed the juggernaut of Ohio high school football, Mighty Massillon. Coach Brown was the one individual whom I wanted to most impress— favorably that is. Through the intervening years, I retained the impression that P.B. from those few seconds forward, harbored a sizable doubt about me. With the incipience of my callow youth near its zenith, I suspected that I had committed a grievous error. The upshot of this back-assward beginning is that, during the succeeding 1942 season, I achieved a rather inglorious position of prominence. I hereby claim that I hold the record for the number of times Coach P.B. found it necessary to interrupt the practice sessions to point out to me in very specific, concise, explicit, well articulated, clearly enunciated, easily comprehended language that everyone on the field or on the sidelines quickly understood. I was going the wrong way, and my performance "JUST WOULD NOT DO". I smartened up by the fall of 1942. I distinguished the front from the back of the shoulder pads with a magic marker, "F" for front and "B" for back.

Dayton, Ohio, is about 35 miles south of Greenville. Sometime in the early fall of 1942, Si Burick, the famous sports columnist for the Dayton Daily News, informed his readers, many of whom were from Greenville, about the composition of the 1942 Ohio State University football team and the origins of the players. Paul Sarringhaus from Hamilton was deservedly recognized, but, my friends, neighbors, or family could not find one lonely, simple sentence in the article that made mention of another "product of the area" on the team their taxes helped to support. Here I was, one of us two players from the entire western side of the state and totally invisible. Si had flatly stated that Paul was the only member of the 1942 team from the Dayton area. Now consigned to total oblivion, a hullabaloo was raised by his Greenville readers. Si hastily penned a very contrite follow-up article, "With apologies to Mr. Rees". Being a lineman, I was not overly sensitive about the lack of media attention as I was too completely involved in trying to survive the pedagogy of the classrooms and the pummeling on the football field. Perhaps his forgetfulness was a kind of Freudian slip as Burick had always been a keen promoter of Dayton sports. Si's Id at some subliminal level prevented him from revealing Greenville's pathetic record from 1937-1940.

"For three long years, a total of three seasons, the Greenville "Green Wave" football team, competing in a fairly well-balanced Miami Valley League tallied exactly NO WINS! Game after game, in the cool crisp air of autumn evenings, with droplets of dew accumulating on the grass, before the world, they were not only defeated, they were unmercifully STOMPED."

The arithmetic of these high school games always intrigued me. With increasing frequency the ball carriers, led by their interference, would wear a footpath over my body. I would then rise and ask, "Just how many head of that herd ran over me?" During one particular game, and failing to stop another stampede through my tackle position, I asked my buddy, hanging loose at End, "How many blockers were on you?" "Three", he replied. Before the next play could be run, I turned to the linebacker and asked the same question. "Three", he also replied, "At least, three". The wheels turned—three on the End, three on the Linebacker, and three on me, that makes ten with the ball carrier. Son of a Gun! do the college scouts know about this super blocker, only one man to handle the remaining eight men on our team? This was the norm for Greenville, not the exception.

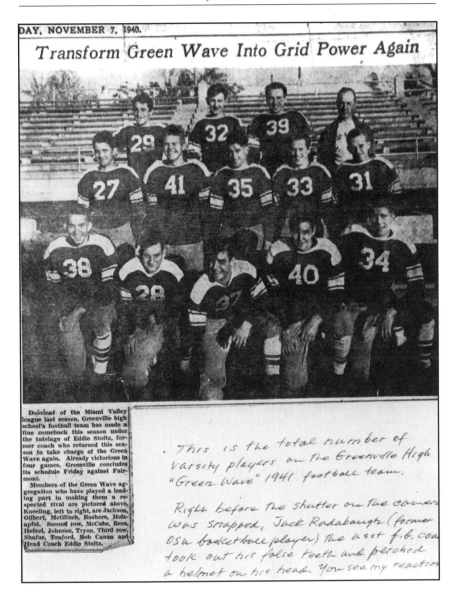

DAY, NOVEMBER 7, 1940.

Transform Green Wave Into Grid Power Again

Doormat of the Miami Valley league last season, Greenville high school's football team has made a fine comeback this season under the tutelage of Eddie Stoltz, former coach who returned this season to take charge of the Green Wave again. Already victorious in four games, Greenville concludes its schedule Friday against Fairmont.

Members of the Green Wave aggregation who have played a leading part in making them a respected rival are pictured above. Kneeling, left to right, are Jackson, Gilbert, McGlinch, Bashore, Holzapfel. Second row, McCabe, Rees, Hetzel, Johnson, Tryon. Third row, Shafor, Teaford, Bob Canan and Head Coach Eddie Stoltz.

. This is the total number of varsity players on the Greenville High "Green Wave" 1941 football team.

Right before the shutter on the camera was snapped, Jack Radabaugh (former OSU basketball player) the asst f.b. coach took out his false teeth and perched a helmet on his head. You see my reaction.

GREEN WAVE
Greenville, Ohio

As a way of manifesting his concern about the effects of these massacres on his son, my father would greet me after a game with the same sort of "encouraging" remark. As a former school teacher, he was given to posing a question in his remarks, "Well, Jim, how did the old Goose Egg team do tonight?" or, "I never saw a team that wanted to give, give, give so much". My mother would then treat me to a malted milk at the local ice cream shop to reassure me that my parents still claimed me as their son.

My senior year, things turned decidedly toward the better. I was switched to Fullback, ran the signals, and the "Green Wave" won four of its eight games. I was named an Honorable Mention in the All State selections without ever scoring a touchdown. To players from teams who are perennial winners, a 4-3-1 record may seem piddling, but at Greenville, we accomplished this record with only 13 varsity players. This made it very necessary for every player to be utilitarian and, as a result, certain perspectives are gained through this needed versatility. To illustrate, the guards and tackles quietly cursed the fullback (all backs) who didn't hit the hole quickly. The defensive tackle damns the end who "drifts" and doesn't jam the interference on off-tackle plays. The defense end, in turn, curses the tackle who does not scramble to the outside on end runs to box in the ball carrier. Thus a player, on such a team as ours, recognizes the necessity for acting cooperatively with his fellow players to overcome the problems they face in a ball game.

The Mysterious Recruitment

There were baffling questions of why an assistant coach would be dispatched to visit one particular small town lad who deviated so greatly from a recruiter's ideal. At seventeen, I was not particularly hefty, my foot speed was unknown, and my academic record was not overly exciting (if you want a thinking player), nor could his possible contribution by measured by his team's record of 4 wins over a span of 32 games. Put in another way, why would Paul Brown enlist an unknown" Jim Who?" from " Where's it at city?" whose teams served so durably as the door mat for a "What did you say, conference?" Forty-five years later, at one of our reunions, I decided to investigate the circumstances surrounding this mystery. Finally, going in the right direction, I consulted Coach Paul Brown. In a warm response, he stated that two of his room mates at Miami University in Oxford were from

Greenville and had recommended me. One was an attorney and the other the editor of the local newspaper. They obviously possessed "language skills" which by sheer eloquence overcame P.B.'s justifiable doubts. The moral of this story is simple and straight forward, "To be there, you first have to get there." I cut it pretty close.

The Giants

As a consequence of the "Miami" connection, my name was included on a special list, a group of some 50 young men the coaches had recruited. The names of these newcomers were called out, including mine, who comprised the bulk of the 1941 freshmen team. I sensed almost immediately that I was associated with some of Ohio's most promising athletes. This was pretty heady stuff for a 17 year old small town boy. Time after time my first insight proved to be exactly on the mark. For two years I never ceased to be awestruck by the exceptional speed, elusiveness, and ability of so many of the players. I was amazed by their fierce determination and pure physical power that they, as a team, consistently exhibited. Strange as it may seem, my teammates became my "heroes". How many college players can say that they played with their heroes. Man, how those guys on the 1942 team could hit and scoot. The heaviest team members, the linemen, hardly averaged 205 pounds. The team members were not big men, but they played like giants.

Just How Tough Was It, Pops?

During the 1941 season, my freshman year, Marvin and Melvin Wucotich, identical twins from Warren, Ohio, had equipment lockers on both sides of mine in the dressing room. I don't know how I got in between "Wookey One" and "Wookie Two" as I called them interchangeably. Following one particularly "engaging" scrimmage, during which I came in frequent contact with Henderson, Broglio, Kingham, and Appleby, the merciless manglers from Massillon, I staggered back to the dressing room, giving silent thanks to the Great Referee above for preserving my life. There I suddenly discovered that the Wucotich twins were actually quadruplets, two on each side of me. I asked both Marvin and Melvin, in turn, what their brother's names were. They didn't say anything, just looked at me in a strange way. Later, under the shower, I pondered the "Wookies" rather peculiar behavior. I finally came to the conclusion that their conduct was due to a "natural reserve"— a tendency to be introspective (sometimes taken as shyness) which all big city players possessed.

Postscript: The above story is all a lie. I just made it up while I was in the hospital recovering from a concussion which Bob Jabbusch or Hal Dean or Cy Souders or some other guy with a sledge hammer hung on me during an intersquad scrimmage. I'm still not clear.

Through Adversity to the Stars

Of all the coaches who had a direct influence upon my play, my brother, John, was the first and most strict. He put me through the "paces", and out of respect for his age and muscularity, I gave him very little argument about the strain and pain. John was a good teacher and generally quite reasonable. However, if I didn't take his admonishments to heart, he taught me another valuable lesson. If I failed to follow his demonstrations or his instructions, and he only said it once, or if a transgression was again committed, the hammer would fall. During the War, John had enlisted in the Canadian Air force and was the instructor to many of the boys who flew in the "Battle of Britain". The official motto of the R.C.A.F. is "Per Ardva Ad Astra", "Through Adversity to the Stars". I was a member of five military and post-war collegiate football teams which established an overall record of 35 wins, 7 loses, and two ties. These were not the "Bandade" teams of my high school years. These were the military and post-war collegiate teams that would fit this honorable slogan.

Occasionally, while watching a televised football game, witnessing the young men whacking one another around, I ask myself, "Did you actually do the same thing"? Although my younger relatives can hardly believe it now, the answer is, of course, yes. But then I have to show them my lasting mementoes as proof, the odd lumps on my balding skull, the shiny scar tissue covering my old cleat wounds, and a "gimpy" leg—all indicate that, Yes, I was "in there" many years ago, playing with the giants, daring to reach for the stars.

THE WINNING EDGE
Dreams of Childhood

The average young man will find himself sitting as a spectator in the stadium rather than a player on one of the teams competing on the field of play. The usual advice given to young people is to put away their childhood dreams and mature into young men in order to cope with the trials of adulthood. These opinions appear well advised but, still, they may have a decided flaw. As we seek to discover the common denominators or reasons that brought this squad of outstanding young men to play for the 1942 Ohio State football team, there was frequently an ever present self-image that began in early in childhood and not forgotten as these formative years passed toward adulthood. I believe Paul Brown recognized these values as he often expressed the thought to his players that they were different from other young men. He would describe this quality as "Blue Steel", the finest grade of steel from the mills of Massillon. These young men were participating on the field rather than sitting as spectators in the stands.

If one were to compare the physical characteristics of the players to the spectators, there would be little difference. Perhaps, one would notice a slightly taller or heavier young man but little more. What would not be seen, however, is each player eagerly accepting the daily pain and physical exhaustion necessary for him to prepare for a future opportunity to be on the playing team. Yet, there was no certainty that he would ever leave the bench on the sideline. Nor would one see the acceptance of discipline from his coaches trying to evoke a better response or effort. A spectator has little appreciation of the pride in being just a member of the team despite never being sent into a game. All of this is born from a positive self-image that starts in early life and is never forsaken.

Perhaps the most convincing argument that this persistent childhood motivation frequently powered the lives of these players is the athletic career of Lin Houston. Lin and Bill Willis were, without reservation, the greatest pure football players that I have ever known. Lin was the oldest child in a family of sharecroppers in the midst of the

Great Depression. As a young child he was convinced that he was destined to bring his family out of poverty. As he advanced through his athletic career, he never lost sight of his family's dire needs. When he accepted a scholarship to Michigan after graduating from Massillon High, one of his requests was a job for his father. When his scholarship to Michigan did not work out, he was given a promise by Ernie Godfrey that with his enrollment at Ohio State, that his father would be given his job back at Republic Steel in Massillon so the family could move from Romulus, Michigan, back to Massillon. Another young man might show little regard for the needs of his family as he pursues his goals.

Les Horvath returned to the football team in 1944. He brought the Ohio State team through an unbeaten season, and was awarded the Heisman Trophy. As a young boy, he weighed barely 100 pounds as a Freshman in high school. From early childhood, he dreamed of playing football for Notre Dame. He lived in South Bend, was Catholic and held on to this dream. Although he became an outstanding halfback at Cleveland Rhodes High School, the Notre Dame staff felt that he was too small to play for Notre Dame. Even his recruitment by Ohio State was rather "left handed". The Ohio State coaches were primarily interested in Don McCafferty and only a passing remark from Ernie Godfrey that "he could come along, too" brought him to Ohio State. His football progress toward becoming an active player was further impeded by Coach Schmidt who had a penchant for large players. One Saturday afternoon, it was raining briskly and the opposing team was about to punt the ball back to Ohio State. Coach Schmidt had over a hundred men on the bench but rarely knew any of their names. Coach Schmidt yelled out, "Is there anyone here who can catch a punt?" Les wasted no time in volunteering, went into the game, caught the punt, and return the ball 40 yards up the field. Les came off the field and Coach Schmidt questioned, "Don't you know it is raining? Don't you know how dangerous it is to catch a slippery wet football in the rain?" Les answered, "Coach, I never drop a football." Schmidt looked at Les who weighted about 150 pounds and said, "Son, you sit down next to me. You're going to play a lot of football." There was never any doubt as to Les's speed, agility, courage and sure handedness, but it was his everpresent childhood self image that powered his talents.

My approach to a childhood self image was more philosophical. I had decided at a very young age that I should do as I was told. It made getting along with my elders much easier than resisting, but more than that, it formed the basis for my being very "coachable". I was convinced that I could carry out any assignment that my coaches wished me to do which was principally blocking and tackling regardless of the opposition. I recall one incident playing against the Iowa Seahawks, the last game of the 1942 season. It was my assignment to move a giant of a tackle who had played for the Green Bay Packers prior to his enlistment into the Navy. The play called was an off-tackle play which required blocking this giant and moving him laterally toward the center of the line. In as much as he was on my outside shoulder I had to drive into his midsection before he could start his drive and my wingback, Les Horvath, could then move him inward. At 187 pounds, against this tackle who was 6'3" and weighed 250 pounds, I found myself, like David, standing over this unconscious Goliath after the play was over.

Bob Jabbusch and Paul Selby had other childhood dreams. Bob adored his Uncle John, a star football player for Lorain High School and the Cleveland Panthers, a semi-pro team. Bob was only five or six years old and he was going to be a football star like his Uncle John. Paul Selby lived across the Olentangy River which separates his home in Upper Arlington from the Ohio State campus. The stadium lies near the banks of the river. His childhood dream was always to play football for Ohio State. His father was a prominent lawyer in Columbus and had urged him to go Dartmouth College after graduation from high school. Near the end of his Senior year in high school, Fritz Mackey, one of the Ohio State coaches, made a chance remark that rekindled his childhood dreams of playing football for Ohio State. Going to Dartmouth went right out the window.

Cecil Souders had an almost fairy tale-like childhood in Bucyrus, Ohio complete with a pony cart to explore the forest near his home. He played all of the childhood games and baseball, but football was the game of his childhood aspirations. Not being able to play football until high school, he organized the young boys to play in a staked out cow pasture. Paul Sarringhaus's childhood aspirations were somewhat more unusual. By the time he graduated from high school, he was one of the most sought after halfbacks in the country with over 40 college scholarships offered to him. All of the universities were correct in their assessment of Paul as he became one of the great power halfbacks in the country. On his return to Ohio State football after service, his picture was featured on the cover of Life Magazine. What decided him on Ohio State was his childhood dream of avenging the 1935 defeat of Ohio State by Notre Dame.

Many of our players could relate similar feelings. They may seem trivial or unlikely reasons to achieve athletic renown, but they were the motivating differences between playing and watching. Playing requires courage, sustained dedication no matter the guarantee of success, acceptance of rigorous discipline, a receptive attitude and very positive self image. Lacking any of these qualities makes one a spectator while the player is fulling his childhood dreams on the football field.

LIN HOUSTON

Football:	Ohio State, 1941, 1942
	Consensus All American, 1942
	Player & Coach Ft. Bragg Bombardiers
	Cleveland Browns, 10 years
	All-Pro, 2 years
Education:	B.A. in Education
Career:	Professional Football
	District Manager of Sharon Steel Corp.
Married:	Edna Mae – 45 years
	Four children & eleven grandchildren
Service:	Artillery in South Pacific

LIN HOUSTON

We were all standing on the porch of the old grey weather-beaten farmhouse to say goodbye to Cousin Homer. Our families had lived close by for five years as sharecroppers in Wolf Lake, Illinois, just north of Cairo, in an area known as Little Egypt. And now, Homer was off for Pittsburgh where his brother had a job promised for him at the steel mill of the U.S. Steel Corp. Dad wished Homer well and shook his hand. Mom stood silently holding the small children away from a hole through the porch from the rotted wood. The sadness of her life showed with more intensity now that Homer was leaving. I stood by my Dad and was the last to say goodbye and wish him well. I was fourteen years old and had helped my Mom care for the farm while Dad worked nights at the Atlas Powder Plant nearby.

We had come to this God-forsaken place during the Great Depression from Tennessee. The Houston family had a great and grand heritage as part of the family of Sam Houston, the first Governor of Texas. Pop had always said that there was a strong family resemblance. Pop had brought his family from place to place ever seeking his fortune and a better place to raise his family. His only resemblance to the other parts of the Houston family was his ability to produce children. Mom and Dad had nine children, and there were seven who survived infancy.

Alone at the depot, Cousin Homer climbed aboard the Illinois Central train bound for Chicago where he would catch the Pennsylvania train for Pittsburgh. The train left Chicago and was lumbering through the farm land of Indiana. The conductor, a tall, thin friendly man, came through the coach collecting the tickets. "Son", he said, "You're not on the right train, we're headed for New York. This is a New York Central train and you have a Pennsylvania train ticket." "But, sir," Cousin Homer replied, "I want to go to Pittsburgh. I've been promised a job in the steel mill there." "Well, I'll tell you what you should do. There is a small town in Ohio named Massillon where you can get off this train and catch the Pennsylvania train that will be coming through there in about three hours." The conductor handed Homer back his ticket, and Homer thanked him again.

Massillon was one of the many mill towns that filled this area of Ohio. Republic Steel Corp. had one of its steel mills here. These mills were the support and masters of the community. Cousin Homer wandered into a saloon, "The Erie Grill", near the depot to await the arrival of the Pennsylvania train that would take him to Pittsburgh. He ordered a beer with a whiskey chaser as was his custom of drinking. Sitting next to him was a dark haired man who was already showing his years well beyond his actual age. He turned to Homer and said, "There aren't many of us who can drink beer with whiskey chasers." "Say", asked the man "What are you doing in these parts?" "Well", answered Homer, "I got on the wrong train in Chicago and I'm waiting for the Pennsylvania to Pittsburgh where I've been promised a job in the mill at the U.S. Steel plant." "What do you want to go to Pittsburgh for? Hell, I'm the foreman of the Republic Steel mill here in Massillon. You just stay put and let's have another beer with a whiskey chaser." Perhaps chance meetings such as this one are common, but this particular meeting of my cousin Homer and the foreman at Republic steel was the beginning of my football career that would bring my family out of poverty.

I had just completed my first year in high school in Illinois, when a letter arrived from Homer. He could get my Dad a job at the mill if he would come to Massillon. Pop didn't do anything about the letter until one night when he was going to work at the Atlas Powder Plant. A great flash and explosion filled the sky. One of the many buildings at the powder plant had exploded and carried my Dad's best friend through the roof to his death. Pop turned back to our home and announced that we were leaving for Massillon, in the early winter of 1936.

Pop started work at the mill, and, I, being big for my age, thought that I, too, should go to work. Mom would have none of this, and I enrolled as a Sophomore at Massillon High School. The only sport that I had ever played was basketball. Paul Brown was the coach of both the basketball team and the football team. He was assisted in basketball by Carol Widdoes and was assisted in football by Hugh McGranahan. That winter we went to the state finals in basketball, only to be defeated in the championship game. One day Coach Widdoes remarked to Paul that he was amazed that I looked like I only weighed 150 pounds but, in reality, weighed 185 pounds. He also remarked that he had never seen a boy as strong as I. Paul left the history class that he was teaching just to see how this could be. The years on the farm had given me enormous lower body musculature. Hugh McGranahan, Paul's assistant coach, at Paul's insistence, always wished to test a player's aggressiveness. He decided to match me against a boy about my size in a wrestling match. I pinned this boy in 17 seconds. Hugh was amazed at my strength and said, "Let's see if you can do that again." This time it took me 19 seconds. Paul Brown introduced me, Lin Houston, to football. In our first game that fall, I was the first string Guard in my junior year at Massillon High, having never seen a football game.

Massillon, with Paul Brown as coach, were the perennial Ohio State High School Champions. We played against the other high schools in Northeastern Ohio all of whom had great football traditions. These high schools were the football nurseries for the major college teams across the country. During my senior year at Massillon, the left guard was injured. Paul asked me if I knew the plays that ran to the right or left. This was no problem to me as they are mirror images of each other in the single wing formations. Paul installed a tackle in the other guard position and I played both pulling guard positions for plays running to the right or left. Little did I realize that Paul and I would have a very special relationship in football that would last for the next twenty years and would be a life long friendship thereafter.

After graduation, I had received over forty invitations to attend universities across the United States as I had been selected the first string Guard in the All State polls. Of all the scholarships offered me, Paul objected to Ohio State as Francis Schmidt was the Head Coach. He liked Fritz Crisler at Michigan and I accepted the scholarship to Michigan. I accepted the scholarship only if they would find employment for my father. Dad was employed by the Ford Motor Co. We moved to a small town outside of Ann Arbor named Romulus. Pop loved his new job, and mom hated the house in Romulus.

My freshman year at Michigan began with great expectations. I was the first string Guard on the freshman team and attended classes. One of the alumni had been appointed to look after my needs. He left for Florida in the fall, and I was no longer able to study as I was assigned to wait on tables in the dormitory while I was still practicing football. No one seemed to care about my circumstances nor the promises that had been made. Disheartened, I decided I had no future at Michigan. Along with my mother's dislike for living in Romulus, I decided to leave

Michigan and look over some of my other scholarship offers. My first stop was at Purdue as I knew several of the players on the freshman team. I didn't like Purdue so I started off on a "Hegira" that brought me to Wake Forest, Louisiana State, and finally to Tennessee. Here, I didn't enroll but I did practice with the football team. Col. Neyland, the Head Coach, offered me a full scholarship if I would return after Christmas vacation and enroll in school.

I decided to return by bus to my family in Michigan by way of Columbus, Ohio. By the grape vine, the athletic department at Ohio State had learned that I had left the University of Michigan. For three days they waited for the bus to arrive in Columbus from Tennessee. When I arrived, there was Ernie Godfrey. He introduced himself, and, with a friendliness I had not received in many weeks, he asked, "Son, where would you like to go to college?" " I want to go to a university where my parents can watch me play football," I replied. He promised to get my Dad his job back at Republic Steel in Massillon and I accepted the scholarship at Ohio State. My Dad was back at Republic Steel in two weeks and Mom was back to her home in Massillon.

Ernie Godfrey was the principal recruiter for Ohio State. The year before Paul Brown became the coach, he had assembled an outstanding freshman team. The annual Freshman-Varsity football game was as tough a game as the Varsity would have all season. His only inducements for coming to Ohio State were his personal love for Ohio State, that it was a fine university for study, and I would have a part time job to help pay my way through school.

The 1941 football season at Ohio State continued the winning spirit that Paul Brown had instilled in us at Massillon. During my years at Massillon, we had never lost a game. Although only a few players had played for Paul in high school, I could easily see the same qualities develop in this team. We remained undefeated until the Northwestern game in mid-season. Some good would result from this defeat in the distant future, but now we were confronted by a Paul Brown in a dimension that went deep into our spines. The Monday conference before going on to the field to practice was a soul penetrating oration against every player regardless of whether or not he had played in the game. He went around the room, row by row, and demolished every player, one by one. We would not lose again. However, we did have one tie game which was really a great moral victory for Ohio State. Except for Tom Harmon and Forest Eveshevski, the 1940 Michigan team that had devastated Ohio State 40-0 the year before, was still intact and predicted to again overwhelm Ohio State and their new coach, Paul Brown. Michigan had to come from behind in the closing minutes of the fourth quarter even to gain a tie with the Buckeyes.

Spring practice in early 1942, brought together the returning varsity players and Paul's first recruited Freshman class. The Ends were Dante Lavelli, a sophomore, and Bob Shaw, a junior. Dante would become the greatest pass receiver in the National Football League during his years with the Cleveland Browns, and Bob Shaw was probably the most talented athlete in all of football. He had great size, great speed, and wonderful hands. In the later years with the Chicago Cardinal's professional football team, he would establish the record for the league by catching five touchdown passes in one game. The tackles were Bill Willis and Chuck Csuri. Bill would be named to both the collegiate and professional football Halls of Fame, and Chuck would receive All American honors for his play in 1942 by several polls taken around the country. The Guards on the team were Hal Dean and myself. I would play offensive guard for the Cleveland Browns for over ten years, and Hal would play for the Los Angeles Rams also as an offensive guard during the years they were the NFL champions prior to the merger of the two professional leagues. I was a consensus All American and Hal, along with Bill Vickroy, our center, were All Conference. Bill Vickroy had outstanding offensive talents and excellent speed and mobility. The backfield was equally talented. Les Horvath would win the Heisman Trophy as the outstanding football layer in 1944, and played pro ball with the Rams and Browns for three years. While he was playing for the Rams, he was starting his dental practice in Los Angeles. Gene Fekete was only a sophomore but held the national rushing record for most of the 1942 season as a fullback. He, too, received All American acclaim in Bill Stern's roll of outstanding players. Paul Sarringhaus was among the first players to wear contact lenses, but his eyesight was only a minor deterrent to his ball carrying and passing skills. It was almost impossible to tackle him in the open field. When he returned to play after the war, his picture was the front cover of Life magazine as the most promising returning player of the coming season. Our Captain, blocking back, and Quarterback in the T formation was George Lynn. No one could have dreamed up a better leader on the field than George. It was predicable that he would become an outstanding coach with Oklahoma and Stanford after the war. During these years when we played both offense and defense during a game, it was common to have a large number of injuries on every team including ours. The players in every position were well schooled by Coach Brown so that there was little if any loss of skill and execution when a substitute entered a game.

By mid-season our 1942 team would be rated as the number one team in the country, until our ill fated week-end at Wisconsin when almost the entire team was afflicted with dysentery. Still, we lost to a very talented Wisconsin team. The following Monday was a repeat session with Paul Brown similar to the Monday after our loss to Northwestern the year before. The rest of the year we were unstoppable. Tommy James went wild against Illinois at Cleveland stadium and we had 20 points before the first quarter was half over. Our Michigan game, to decide the championship of the Big Ten, was a classic struggle that lasted into the fourth quarter before the game was finally decided. Our last game against the highly touted Iowa Seahawks and Bernie Bierman was probably the best game we had ever played. We were almost faultless in execution both on defense and offense, winning 42-10. The following week, Ohio State was acclaimed the National Champions. This was Ohio State's first National Championship team.

Our 1942 season was marred by a personal tragedy in my family. Of my six brothers, Howard, was developing as the best football player in the family, including myself and three others who would gain national prominence as football players both in college and professional football. I received an urgent call from my mother that Howard had had a serious accident. Both of his legs had been crushed in a truck accident. They had to be amputated below the knee. Here was a boy who could throw a football almost a hundred yards, pass with uncanny accuracy, and run equally as well. I returned home to see a young man so devastated that he threatened to take his life. No matter what hope we held out to him, it was to no avail . He just laid in the bed with his face to the wall and refused to talk with anyone. One day, a man named Spivak knocked on the door of our home. He was a rather short man with an expression of conviction in his eyes. He asked to speak with Howard. My mom brought this stranger into the bedroom to see Howard. He asked mom to leave him alone with Howard. He closed the door behind my mother and began to sing and dance in front of Howard who lay despondently in bed. "Get this maniac out of here!" screamed Howard. "Get this maniac out of here!" The man unfastened his belt and dropped his trousers. Standing in front of Howard was a double amputee. Mr. Spivak had come from Youngstown where he made artificial limbs. He told Howard he would have him walking without any type of assistance in six weeks. This miracle, embodied in this stranger, enabled Howard to have a new lease on life. He put football and other sports behind him and became a self-sufficient man that we have admired all of our lives.

Early in the Spring of 1943, the President of the Ohio State University, the members of the athletic department, the coaches, and some of my closest friends, gathered near the entrance of the stadium just east of the open end of the stadium. There is a small triangular patch of grass where several Buckeye trees are planted. These trees with a small bronze plaque at their bases are Ohio State's recognition for the greatest football players that have attended the university. The university had planted a Buckeye tree with a Bronze plaque at its base that read, "Lin Houston, All American 1942". Ohio State has had many outstanding players but only a few have been offered such a prestigious honor.

Soon after, the war descended on all of us. I was drafted and sent to Ft. Bragg, North Carolina, for artillery training. During the fall, we organized a football team to entertain the troops with games against other service teams and large universities in the East. I was the Head Coach and Don McCafferty, our number three tackle on the 1942 OSU team was the Assistant Coach. We were playing members of the "Bombardiers" as well. This began the outstanding coaching career for Don as he would become the Head Coach of the Balitmore Colts in the National Football League. In his first year, the Colts would win the Super Bowl. Unfortunately, Don McCafferty died suddenly just before he was to open his second season as Head Coach of the Detroit Lions.

Some months later, our contingent at Ft. Bragg was shipped overseas to the South Pacific. For five months we fought almost continuously against the Japanese as we fought island by island back towards the Philippines. During this time, I received a letter from Paul Brown. He wrote that he would not be returning to Ohio State. He had decided to enter professional football, coaching a team in the newly formed All American Football League to be called the Cleveland

Browns. He offered me a contract and agreed to pay me $200 a month while I was in service, if I agreed to sign with the Browns. Compared to my service pay of $30 a month, $200 a month seemed like a fortune for doing something that fulfilled my young ambition. The war ended and I was again united with Dante Lavelli, Bill Willis, Tommy James, Gene Fekete and Les Horvath. Other Ohio State players closely related to the 1942 team were George Cherokee, Horace Gillam, Lou Groza, Tony Adamlee, and Bob Gaudio. This was largely the nucleus of the Cleveland Browns teams who were to completely dominate the All American and later the National Football League for ten years.

The majority of the other players that Paul had signed for the new franchise in Cleveland were players who had stood out in games against the 1941 and 1942 Ohio State teams. Paul had a real appreciation for their individual capabilities. In reference to our loss to Northwestern in 1941 was one such player, Otto Graham. Paul was convinced that here was an outstanding quarterback with peripheral vision that was unmatched by other quarterbacks and an equally outstanding passing arm. He was among the first players who agreed to sign with the Browns. Lou Saban, Marian Motley, and several other players from Great Lakes and Notre Dame joined with us. Unfortunately, Gene Fekete injured his knee early in his first year and was replaced by Marian Motley from Canton McKinley High School and the University of Nevada. Most of these players would become legends in the history of football for the coming generations of young men.

My professional football career would last for ten years. In our first year in the National Football League, we would win the National Championship beating the Philadelphia Eagles 35-10. For seven of these ten years, we would be the champions of the All American or National Football Leagues. Of the other three years we were the runners up. Twice I was named an All Pro Guard. I had known only one coach from high school onwards. My retirement from football was emotionally intolerable. I went to see Paul with my football shoes around my neck, and he agreed to one more year. I think I had my greatest football season that last year. The following year I was offered the Head Coaching job at Massillon High School. The contract only guaranteed one year which was not much security for my future. They refused to consider a longer contract so I entered business with the Sharon Steel Corp. I became the Regional Manager for the corporation and despite a small geographical working area we were among their top sales producers. I spent thirty-two years with the Sharon Steel Corporation and finally retired.

Edna Mae and I have been married for 46 years. We now have two sons, two daughters, and eleven grandchildren. We spend a lot of time traveling about the country seeing our families and our brothers' and sister's families. Oftentimes on Fridays before an Ohio State home game, we meet in Columbus with Gordon Appleby and several other players from our 42 team and play golf and reminisce.

Our family, sharecroppers from Illinois, started with little or nothing. Football gave me the opportunity to help my family. There are few families that can equal to football records set by the Houston brothers. My brothers, Jack and Walt, played football for Purdue and Jim and I for Ohio State. Jim spent ten years with the Browns and was the team captain. Walt played with the Redskins in Washington but Jack was unable to play pro ball due to a knee injury. After football, all of my brothers and sister have had outstanding careers in business. Paul Brown, our educations at Ohio State and Purdue, and the enduring friendships of my team mates that have lasted a lifetime is, in my mind, the essence of America.

LES HORVATH

Football: Ohio State, 1940, 1941, 1942, 1944
            All American, 1944
            Heisman Trophy, 1944
            Los Angeles Rams, 2 years
            Cleveland Browns, 1 year

Education: Bachelor of Science
            Doctor of Dentistry

Career: Dentist

Married: Shirley – 23 years – Passed away
            Ruby

Service: Naval Dentist

LES HORVATH

Every young man looks forward to a successful occupation, and there are countless occupations for him to pursue. However, every young man frequently dreams of becoming a sports hero. He will often dream of emulating a sports hero of the past. There are heroes in every sport long remembered for their outstanding play or rising to that single occasion that will bring them lasting fame. The ultimate recognition in collegiate football is to be awarded the Heisman Trophy. This trophy is presented to one player each year from all the football players in the country. I think it is important to begin my autobiography in this way so that young men in the future will have a clearer conception of how this trophy came to be awarded to me.

When my parents came to the United States from Hungary, they settled in South Bend, Indiana. My dad established a small pharmacy after graduating from Ohio Northern University, a small university in northwestern Ohio. While I was in grade school, I dreamed of Notre Dame football. I was going to be a football star for Notre Dame. This was some dream for a boy less than five feet tall and weighing less than 90 pounds when I reached the eighth grade. However, I may have been short and light, but I soon noticed that I was fast, agile and sure handed, much more so than the other boys. My courage and my dreams were the attributes I would carry throughout my athletic career. Oftentimes I would be playing against men who were twice my size. My courage was also needed to continue my quest of overcoming a multitude of obstacles and disappointments. This goal seeking eventually allowed me to attain the status of playing football for a major university rather than accepting a scholarship to a small college as many of my advisors had suggested. In my estimation, these qualities were far more important than good fortune or fortuitous occasions.

As I recall, among the many choices I would have to decide upon during my collegiate career, there was only one that truly stands out from all the others. I had to make this decision just before the 1944 football season was to start at Ohio State. I had the opportunity to turn professional with a very lucrative contract to play for the Cleveland Rams before the franchise was moved to Los Angeles. Or, I could stay at

Ohio State and play collegiate football and graduate with my doctorate degree in Dentistry as I was already a senior in the Dental College. I am sure I made the correct decision to stay in school.

My family had moved to Cleveland where I attended Cleveland Rhodes High School along with Don McCafferty and several other excellent football players. After the season was over my Senior year, we were actively recruited by many universities. I had many offers of athletic scholarships from small colleges and universities, but my only desire was to play for a major university. Having been selected an All City halfback, my aspirations rose until the Notre Dame recruiters decided that I was too small to play for Notre Dame. Coach Ernie Godfrey, Ohio State's chief recruiter, came to Cleveland with his eyes on Don McCafferty, Bob Harris and two boys from West Tech High School. West Tech had beaten Rhodes for the city championship that year. For some reason unknown to me, each time the Ohio State recruiters would come to Cleveland, they invited me to go to dinner with them, but all the attention was paid to the other boys. Surprisingly, at the end of one of the evenings, they asked me to come to Ohio State. And so my college career began with less than a whimper. My father's attempt to influence Notre Dame had failed to impress them, and I came to Ohio State as a kind of afterthought of Ernie's and the other recruiters.

Athletic scholarships in 1939 had a different concept than they have today. Ernie's Cleveland contact for inducing players to come to Ohio State was a Mr. Harry Hollaway, the President of the Republic Steel Corp. Mr Holllaway was an ardent Ohio State fan. That summer we were employed at Republic Steel working alternately on the three shifts six days a week. The job paid $100.00 a month. At the end of the summer, Don McCafferty and Bob Harris who were the first string Rhodes tackles, Bill Giel, our Center, and I headed for Ohio State with the money we had saved from our job with Republic Steel. Mr. Hollaway personally drove us to Columbus to his Delta Tau Delta fraternity where we were pledged as entering freshmen and where we would live. The fraternity brothers made a deal with us for our board and room. It would be reduced to $35.00 per month if we would help in the kitchen. And so the future winner of the Heisman Trophy and the first professional football coach to win the Super Bowl in his first year as the Head Coach of the Baltimore Colts began in the kitchen of the

Delta Tau Delta fraternity house peeling potatoes. By the end of the first quarter of school, Harris, the two boys from West Tech left school and Geil had enlisted in the service. For all of their recruiting efforts only Don McCafferty, who they really wanted, and I, who they were not so sure about, remained in school.

Freshman football practice at Ohio State was carried out on an immense field that was approximately the size of five football fields. On one of the fields were gathered the forty or so freshmen who had been recruited by the coaches. Far off on another field were the boys who were "walk ons" or just wanted to practice football to satisfy their physical education requirement. There were approximately 150-200 of these boys. The first week of practice brought my first real crisis in college football. I sprained my back and was unable to practice for two weeks. When I recovered from this injury, I was forgotten. From the time I was in the eighth grade and all through high school, I had always been the starting halfback, and now I stood about watching all of the other very talented athletes. I was never asked to scrimmage, and, for the first time, I began to have doubts as to my capability to play Big Ten football. One day I wandered over to the other practice area where the "walk on's" were now reduced to 30-40 young men. They were having a scrimmage and at one point the coach called out for a halfback to join in the scrimmage. Since these boys had such limited experience in football, I had a field day. The coach immediately recognized that I did not belong with this group and sent me back to the recruited freshman squad. At first, I declined as I was so disappointed that I had decided that, perhaps, I had made the wrong decision and should have gone to a small university, as I was too small for Ohio State. The next day as I was dressing to practice with the "walk ons", my name was called as the starting halfback for the recruited freshman scrimmage. I had successfully negotiated another hurdle.

The Head Coach of the varsity football team was the one and only Francis Schmidt. He had the most violent temper and the most vile mouth of any coach in football; but, more than that, he was a genius in college offensive football. He had little talent for organization so teaching fundamentals or the timing of play execution escaped him. These capabilities you had to have before you reached the varsity team. During the 1940 season, as a sophomore, I played in enough games to earn my Varsity "O". I was the only sophomore to do so. Although I had played in almost all of the games, there was one game that sticks in my memory about Coach Schmidt. We were playing Minnesota who were contending for national recognition as the best football team in the country on a raining Saturday afternoon. Minnesota had failed to make a first down and were in their huddle ready to come to the line to punt the ball back to Ohio State. Coach Schmidt suddenly called out, "Is there anyone here who can catch a punt?" I said, "I can." He sent me into the game as the safety man to catch the punt. Probably due to the wet ball, the punt skidded off the side of the punter's foot and flew in a low trajectory. I was able to catch the ball on a dead run and advanced the ball up the field forty yards. Schmidt was furious when he pulled me out of the game after the punt return. "Don't you know who we are playing?" "Yes", I replied." Don't you know it is raining and how slippery the ball is? It was a short punt, and why would you try to handle a slippery, wet football?" Coach Schmidt was a large man and towered over me. I answered him not out of fear, but out of honesty. I said, "I have not been hit that hard in the Big Ten and I am sure that I will never drop a football I can get my hands on." After hearing my reply, he put his hands on my shoulders and said, "Your going to play a lot of football." I guess I became a sort of good omen to him as he always wanted me to sit next to him from then on. He always had trouble remembering my name and referred to me as "the little guy". He did keep his word and I played in every game thereafter.

All coaches had a penchant for making players in the same position constantly competitive as a device to improve their performances. Whenever I thought that my future was secure on the starting team, I might overhear him telling another halfback to run the signals in practice instead of me. It was rather disconcerting but I survived, although at the time I did not understand his motivation. The 1940 season was very satisfying to me as I had become the starting halfback, but, on the other hand, was a disappointment as we were picked to have the best team in the country pre-season and ended the year with only a .500 average.

After the season ended, I returned to Cleveland at the end of the school quarter. Since I had become somewhat of a celebrity in Cleveland, I was interviewed one afternoon by a sports reporter from the newspaper. This interview consisted merely of yes and no answers and I had never made any adverse comment about the coaching or the team. The next day the sports page was filled with an article written about my interview with this reporter. One of my replies to his questioning was to the effect that we had a lot of talent but frequent and lingering injuries had prevented the team from performing at its best. This statement had been distorted in print, reading,"Horvath says Ohio State had all of the talent it needed to be National Champions but coaching destroyed the team!" This type of sensationalism is very common in newspapers, but, at the time, I was certain my career at Ohio State was over. Although Coach Schmidt was fired at the end of the season, he was an outstanding coach for his time and a genius in offensive football.

Before the end of the year, Paul Brown replaced Francis Schmidt as the Head Coach at Ohio State. The contrasts between the two coaches were soon very apparent. Paul was quiet and intense, in contrast to the bellicose approach of Schmidt. Complete organization in every phase of the game was a hallmark of Paul's coaching. His thorough coaching methods replaced the placards of new plays held in the air by Schmidt at almost every practice session. Where Schmidt had over 300 plays, Paul had very few. However, these few were gradually expanded into groups that required each player to know the assignments of the other players in each offensive play or defensive alignment. Blocking techniques, exact timing in the execution of plays on offense were taught both on the practice field and in our pre-practice conferences. In addition to athletic talent, Paul demanded intelligence, courage, and dedication. The pre-practice sessions were much like a college classroom, and there was no haphazard activity on the practice field. Each day we practiced our fundamentals as they related to our positions. Then we gathered into groups to refine our roles on offense or defense. During the last period of the practice, we would form into teams to scrimmage or to improve the timing of a play so the ball carrier would hit the hole in the defensive line made by the blocking linemen at exactly the right instant. Every player on the squad was in constant participation—there was no standing around by anyone. In essence we were a team that would "play like it practiced".

The 1941 season, Paul's first at Ohio State, was not a great year for me personally. Paul's approach for competing for each position throughout the year was very trying on me emotionally. I did not play at all in our opening game, and was not sure I was even going to make the traveling squad for our second game in Los Angeles against Southern California. Surprisingly, he started me and I played the entire game which we won 33-0. I felt that I had played well in our upset of Southern Cal, but I played only occasionally in the next few games. Again my emotional level was returning to a new low, when Paul returned me to the starting team for the remainder of the season except for the most important one, our last game against Michigan. He told me that I had earned the starting position for the game, but since Tom Kinkaid was playing his last game as a senior, he would start. For the second time in my football career, I sat on the bench the entire game. My disappointment was more than I could handle. I went to see Paul in his office early the next week, and told him that I did not expect to return for the next season. I was entering dental school in the fall and I would be giving up football. He tried to talk me out of this, but I left his office convinced that my football playing was over.

The 1942 season was approaching and my desire to play football was overwhelming. I asked Coach Brown if I could return to the team. Of the two halfback positions, I preferred to be the left halfback. Paul was uncertain about this as he had Paul Sarringhaus, Tommy James and George Slusser already slated for this position. When we had our final scrimmage before the opening game, I was in the third string backfield, but I had a great day running for three touchdowns and passing for two more. There were no other reasons for being on the starting team other than being the best in that position. After the scrimmage, Paul said nothing until the following Monday. He said that I had earned the right to start in the left halfback position. He asked me if I would be willing to play the right halfback position since we had so much running and passing strengths in the other halfbacks. Even before the season started, he told me we could be National Champions if I were willing to make the change. I like to feel that my willingness to make the change made the difference when we were acclaimed the National Champions in 1942. However, this team, unknown to the rest of the football world, was loaded with talent. Almost every player on the first two teams and even into the third team would eventually be All Conference, All Americans, and would fill the professional ranks with 17 players from the 1942 team. Many of them would individually be dominate players in the National Football League for a decade. Several players would be placed in the Intercollegiate Hall of Fame and the Professional Football

Hall of Fame. Paul was never one to pass out compliments to individual players, but he did remark that he thought I was the best right halfback in the country in 1942. This 1942 season made enduring memories and lifelong friendship between the players.

The World War decimated the athletic program at Ohio State in 1943. I was still in Dental School in the Army ASTP program that prohibited participation in intercollegiate athletics. This policy was the opposite of Naval university programs that allowed intercollegiate participation. This resulted in a marked imbalance between the athletes available to play for Ohio State and the opposing teams who were loaded with experienced university and professional football players. As I was in Dental School at Ohio State, it was an emotionally very trying time for me not to be able do my part in 1943 as the rules had been changed to allow participation for four years. Paul did a remarkable job of coaching only freshmen and a few players who were 4F for medical reasons. Paul Brown left Ohio State at the end of the 43 season when he entered service as an officer at The Great Lakes Training Center. The linemen on the "Baby Buck" team laid the foundation for the 1944 season.

Just before the 1944 season was to begin, the Army discharged its students in the Dentistry and Vet Med Programs. I was to begin my senior year in Dental School and I still had this fourth year of eligibility. Since my undergraduate class had graduated, the Cleveland Rams approached me to turn professional. In addition to a very lucrative contract and bonus, they said if I would get back in sound physical condition and learn their offense, they would fly me into Cleveland each Sunday and then fly me back to Columbus after each game. Carol Widdoes, Paul's assistant coach, had been appointed Head Coach at Ohio State. Widdoes was a quiet religious man. Both he and Ernie Godfrey, who was the epitome of love for Ohio State, came to see me at the Dental School. I told them of my offer from the Cleveland Rams, and, without undue pressure, they thought it might be better if I stayed to play for Ohio State. They felt they had three outstanding freshman backs to compliment the excellent line that Paul had developed. This line was largely composed of players from the 1942 team and several sophomores from the 1943 team. If I could get in good physical condition after a year away from football, they would build the offense around me. Thus I would be most effective as the quarterback, or the right or left halfback depending on the play being called. Their honest motives created a challenge to me that was irresistible. I would stay at Ohio State and play the 1944 season rather than turn pro. Their impressions of the freshmen Kline, Brugge, Flanagan, and Keane were everything Carol and Ernie said they were. This team was a repetition of the 1942 team with the only difference being we were undefeated. Again, All Conference and All American selections were in almost every position. This team was ranked second behind Army's team with Davis and Blanchard that had captured the country's sports fantasy. I reached the pinnacle of intercollegiate recognition being awarded the Heisman Trophy.

After my graduation from Dental School in the spring of 1945, I enlisted as an Ensign in the Navy and was assigned to The Great Lakes Training Center. Since officers were not allowed to play football at this base, Paul requested that I be assigned to his coaching staff. At the end of the season, I was transferred overseas with my eventual destination, China. We stopped in Hawaii where I was stationed at the Marine Headquarters. The base was small having only 600 men, but they wanted a football team. As I had the only football experience, I became the coach. Our season was a successful one losing only our first game. I had no war experiences and was discharged in July of 1947.

After my discharge, I returned home. As with the rest of the 1942 team, football was still a dominant factor in our lives, despite the fact that I had intended to start my dental practice. I was signed by the Rams who, by then, had moved to Los Angeles with Bob Shaw and Hal Dean from our 1942 team. My professional football career spanned three years, two with the Rams and my last year back in Cleveland with the Browns whose nucleus was our 1942 team. Through these years, I noted a marked difference between intercollegiate and professional football. Granted that each position on the squad was played by a noted player, the attitude of the owners, coaches, and players was guided by anything but the spirit of football as a sport. This spirit that I had known and respected through the years in high school and college was relegated to one of low importance. One of my experiences with the Rams still makes me wonder what they were thinking of. I had signed a year's contract of $10, 000 to play for the Rams. I had decided that I would like to set up a dental practice in Los Angeles and went to them for an advance on my salary so that I could buy the equipment needed to furnish an office. Instead of recognizing the importance of assisting me and thus receiving my gratitude for their help, they agreed to give me the money but at the same time reduced my salary. The coaches and players seemed to have only a financial interest in football so the actual fun one attaches to team play loses its importance. This was true of the Rams but much less so with the Browns as Paul always recognized the importance of what one might call the "collegiate spirit" behind playing winning football.

On one of our transcontinental flights, I met one of the stewardesses. She was beautiful with a sparkling personality. We would meet as often as possible when she had a layover in Los Angeles. We were married in her home in Detroit and had a wonderful married life for 23 years. As fortune would have it, Shirley was stricken with cancer of the ovary and died in 1973. We had no children, but I have always had beautiful memories of those years. Several years later, when I was vacationing in Hawaii, I met and courted my present wife, Ruby. The cost of long distance calls and frequent plane flights to Hawaii were getting more than a little out of hand. I enticed her to return to California. Ruby is a beautiful perceptive woman who has one son from a previous marriage. Her son now has seven children so I have a "built in" family. After my father passed away, my step-mother has come to live with us. We have just completed a second home in Virginia where Ruby's family lives. We will probably retire there if I ever quit working. At the present time we have a home in Glendale, California, on the top of a hill overlooking Los Angeles. At night the view is quite spectacular.

I think that I have received every honor an aging athlete could ever expect. In 1977, I was elected to the Intercollegiate Hall of Fame and the next year to both the Cleveland and Ohio State Halls of Fame. Besides wonderful memories, I have made many wonderful lifelong friendships. One of the most memorable was my friendship with Don McCafferty. We were together through high school and college. We always kept in close contact while he was coaching the Balitmore Colts for over fifteen years. He had every quality one would want in a close friend.

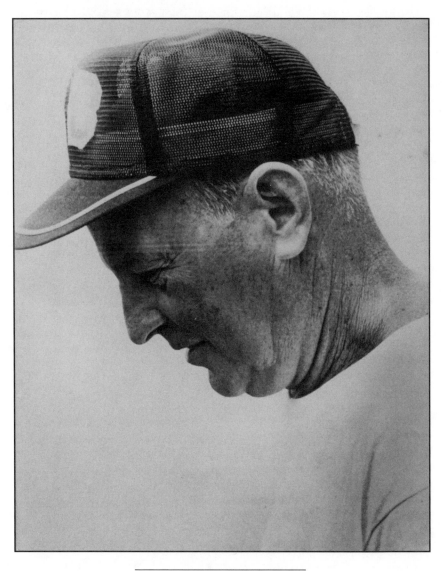

PAUL BROWN

THE PSYCHOLOGY OF WINNING
A *Player Views His Coach*

In the realm of intercollegiate athletics, the most successful coaches are not those who collect the largest number of outstanding athletes. Every coach has a number of fine qualities, but the coaches who are most successful are best able to select and mold their players into a team, not only willing, but eager to follow their directions. A winning coach's most outstanding quality may be in attaining continual dedication from his players. Another coach's major asset toward success may be unusual perception. Others provoke performances that are greater than could be expected from the abilities and talents of his players. Regardless of his coach's qualities, the coach will leave a life long impression on each of his players—one that is almost always positive.

Team play differs markedly from individuals who participate in a sport where winning is one of an individual's performance such as swimming or track. In these situations, the athlete involved in an individual performance must have outstanding innate talent coupled with rigorous training. While sitting next to Mike Peppe, the great Ohio State swimming and diving coach, I asked, "Mike, these boys who practice swimming hour after hour each day, won't they become outstanding by making this super effort?" Mike replied, "Not if they have two left feet. They could practice forever and not be able to go beyond a certain point of achievement". Team play differs markedly from this situation. Singular efforts are welded together to develop a winning team with players who can express their individual assets but each may not have every talent a coach could wish for. Every position in football calls for more than one type of capability. An End, for example, must be courageous and strong enough on defense to strip a ball carrier of his interference. This interference may be two or three opponents, all of whom are as large or larger than the defending end. On Offense, the End must be able to block an opponent who is by far the largest and strongest man on the opposing line in several different ways depending on the play being run and the position on the line of the opposing

Tackle. The End, of necessity, must "beat" the Tackle in their charges at each other so his speed at contact will overcome his size and weight. Lastly, the End must be able to catch passes. In this position, all of the Ends on the team vary in their ability to perform all of these assignments. The coach must select among his Ends, the two who best fit all of these requirements. Each player in each position can then be molded by the coach into the unified action of team play. The skilled backfield players depend on the courage, heart and strength of the linemen. The greatest halfback in the world is not going anywhere without a perfectly functioning offensive line.

To define the psychology of success, in this case, winning, is well beyond anyone's capability. But, still, there are parameters that one can use to measure the extent of individual success. The duration of a coach's service to the university or the number of championships achieved by his teams are good examples of these parameters. For those who strive toward the pinnacle of their ambitions, the road is well marked. The one coach who best exemplifies this type of person is Paul Brown, our head coach in 1942 at Ohio State. Among the obvious qualities of thoroughly understanding his goals are dedication, organization, and innovation. But more than these are indefinable qualities that set him apart from almost all other coaches. Good fortune or hoping for success are never reasons to "fit the stride" of such a man as Paul Brown. He always had a complete understanding of his goals and the manner in which he could reach these goals.

When Paul Brown arrived at Ohio State, he had inherited a group of players whom he had not recruited. The 1940 Freshman team had been largely recruited by Coach Ernie Godfrey whose deep affection for Ohio State football was able to overcome the almost chaotic situation in the football program at the end of Francis Schmidt's coaching career at Ohio State. There were many outstanding upperclassmen with excellent football talents, but they were largely an undisciplined squad who mentally questioned the ability of the "high school" coach who had been selected as the Head Coach in this heady atmosphere of Ohio State football.

In the days prior to starting spring practice, while the weather was still winter like, we trained in the gym. Paul identified his starting team as a basis for beginning spring practice. Whether you were one of these select players or not, everyone was very involved from the first day.

There were techniques to be learned and refined. There was a progressively increasing intensity of conditioning. We were groomed in his phraseology such as "Blue Steel" and" You play like you practice". Blue Steel defined you as different from other men in the university. You play like you practice will always reflect your performance in a game.

Paul had selected punctuality as the first rule never to be violated. He had set the time that we were to dressed in our practice uniforms and seated in the conference room of the stadium for our first practice in the spring. He said, without much emotion, that he wanted us to watch a movie of his Massillon High School football team. Despite the murmuring of some of the upperclassmen, we viewed the type of team that Paul wanted us to become. The speed and precision of this team could only be admired, and one could feel that Paul was establishing his leadership among players who, for years, had known little organization or leadership. By the Fall of 1941, the ingredients instilled by Paul Brown, had ingrained the desired concepts for this team to become a Paul Brown team. We lost to Northwestern which was our only loss and tied Michigan which was a great moral victory for Paul's first year of coaching at Ohio State. On Monday, after our loss to Northwestern, Paul displayed a side of his psychology of winning which set him apart from all other coaches, as we shall see.

One of the obvious attributes of a coach is to be able to recruit and develop players of his own choice. The number of truly great football players who Paul had coached in high school, at Ohio State, or with the professional teams at Cleveland and Cincinnati are so numerous that it is difficult to separate selection from coaching. Truly it must be a combination of both. Many of the Massillon players became All Americans at universities across the country. The 1942 team at Ohio State was only a squad of 43 players. Yet 16 of them played professional football after returning from the service. Several other players on this team were also sought after to pursue a professional football career. During their years in college, there were 8 All Americans. Frequently, there were All-Pro designations as well as entrance into the Professional Football Hall of Fame. For those who are interested in the academic achievements during college, for four years a player from the 1942 team was named the outstanding Scholar-Athlete of the year in the Big Ten from all of the athletes at Ohio State in all sports. The 1944 Ohio State team that won every game and ranked behind Army that year as the best team in the nation, was an outstanding tribute to Paul Brown. He had coached the 1943 "Baby Bucks", an aggregation of players with little or no football experience except for a few players who were still in school from the 1942 team. The line for the 1944 team had largely been trained and developed by Paul. In 1944, this line, along with three outstanding backs were led by Les Horvath to an unbeaten season. Most of the 1942 members of this line were declared All-Americans along with Les. The basic ingredient of this team was Paul Brown's coaching. Paul wanted, in each of his players, courage, speed, lower body strength and the willingness and intelligence to be coached.

The comprehension of the concepts of football are fairly basic to all coaches. However, they must be tempered by each coach's innovations. These innovations are not those of unexpected surprises that overwhelm the opponents on any particular play. They are the result of studying the defenses, offenses and techniques of the opposing coaches and the qualities of his players. In any game, a knowledgeable person can often analyze the outcome of a game as football games are much like chess matches between the coaches. All of the detailed study by the head Coach, with the aid of his assistant coaches, becomes incorporated in a "game plan". During the week prior to the upcoming game, the offense and defense is geared to this game plan so the weeks and weeks spent in preparation prior to the start of the season will result in winning. Paul often remarked," You play like you practice" which could then be tempered by his guidance and innovation. If these features escaped the comprehension of a player, they were substituted by absolute obedience. Frequently, in modern day football, teams appear to be "up" or "down" emotionally for an upcoming game. Oftentimes, the blame for losing is placed on the team believing the admiring headlines they read in the newspapers about themselves and the supposed weaknesses of the opponents that results in defeat. Our 1942 team would have none of that. We were geared only to winning. We were geared only to Paul Brown.

When a spectator watches a football game, ordinarily he focuses on the ball carrier or attempts to follow the exchange of the ball in the backfield. A coach, on the other hand, has a wide field of vision which enables him to see the activity of the men on the line who are the principal reasons for the success or failure of a play. When a player misses his blocking assignment or a player makes an error in judgment, it is immediately apparent to the coach. Paul's perception in this area was extraordinary. A player who missed his assignment or used bad judgment was immediately replaced in the game. He was corrected by Paul in a manner that was quiet but mentally penetrating, not a diatribe that is so common to lesser coaches. A mental mistake was particularly intolerable to Paul Brown.

Much of a coach's time is spent developing dedication in his players. There are many methods available to a coach to develop dedication. By far the most common is one that develops the ideal that he will be a better person by being a member of a winning team. Contrary to the perceived attitudes about young people in their formative years, this method of developing a positive attitude works. During my Senior year in high school, I was very close to receiving an appointment to West Point. The attitude toward dedication that I had already developed from athletic team participation would have easily molded me in the traditions of total obedience of army officers.

Acceptable performance at one's first opportunity was an axiom of a Paul Brown team. In 1941, an All Ohio halfback was substituted as the Safety man on defense against Otto Graham and the Northwestern "Wildcats". Otto promptly threw a pass over his head for a touchdown. He was taken out of the game and never got off the bench thereafter. In 1942, I was the third string End behind Dante Lavelli and John T. White. Dante would become the most successful receiver in the National Football League, and John, who transferred to Michigan's V-12 program during the war, became an All Conference player. Both players were injured before our first game in 1942. On Tuesday, Paul walked up to me and said, "You are starting on Saturday". From that point on, except when I could not play due to injury, I remained the first string End. For people who sat in judgment of Paul Brown, these decisions were hard for them to understand. People who had no connection with the team and newspaper reporters would frequently question his judgment or compassion. They could never appreciate the forces that drove Paul Brown.

The success of any of his teams was always the play of the entire team. No single player was ever the reason for winning or losing. The greatest passer in the world needs time for his receivers to run their pass patterns. This time is provided by the offensive line. Any breakdown by the men in the line results in an incomplete pass or a quarterback sack.

Dante Lavelli, the great Hall of Fame receiver for the Cleveland Browns, remarked quite poignantly that Paul's concept of team play always disregarded the public fame and record setting performances of any of his individual players. Dante was approaching the longest individual pass catching record in the NFL when "Greasy" Neale, the coach of the Philadelphia Eagles, remarked that the only way the Browns could beat the Eagles was through the passing of Otto Graham. The Browns defeated the Eagles that Sunday without throwing one pass the entire game.

What Paul was always very concerned about was the players' safety. In 1942, the second and third team players entered the game as soon as the outcome of the game was assured to prevent useless injury. Gene Fekete, our first string fullback, led the nation in rushing yardage for most of the 42 season. If he had played more time in each game he could probably have set a record for rushing yardage which may be still standing today. Paul never paid attention to the accolades directed to individual players. Safety was much more important to Paul than any record.

With all of the details that Paul insisted upon in his coaching methodology, we were a happy team. We thoroughly enjoyed one another as well as our coaches. On trips, all of the people who were involved with the team went on the train with us. The President of Ohio State often accompanied us along with members of the faculty and friends of the university. One has only to attend a sports banquet in his community to appreciate the uniqueness of sports humor. In 1942, the Cleveland Baseball Stadium was the visitor's home field for our game with Illinois. We arrived on Friday and went directly to the stadium for our light Friday afternoon practice. In every baseball stadium, the grass is the pride of the groundskeepers. The grass must be full and luxurious and cut so that every blade is the same exact height. Our groundskeeper for the Ohio State Stadium, in Columbus, was one Tony Aguilla. He approached the Cleveland stadium groundskeepers and without batting an eye, in his full Italian accent, declared, "I'm a Tony. I take over." Every five years this team gathers together in a reunion to renew past friendships that bonded us so closely together. One of the incentives for this reunion is the pride of having been part of this team. Loran Staker, one of our four seniors had been a high school star halfback but was a fourth string halfback on this 42 team and rarely played in a game. He was always filled with the pride of having been a part of this team. Paul had always made each player feel that he was truly needed.

Paul had another quality which all of his players sensed from one time or another. His eyes seemed to convey a subliminal message to you. He was well aware as to your capabilities. The message seemed to say that you should know your capabilities and what he expected of you.

Many coaches have all or most of the above ingredients to be a successful coach. However, there was one aspect to Paul Brown that separates him from all of the others. It was something his players could recognize. Even as a young man, he had no other alternatives in his mind. He would win and only win. It was most apparent in 1941 after our loss to Northwestern. This rather shy taciturn man stood before us in the conference room the following Monday. It was not so much the remarks of criticism he made to each of us, whether we had played in the game or not, it was this concept of "only winning" that pervaded the atmosphere of this meeting. It was truly inconceivable to him that we could lose. My mother was of this nature. She had ten children, five boys and five girls. Of necessity, she raised her family always on the border of poverty. She refused all and any assistance outside of her family and had only one concept in her mind for her sons. They would be physicians and only physicians. Of the five boys, three would become Surgeons and one a dentist. The eldest son and the eldest daughter made it possible for my mother to begin fulfilling her self restricted ambition for her sons. There is much to be said for this "narrow" visionary concept for very few people in any walk of life restrict their ambitions in this manner. But it sets a man apart from all others, as it set Paul Brown apart from other coaches.

DANTE LAVELLI

Football:	Ohio State, 1942
	Ft. Bragg Bombardiers, 1943
	Cleveland Browns, 10 years
	All-Pro, 7 years
	Professional Football Hall of Fame
Education:	B.A. in Education
Career:	Professional Football
	Owner, Appliance & Furniture Store
Married:	Joy – 42 years
	Three children
Service:	Infantry – 28th Division
	"Bloody Buckets" Division

DANTE LAVELLI

Like almost all of the other players on the Ohio State 1942 team, my parents migrated from Europe in the early 1900's. They came from the small town of Manevra about 14 miles from Florence, Italy. Mom and dad really didn't know one another while they lived in Manevra. They even came to America in the Steerage of the same ship without having met. Their love affair started under the clock in Grand Central Station in New York while they were waiting for the train to take them both to Cleveland. My father was one of the handsomest men I have ever known, so it was understandable that it would be love at first sight.

Dad was first employed as a worker for the street car system in Cleveland, but, later, he moved our family to Hudson, Ohio, a small town south of Cleveland. He became a blacksmith to shoe the horses of the farmers in the surrounding area. It may sound comical but that there really is a Hudson High School to correspond to the radio program, "Jack Armstrong, the All American Boy" that was so popular with the boys and girls during the time I attended high school.

During my high school years, I played all of the major sports, football, basketball, and baseball. My high school coach contacted Notre Dame when I was a senior. Since I was Catholic, he thought that Notre Dame should be the university I should attend. Our high school was so small that there were no polls the newspapers could use to the judge the quality of our athletic talents as in the larger schools. I was "successfully" recruited by Notre Dame and even had my room assigned in Angel Hall. I was introduced to Eddie Prokopp, who would later star for the New York Yankee Football Team. He was one of the fifth string backs at Notre Dame. I knew of Eddie's ability, and this chance meeting steered me away from Notre Dame. If Eddie Prokopp were only a fifth string player, I was not one to sit on anyone's bench.

This was the year that the Ohio high school coaches insisted that Ohio State make Paul Brown the Head Coach after the departure of Francis Schmidt. With their insistence, they also promised to send their best players to Ohio State. This unusual promise also influenced the high school football referees. One of the game officials was Mike

Polarmo who thought I would be well suited to play for Paul Brown. Mr. Polarmo's recruiting and the hiring of Trevor Rees to be the freshman football coach brought me to Ohio State. My freshman year at Ohio State could well have suited a question for Ripley's "Believe It Or Not". "Name three players who would room together at Ohio State. One would win the Heisman Trophy as the most outstanding football player in the country. One would win the National Football League Super Bowl his first year as a head coach. The third would be named to the National Football League's Hall of Fame". Yes, we were roommates my freshman year—Les Horvath, Don McCafferty and myself.

My collegiate career was marred by injury, although I was the first string End with Bob Shaw for the 1942 season as a Sophomore. Just before the opening game, I was suffering with a bad charley horse in my thigh and John White, the second string end, was also injured. We were replaced in the starting line up for our opening game against Ft. Knox by Don Steinberg. Paul was pleased with his overall play and he started the next game against Indiana. However, he too was injured late in the fourth quarter of the game. By the next week, I was now well and played against Southern California. Late in the game, I went up for a pass on the one yard line and was hit in the knee by one of the defensive backs fracturing a bone. This severe injury would sideline me for the remainder of the season. Although I fractured a small bone in my foot playing professional football with the Cleveland Browns, this was the most severe injury I would ever sustain. Through the years, I had played in over 110 games for the Cleveland Browns.

My college career ended after being drafted into the Army. I was assigned to the famous 28th Division of the U.S. Army for the entire War. This division's history goes back to the Revolutionary War with its formation in Pennsylvania by Benjamin Franklin. After basic training we were transferred to various Army camps for specialized training. We were trained for sea-land assaults and direct assaults on heavily fortified positions of the enemy. This was to be our plight beginning with the invasion on to the beaches of Normandy. We continued east battling the Germans across France to Paris. We entered Paris to parade in the celebration of its return to freedom. After Paris, we fought across eastern France, across the Rhine, and finally to the defense and victory at Bastogne in the Battle of the Bulge. Throughout history our division was know as the "Bloody Buckets Division" and a more appropriate name could not have been given. From the invasion in May to the victory at Bastogne, we were in continuous combat against the cream of the German Army. At one time or another 75, 000 American soldiers fought with the 28th. One out of three of its soldiers were killed or were casualties from battle or illness. One out of five would not be returning home.

Following my discharge from service, I was recruited by the Detroit Tiger Baseball Team. I was ready to sign my contract with the Tigers, when I received a call from Fritz Heisler, an assistant coach of the newly formed Cleveland Browns in the All American League. My first love was football and nothing could stop me from the opportunity to join the Browns and my many football friends from Ohio State.

For ten years, the Cleveland Browns were the champions of professional football both with the All American League and later, after the merger, with the National Football League. The team was built around the 1942 Ohio State team and the players from other universities who were able to star against the 42 team. The National Football League has never acknowledged our outstanding records in the All American League, but, taken together with the NFL, no professional team could equal the Browns as a team or Paul Brown as a coach.

I have always known Paul Brown to be both very shy and also totally devoted to football. I don't think that anyone who has not played for him could ever fathom the depth of this dedication. There have been many coaches who were very successful and the same time very flamboyant, but not Paul. He always perceived his players as an integrated team and not as a collection of individual star athletes. Every aspect of the game had been conceived and developed by Paul. The type and temperament of the players he selected, the classroom atmosphere and play book, the progressive development of the offenses and defenses were totally Paul's. I think this was true from his beginning in coaching from Massillon to Ohio State or in professional football. Oftentimes, in the press, he was criticized for "calling all the plays" while the other teams' quarterbacks were allowed to make these decisions. Paul always felt the quarterback should not be burdened with this duty when he had so many other things to do. The basic call was Paul's and the variations could be made by the quarterback at the line of scrimmage adjusting to the defensive alignment.

Paul always abhorred bad habits such as drinking, smoking, and breaking training rules. He had less control over these aspects of the lives of professional players than at Ohio State. Oddly enough, those players who had "grown up" with Paul and there were many of us, maintained these rules naturally.

Paul, Otto Graham, MacSpeedie and I developed several passing options that were new to football and later would be copied by other teams. The most famous of these was "the come back toward the passer" option. After it appeared that a pass pattern was not going to be successful, the End would break his pass pattern and turn back toward his passer. It would take another second or so for Otto to hold the ball before passing it, but it proved a valuable addition to our offense. Another innovation that we developed was called "breaking the pass pattern". Otto had such an amazing peripheral vision to survey the entire field that we worked out this scheme on long passes. The receiver could break out of his pass pattern if he was certain he was covered and strikeout for the opposite sideline and be free to receive the pass. If this maneuver was successful, it invariably resulted in at touchdown. Lastly, we developed a novel use of the goal posts which were on the goal line in pro ball rather than ten yards back as in college football. One afternoon, when winter ice and snow often covered the area near and in the end zones, I ran a pass pattern with Otto's knowledge in which I grabbed one of the uprights of the goal post, twisted around the pole to change my direction while the defensive back slid by and was unable to cover me.

My football career with the Browns lasted ten years. I was selected All Pro seven of these years and some time later was installed in the National Professional Football Hall of Fame. I have had many, many wonderful experiences and honors. During these years, we had a streak of 29 winning games before we were beaten by the San Francisco 49ers. From 1948 through 1950, there were no rookies who were able to break into our roster. My passing catching streak of 23 games was ended in one of our games against the Philadelphia Eagles. Greasy Neale, the coach of the Eagles, was still chafing from his defeat by the Browns in their championship game in the year of the merger of the two leagues. He questioned, in the newspapers, the prowess of the Browns as an NFL "running team" in contrast to its reputation as a "passing team". Paul decided to accept the challenge. "Out the window" went my pass completion record. We beat the Eagles 7-0 without throwing a pass!

For the most part, the Browns were a happy team. The comic antics of George Ratterman, the backup quarterback to Otto Graham, are legendary. Morrie Kono, the equipment manager, had replaced a midget that Paul had hired early in the franchise. He would do imitations of Paul that would bring the team to its knees in laughter. Marian Motley, the hugh fullback, had the habit of falling asleep in his chair during our pre-practice conferences. He would often sit in the back row of chairs in the room to be less obvious to Paul. One afternoon, Paul let fly a wet towel filled with ice water into Marian's face. From then on, Marion was assigned to the front row.

Much has been said and written about the social distance Paul kept from his players. I think it is extremely important for a coach not to be too familiar with his players. It may cause many embarrassing moments, especially at the end of a player's football career. The average number of years for a pro player in the NFL is less than four years. With the Browns, there were players who had been with Paul from Ohio State and even at Massillon. Lin Houston had never known any other coach. For Lin, football began with Paul and football ended with Paul. Tommy James, except for one year after the war with Ohio State and one year with the Lions was in Paul's football family from Massillon. In every respect, Paul Brown has always been a very fair person. I don't think that he has ever made a decision where his own benefit held precedence over the good of his team. Paul Brown is a very rare person for he has lived his life by an expression of moral correctness he has always used, "Honesty."

I was introduced to Joy, my wife, early in my professional football career. She is a very beautiful perceptive woman who has had to tolerate the grandiose acclaims I have received, the overly enthusiastic business projects I have become involved in, and my frequent absences from home when games were played out of town. Since then there have been innumerable speaking engagements that also required being away from home. We have two daughters and one son. Through all of this never ending excitement for me, our marriage is in its 42nd year.

After my years in football were over, my only relationship with coaching was the All Star game in Chicago. Otto Graham was the coach for six years and I assisted him. Near the end of my years with the Browns, I started a furniture and appliance business which has been my livelihood. As I look back, professional football requires an absolute devotion, and any enterprise that takes your mind off of football will decrease your effectiveness. Football may seem to be primitive mayhem to the uninformed, but it is a very exciting and exacting game. It was a never ending thrill to have played football for Paul Brown. To the public I became know as "Glue Fingers". Paul, who felt that I repeatedly had been successful in difficult football situations, referred to me as "Mr. Clutch".

ROBIN PRIDAY

Football: Ohio State, 1942

Education: B.A. in Education – Graduated Cum Laude

Career: Secondary Education
Coaching and Teaching
Principal of Junior High School

Married: May – 37 years – Died from Cancer
Carol and Robin have two children
& sixteen grandchildren

Service: Bomber Pilot in Europe – 63 Missions
Air Force Reserve Outstanding Commander, 1946
Historian 387th Bomber Group

ROBIN PRIDAY

It is very likely that the first Priday to move to Ohio was an English emigrant, Henry Priday. He swam ashore from Lake Erie near the town of what is now Willoughby, Ohio, in the early hours of June 17th 1850. Henry was one of the few survivors of the paddle wheel steamer, "Griffith", that caught fire and sank while bound from Buffalo to Cleveland. Henry's wife and daughter, who had accompanied him from Quedgely, England, were among the 219 victims.

One can assume that Henry was my great Grandfather as he settled in the area, remarried, and sired nine children. I am sure Priday Ave. in Euclid is named after Henry or one of his offsprings. According to the author, Dwight Boyer, in his book, "True Tales of the Great Lakes", Henry in his later years continued to embellish on his version of the Giffith disaster until he became known as, "The Great Prevaricator". At any rate, it is a matter of record that my father was born in Euclid.

The wanderlust of the Priday family seemed an inherited trait as my Father moved from Euclid, Ohio to Omaha, Nebraska to Ames, Iowa, where he spent a year at Iowa State University. There he met my Mother prior to the outbreak of World War I. They were married just before he was sent overseas and when the war was over he returned to continue his quest westward to Spokane, Washington. It was in Spokane that my brother and I were born. The Great Depression suddenly arrived and my father moved his family to Columbus, Ohio, where he had been promised a job. When Roosevelt became President, a bill toward assisting people who wished to return to farming was passed and from then on my father was an ardent Democrat in a county of staunch Republicans. We had moved to the country near West Jefferson, Ohio, and I entered West Jefferson High school in 1937. Despite a small enrollment, the school included football in its sports program and I had my first opportunity to play on an organized team. During my junior and senior years, our teams were undefeated and the resulting publicity attracted the recruiting coaches at Ohio State. Gomer Jones, the great All-American Center, and Sol Maggied who was a former OSU player and now an official at some of our games initially talked with me about coming to Ohio State. When Paul Brown became Head Coach, he assigned Fritz Mackey to monitor recruiting in our area and Coach Mackey continued to encourage me to come to Ohio State. Their sincere interest made a deep impression on me.

In the Fall of 1941, I entered the Ohio State Univiersity College of Education to begin my preparation for a career in teaching and coaching. Our freshman squad included nine starters from Paul's state championship Massillon team as well as many other future outstanding players including Gene Fekete, Dante Lavelli, Bill Willis, Bill Hackett and Jack Duggar, Tommy James, Horace Gillom and George Slusser, who had transferred to OSU from Dartmouth. To put it mildly, the competition on this freshman team was intense as Paul Brown insisted on dedicated competition to bring out the best in his players. When the spring practice in 1942 arrived, those remaining Varsity players from 1941 and these fiercely competitive freshmen were joined together. By the end of spring practice, an intrasquad game was held that pitted the best of one half of these competitors against the other half. Paul wanted each of us "lean and hungry".

At the beginning of the Fall practice in 1942, the players reported in remarkably good physical condition. The rugged "two a day" drills were meticulously planned by Paul and his assistant coaches. These drills developed the additional strength, stamina and quickness that would characterize the play of this team. A very high level of mutual respect developed between the players and we became a thoroughly congenial group. Our confidence in our coaches and our experience and ability made us feel we could compete on equal terms with any team in the country.

Paul Brown was a demanding perfectionist who had little patience for mental errors or less than our best effort. He was a keen student of the football and placed great emphasis on individual techniques and team coordination. Players were expected to perform as parts of "a well oiled machine". However, he was quick to praise as he was to criticize and displayed a remarkably controlled temperament in a profession, which in recent years, has been characterized by petty tyrants and sideline "Hot Dogs". Although a strict disciplinarian, Coach Brown possessed a great sense of humor and was able to relate to his young athletes on a personal level.

One incident, in particular, remains very clear in my memory. On a bleak and rainy November afternoon, during the week we were preparing to play Michigan, Coach Brown had carefully set the stage for a trial run of a special play he had devised for this crucial game. George Slusser, a substitute halfback, but an excellent ball handler, was unobtrusively inserted into the backfield to carry the ball on a sweep to the left and then hand the ball off on a delayed reverse to Paul Sarringhaus, one of the nation's premier power running backs. Paul was to circle back from his left wingback position and receive the ball from George running "full tilt" to the right, picking up blockers and streak down the right sideline. At that time, George probably weighed all of 165 pounds and Paul Sarringhaus weighed at least 210 pounds. The combination of a muddy field which made the footing treacherous, the slippery football, and the fact that this was the first time the play had been practiced against a "live" defense resulted in George and Paul colliding head on and the ball popped loose and rolled on the ground. George had played three years at Massillon for Paul Brown and had completed his first year at Dartmouth before sacrificing a year of college eligibility to return to his coach when Paul came to Ohio State. As George picked himself up from the ground, wiped the mud from his face and eyes, he looked at Coach Brown and said, "P.B., you can take that play and stick it up your ___!" Those of us who were grouped behind Coach Brown were incredulous. No one ever talked to a coach like that, what's more Coach Brown. I fully expected the clouds to part and a bolt of lightening to strike George down before our eyes. Unbelievably, Coach Brown doubled over in laughter. When I related the experience to him many years later at our 1987 reunion, he chuckled and said, "You know, George and I had a very special relationship."

During the season, I played as the substitute Quarterback for our Captain, George Lynn, an outstanding athlete and team leader. In those days, the rules precluded coaches sending in plays from the sideline and the Quarterback actually directed the team on the field. Phil Drake and Paul Selby were the other backup Quarterbacks. We were primarily blockers but with the introduction of the T-Formation we became ball handlers and potential running backs, as well. Because of the limited substitution rules, we were also defensive backs.

Just after the United States was plunged into World War II, several of us enrolled in the Army Aviation Cadet Program. In early 1943 we were ordered into active duty. I completed pilot training in March 1944 and was assigned to a B-26 replacement training unit as a co-pilot. In July 1944, our crew flew a new B-26 to England and shortly thereafter, became part of the 387th Bomber Group(M), the first such unit to move to France following the invasion. From our bases in France, we flew missions in support of our ground forces during the most bitterly contested battles of World War II. On other occasions, we would strike deep into Germany and attack strategic targets. I checked out as a first pilot early in 1945 and completed 63 combat missions by the end of hostilities on May 8, 1945. We celebrated VE Day in an orchard near Mastricht, Holland in a tent beside our steel mat air strip.

Although I received a letter from the Green Bay Packers in the Spring of 1945, while still in France, I was eager to return to Ohio State following the War. I was discharged in September just one week before the first game of the 1945 season. We lost only two games in 1945, but it was not a satisfying experience. The absence of Paul Brown, I am sure, was a major factor. In addition, there was the lack of physical conditioning among the players who had just returned from service, insufficient practice sessions, and a lack of cohesiveness so necessary to a winning team. Late in the season, I suffered a knee injury which did not appear to be serious. In spring practice for the 1946 season, the knee was re-injured and I was forced to accept the reality that my playing days were over. Coach Bixler allowed me to serve as a student coach and elevated me to Junior Varsity Line Coach during the 1946 season. This was a great opportunity and invaluable experience for me as I had chosen teaching and football coaching to be my career.

I graduated "Cum Laude" from the College of Education in the Spring of 1947. For the next 31 years, I was deeply involved in high school coaching, teaching, and, eventually, Junior High School Administration. During that period I had the opportunity to work with some fine young people both on the field and in the classrooms. I truly believe that those particular years were the "Golden Years" of Secondary education.

May and I were married during the war, and we were blessed with a daughter just before my graduation from Ohio State. We also had a son born two years later. Jan is a graduate of Ohio State and now lives in Athens, Georgia, with a family of seven children. Our son, Robin, went to North Carolina University and now lives in Columbus, Ohio

I maintained my interest in military aviation as a member of the

Air Force Reserve. This is a demanding program with air crew members required to train at least two weekends a month and two weeks annually in a tour of active duty. In 1966, I was named the outstanding Air Craft Commander in the U.S. Air Force Reserve and was duly honored at our convention in San Francisco. Due to my increasing duties, I had to resign from the reserve when I became a Junior High School Principal in 1969.

My interest in the Air Force has provided a satisfying activity since my retirement. We organized an association about ten years ago to keep in touch with one another. We now have over 200 members who receive timely newsletters and plan frequent reunions. A spinoff from this activity, with an OSU connection, was my effort to have some recognition of Don Scott's athletic and military achievements. Don was an All-American Quarterback in 1940 and was a member of our 387th Bomber Group. He was very involved in the training and development of this Bomber Group. Don was killed during the War. At the ceremony of naming the aviation field at Ohio State, The Don Scott Airfield, a plaque was placed in the administration building of the airfield by Don's commanding officer which reads, "As a fitting commemoration of his life and service". At the persuasion of Jack Graf, one of Don's teammates and the Varsity "O" Alumni Association, a display case of Don's athletic and military memorabilia are displayed.

Another project that is especially enjoyable is serving on our committee that organizes our five year football reunions. Web Schneider and Gene Fekete and I plan and develop the details for each reunion that are always rewarding successes. Our planning for our 50th Reunion in 1992 is already on its way.

As part of my plans for retirement in 1978, May and I built a home in the country on a portion of our family farm that President Roosevelt had aided my father in acquiring. It is an extensive recreational facility that Don Steinberg likens to a Boy Scout Camp complete with a swimming pool, activities building, play areas, etc. in addition to our home. It is a great place for summer socializing and year-round country living. Unfortunately, May became a victim of Lung Cancer and enjoyed our new home for only seven years. In 1985, I married Carol, a lovely woman with four children. Between us we have sixteen grandchildren so the recreational facilities are always being used in the summer.

In retrospect, being a part of the 1942 Ohio State Football team was one of the great learning experiences of my life. Certainly my philosophy of coaching and teaching was greatly influenced by Paul Brown and his assistants. The comradeship which developed among our squad members continues to this day and the bonds which were formed become increasingly meaningful, "How Firm Thy Friendship, Ohio".

A PAUL BROWN
FOOTBALL TEAM

On the first day of practice in the fall of 1942, we gathered in the conference area of the dressing room for our first meeting with Paul. This conference area is a rather large room with rows of chairs that have a writing surface on one arm which are often used in school classrooms. This area is on the second floor of the most imposing stadium in Football. He welcomed us but there was no pep talk or "spiritual incantations" in his approach to the coming season. Each player received his playbook in which was to be written the description of our activities for the year. It was a large blue looseleaf notebook with thick substantial covers and filled with about fifty pages of blank paper. As Paul spoke of the fundamentals, we were expected to take notes on the points he would emphasize about a particular block or tackle. Each day he would add a new offensive play or defensive alignment. These sessions were as detailed as any lectures we would have in our college courses. He would insert special phraseology to emphasize speed, execution, or dedication as they applied to each of these fundamentals. He described, with added emphasis, the objective of each new play. As I look back on these meetings, it is now obvious that he was, not only describing the details of our offenses and defensive techniques, he was inserting a part of himself into each of us. We never had a pep talk the entire season except before our opening game against Ft. Knox. All he said was, "I don't know how good a team you are, but I don't know one that is better."

The first day or so of practice we were fitted with our practice and game uniforms. Newspaper reporters and photographers from the university and area newspapers introduced us to the public. Photographs were taken in a variety of poses such as stance, running, pass catching, etc. The expected first team, the group pictures of the players in the same position, and individual standing and action shots were taken for future use. Except for very special circumstances determined by Coach Brown, this was the end of our contact with the media for the season. One may question the usefulness of this policy, but it was very

Buckeye Plot Trouble

COACH PAUL BROWN attributes precision to part of the success of his Ohio State football team, which today ranks as the No. 1 team of the country by the nation's sports writers. With practice togs on, members of the team are shown studying formations.—(Associated Press Wirephoto.)

From Seattle, Washington newspaper

THE CONFERENCE
BEFORE PRACTICE

understandable to us as Paul guided us under his total leadership. In our present day of unlimited self expression, it may be difficult for one to visualize this type of discipline but it is absolutely necessary in developing the concept of "team". I am sure from his past experiences, he wished to keep away any misunderstandings that so easily arise concerning newspaper comments of coaching decisions or a player's progress. There was only one exception to his rules concerning contact with the media. Paul had developed a very close relationship with Paul Hornung, a sports reporter for the Columbus Dispatch. I believe that their personal friendship was of mutual benefit for Paul could honestly express his feeling to Paul Hornung and Paul Hornung could also bring situations to Paul's attention that might be otherwise misconstrued.

Before we returned to the university to begin fall practice each of us received a letter from Coach Brown that set the tone for what would be expected of each of us. Paul Matus has saved this letter for over fifty years. Being physically prepared to participate in the rigors of two a day practices for the first two or three weeks, and being prepared to accept the rules that Coach Brown laid down for us were stated in this letter. One had no need to read between the lines.

August 14, 1942

To All Candidates for the 1942 Ohio State University Football Team:

This notice represents an official invitation to you to report for football, at the Stadium, Sept. 5th, at 8:30 A.M. I would advise you to get to Columbus the preceding day.

The morning of Sept. 5th will be spent fitting uniforms (both game and practice). I must personally approve all fitting of suits—you must absolutely feel that you are equipped to do your best. We provide you with the best equipment money can buy, and we want to be better for it. Dr. Duffee will give you your physical examination just before you start to be fitted up.

Lunch will be served at 11:30 A.M. at the training table in the Ohio Union. This will be the first meal served. This will be an hour earlier than usual because we want a full afternoon for photographers.

On Sunday, Sept.6, at 1:30 P.M. we will meet as a squad to distribute our notebooks and to get organized for our dressing room procedures. Practice will start on Monday, Sept. 7, 1942. You are to be dressed and in your seat in the conference room at 9:30 A.M. and 3 P.M. daily.

We will have twelve days in which we practice twice daily. This will leave us five days of "once a day" work as we taper off for the Camp Knox game. On Sunday afternoons of Sept 13th and 20th, we will take hikes. We'll fight it out, for better for worse, as just one solid group.

We are faced will a long and most difficult schedule. A great experience awaits you–you must be at your best, both physically and mentally. It is absolutely imperative that you work out daily. If you report out of condition you simply do not represent our type of man–and we cannot use you. You have so much at stake–plan for it–enjoy it–look it right in the eye knowing you have gone "all out".

Training regulations will be enforced exactly as you know them. If you feel you cannot carry out these rules please do not report this fall. For the next three months we will dedicate everything to the success of our team. As a coaching staff, we dedicate our living for the next few months to the success of the Ohio State football team. We hope it means just as much to you.

> *Sincerely,*
> *Paul E. Brown*
> *Director of Football*

Two-a-day practices meant practice for about two hours in the morning and two hours in the afternoon. There is a marked difference between physical conditioning in 1942 when players were expected to be able to play the entire game if necessary and conditioning as it is known today with the two platoon system. Each player had to be trained in practice to respond on both offense and defense with an almost conditioned reflex during a game. The correct response in each situation during a game is required to be almost instantaneous. These responses could only be developed through individual intelligence, repetition, and devotion to your coaches during practice. I recall on some very warm days in September losing as much as 7 or more pounds of sweat in a single practice. One of the fine qualities of Paul's coaching was his ability to know when to end a practice session. Each day began in the conference room where time was devoted to the schedule of the day's activities and the new plays and formations would be presented to us. It was very important for us to know the entire play and what each

THE COACHING STAFF

Treveor Rees, Carol Widdoes, Fritz Mackey, Head Coach Paul Brown, Hugh McGranahan, Paul Bixler and Fritz Heisler.

play was expected to accomplish as the timing of each player's action was essential for success. What started out as simple in our opening sessions, soon became more and more complicated as we learned dozens of offensive plays using multiple formations to be altered by the number of defensive players opposing us on the line of scrimmage.

As the Saturday for the first game of the season neared, the practices were held only in the afternoon. School was about to begin and the only time available would be in the afternoon starting at 4:00 o'clock. Punctuality was an absolute rule as the time to accomplish the daily schedule was restricted to the late afternoon. Almost every evening, Paul and his assistant coaches would meet to prepare for the next day and to evaluate the progress being made by the team and the individual players. The starting team that was selected very early in the spring carried into the fall pre-season practices. However, there was a constant motivation devise by Paul for the members of the second, third and fourth string to challenge the first stringers for their positions. There was no other criteria for a starting player than to be the best in his position. This competition was necessary since injuries were so common during the season. It was of utmost importance that there would be no loss of effectiveness with substitution, for whatever reason, during a game. Oftentimes during a season, a team may lose a game and the excuse is often given that a star player or two were injured and were unable to play. In Paul's self discipline the "team" was the primary consideration. The loss of any player for a particular game was so minimized. The only exception was our game in 1942 against Wisconsin when most of the team was devastated by gastroenteritis. Rarely, would Paul laud any of his players individually. It was always the play of the entire team that occupied his attention.

Football teams are never composed of only eleven players and a few additional players who enter the game as substitutes due to injury or special situations. A team is largely composed of players who practice religiously day in and day out, in the rain, in the cold, and never or rarely have an opportunity to play in an actual game. They are an essential part of every team and challenge the first string in scrimmages to prepare for the upcoming game. Everyone is physically and mentally involved in this preparation. For those players who would not be playing in an actual game, the practice is jokingly referred to as "Character Building". But character building, it was.

The information concerning the upcoming opponents comes from scouting reports made by the assistant coaches. They attend the opposing team's games prior to our scheduled game with them. They study their offenses and defenses. They evaluate the strengths, the weaknesses, the speed and the playing tendencies of individual players. This information is gathered together in the scouting reports that are given to the team in written form with appropriate diagrams at the first practice on Monday. The usual reports are about four to six pages long, except for our scouting report about Michigan. This scouting report was almost sixteen pages long! Mondays, usually light practice days, are detailed discussion days preparing for the remainder of the week. The next three days were filled with intense calisthenics, body contact drills, and scrimmages to refine our offense and defense for the coming game on Saturday.

Our first game of the season was against a service team from Ft. Knox. Except for the starting eleven, the rest of the team had gone on to the field. Coach Brown went over the first offensive plays we would call if we won the coin toss at the beginning of the game, or which defenses we would use if we were to kickoff to the opposing team. This, he said, enables our coaches in the press box to determine the offenses and defenses that our opponents would be using. He ended this session by remarking about not knowing how good we were, but did not know a team that was better. There was little frivolity or expressions of over confidence from any of the players as we walked down the steel staircase to the field. There was just a very sober buildup of adrenaline.

ROBERT FRYE

Football:	Ohio State, 1942
Education:	B.S. in Education
Career:	Secondary Education and Coaching Several of his teams were high school state champions.
Married:	Maxine Two children & six grandchildren
Service:	Field Artillery in South Pacific Forward Observer Multiple Island Invasions

BOB FRYE

The similarity between the lives of many of the members of the 1942 Ohio State team is almost uncanny. It seems more than co-incidental that after our championship 42 season, our service careers, our post service completions of our educations, and our occupations that we would so often match one another. Bill Vickroy and I were both forward observers in the artillery in the South Pacific. We participated in several island invasions and also in the recovery of the Philippines from the Japanese. There was no question that completing our educations after service was the top priority in our lives along with marrying our high school sweethearts. Robin Priday, Bill Durtschi, Gene Fekete, Cy Lipaj, and I all returned to teaching and coaching in high school. In my case, I had attempted an ill-fated business partnership after discharge from service before Hal Dean induced me to return to the university to complete my degree in education. Our coaching careers often closely resembled Paul Brown's winning statistics at Massillon. As for myself, I would attribute much of my success and happiness to Ohio State and Ohio State football under Paul Brown.

My sister, brother and I were raised in Crestline, Ohio, a small town just west of Mansfield. We were a Class B high school with a total enrollment of only 200-300 students. In spite of our small size we had a good sports program that included football, basketball and baseball. My senior year we were undefeated and named the "mythical" State Champions of all the Class B schools in the state. As a halfback, I was one of the leading scorers in the state.

Having achieved some degree of notoriety, I was recruited for Ohio State by Jimmy Hull, Ohio State's All Conference basketball player and Ernie Godfrey. My Freshman year in 1940 found the football program very disorganized. It was probably one of the best choices ever made by Ohio State to decide to hire Paul Brown to be the Head Coach. It only took a few months after his arrival to see that disorganization change into an organized and disciplined administration on and off the field.

One of my fondest memories was being a member of the Ohio State 1942 team. Coming from a small town, I could never even imagine the treatment we received whenever we traveled to another university. The hotels we stayed in were like a dream to me. However, the most memorable occasion, was our being named National Champions. My only regret occurred in our seventh game against Pittsburgh when I fractured my ankle which ended my athletic career.

Shortly after the end of the season, I entered the service. I spent three years with the 96th Division as a Forward Observer in the South Pacific. We fought in Leyte and Mindanao in the Philippines and Okinawa in the Ryukyus. After the end of the War, I returned to Ohio where I worked a short time in a business partnership. During a trip to the west coast to see some of my friends, Hal Dean convinced me to enroll at Southern Cal and complete my education and obtain my degree in education. We had been roommates and fraternity brothers at Ohio State. Hal was still playing football for the Los Angeles Rams while he was completing his master's degree at Stanford in oil geology. He contacted a friend of his at Southern Cal whom he had know from his hometown of Wooster, Ohio. His friend convinced me to return to complete my degree. It took all of twenty minutes to do so.

After my graduation in 1951, I began my teaching career in secondary education and also coached the football team and track team in Yuma City, California. I think it was homesickness that drew me back to Ohio. My teaching and coaching career continued as the assistant football coach at Mansfield Senior High. Mansfield Senior was a state class A powerhouse who played in the Greater Ohio conference against the best teams in the state. In 1958, I was offered and accepted a new challenge. St. Peter's in Mansfield had built a new high school and wanted to start a new sports program. For a high school that had never had a sports program, we slowly began to attract the attention of the boys in the high school. We started with blackboard conferences reminiscent to my days with Paul Brown and established the same rigorous rules that Paul had used at Ohio State. We had over 600 students at St. Peter's so we qualified as a class A school and scheduled teams like Mansfield Senior. It only took us two years to establish a winning basketball record. In 1968 we became the first team in Mansfield to ever win a state championship. During the span of years that I coached basketball we had a record of 259 wins and 65 losses and three of my players reached All American status in college. I finally quit coaching in 1971 and stayed on as the Athletic Director until 1984. I have received many honors during my coaching career which included being named to the Ohio High School Coaches Hall of Fame.

Paul Brown looking over Bob Frye's coaching play book.

The crowning award was just last year when St. Peter's High School named their basketball arena in my honor, the Robert Frye Spartan Gymnasium. The journalism class at St. Peter's sponsored a trip to Cincinnati to video tape an interview with Paul Brown and myself at the Cincinnati Bengal offices. Paul was very gracious and complemented the students on their efforts to place my career in closer relationship with Paul Brown. I shall always cherish this video tape as it brought a clearer understanding of player and coach to the students. After 50 years of success in sports and teaching, I am sure I owe most of it to my loving wife Maxine. Her patience and raising our family during my frequent absences were the real reasons for my success. We have two children and six grandchildren. We spent as much time as possible with our children in Williamsburg, Virginia and when we are not traveling, I wile away the hours at a little cottage we have at Lake Mifflin just outside of Mansfield. It is a great place to boat, fish and just plain loaf.

As a closing remark I believe my greatest disappointment was the breakup of the 1942 team at Ohio State due to the war. We were developing a true football dynasty. This may be an over-emphasis to many people, but to a man who has spent a lifetime in playing and coaching it is very important.

THE ROBERT FRYE
SPARTAN GYMNASIUM

Named after Coach Robert Frye on November 24, 1990, in recognition of his dedication to the St. Peter's Athletic Programs and School and in gratitude for the statewide respect and honor he brought to our school and parish community.

THE 1942 FOOTBALL SEASON

The fall of 1942 found the entire United States engaged in a military and industrial expansion that made all previous war efforts pale by comparison. Nine months had passed since Pearl Harbor. The naval forces in the Pacific were already beginning to turn the tide of battle in favor of the United States. Major naval engagements had begun to cripple the Japanese Navy. The island invasions of the South Pacific were already progressing back toward the Philippines. Mammoth convoys were carrying military supplies across the Atlantic to help England and Russia stem the Nazi advances. The invasion of western North Africa to establish a second front against Italy and Germany had begun.

At home, the growth of the military services was as phenomenal as the conversion to a total war effort by the American factories. Gigantic Army, Navy and Air Force training facilities were planned, built and activated within months. Many of the training bases had 50,000 or more men in training simultaneously. There were camps organized for infantry training, tank training, artillery and a host of other activities that had to support the soldiers, sailors, and air force in battle. The camps were often started with only broom sticks for the infantry, but they were quickly equipped with rifles and all the other needed equipment. This conversion and expansion was true in all of the divisions of the services. Many of these camps supported athletic activities to entertain these troops during the course of their stay at the military instillation. The principal sport was football.

Except for voluntary enlistments, the draft had not yet reached into the student bodies of the universities. Just as the national industrial complex was gearing to a total war effort, the universities across the nation were developing service training programs to assure trained personnel for the very complex requirements of the services. Men and women who had the educational background for these particular skills and knowledge needed by the services, were sent to universities as enlisted men or officers.

In order to maintain a national cohesiveness, sports, football in particular, were continued and often enhanced. Football programs were encouraged at the major universities and service football teams were organized to entertain the stateside troops at the larger military bases. The playing personnel of these service teams were frequently current college players, recently graduated players, or professional football players. Oftentimes change of duty papers were delayed until the end of the season on many of the service teams. Or, at least, that was the frequently heard rumor. The most prestigious of these service teams was the Iowa Seahawks coached by the legendary Bernie Bierman of the University of Minnesota, now Colonel Bernie Bierman. The Iowa Seahawks were scheduled to play all of the Big Ten teams as well as Notre Dame. The Seahawks had gathered together a formidable number of college stars and All Americans as well as a goodly number of the players from the Green Bay Packers.

Nonetheless, the Big Ten and Notre Dame in 1942 were not to be overwhelmed or out-manned by this service team. By an unusual coincidence, almost every Big Ten team, Notre Dame, and Georgia were "loaded". All of these teams proved to be the major teams seeking national recognition as the number one team in the country. Many of the legendary players and coaches from each of these universities who are still revered today for their athletic prowess and coaching were competing in the 1942 season. Almost every Big Ten coach was quoted as saying that his team had the best personnel that he had ever assembled in a single season.

September, 1942 was not only the start of the football season, but this month also marked the end of the baseball season and the World Series. The enthusiasm of the men and boys across America and overseas was reaching a frenzied pitch by the New York Yankees vs. St. Louis Cardinals World Series. Here, too, the playing personal of both teams were outstanding with players still cherished in the memories of people today. The Yankees won the first game and then were overwhelmed by the Cardinals by four straight wins. The series was barely over when the attention of the sports writers filled the newspapers with accounts of the coming football season.

Before the season even started, the sports writers of every city in the mid-west and Chicago were evaluating the players and their teams for possible rankings and recognition during the coming season. Coach Bierman had left for the service after five unbeaten seasons and two national championships at Minnesota. Most of the previous year's players were returning to The University of Minnesota for the 1942 season led by Bill Daley, their All American halfback. It was the opinion by most of the sportswriters that Minnesota would repeat as the champions of the Big Ten.

Across the border from Minnesota at Madison, Wisconsin, Harry Stuhldreher had vastly improved his personnel from the previous season. Stuhldreher had been raised in Massillon, Ohio, and was one of the famous "Four Horsemen of Notre Dame" under Knute Rockne. Among his starting eleven were Elroy "Crazy Legs" Hirsch, Pat Harder and Dave Schriner, the All Big Ten End from the previous year. All of them were of All American caliber and to this day are remembered in the annals of the University of Wisconsin football. They also had an outstanding line and made no bones about considering themselves as the number one team in the country.

Bob Zuppke had just retired as coach of the University of Illinois and had turned the coaching reins over to Bob Eliot. This team would establish themselves as contenders very early in the season against Minnesota when Alex Agase, their All American Guard, would create football history by scoring two touchdowns as a lineman and beat Minnesota. This game was no fluke. Illinois had an excellent team with personnel equal to any in the Big Ten. One had only to see their line opening holes for their Olympic class sprinters at halfback, to realize the talent on this team.

Michigan's reputation as The Champions of the West continued into the 1942 season. Fritz Crisler had again brought together a squad of championship caliber. As usual his line was the envy of the conference centered around Merv Pregelman, John Franks, and Al Wistert. His backfield was equally talented with Bob Chappius, Al Wiese, Tom Kuzma, and John White's younger brother, Paul. During the previous five seasons, his only nemeses were Minnesota and the 1941 tie against the Ohio State Buckeyes.

Bo McMillan, the Indiana coach, was extremely confident that he had, in 1942, the best team that he had ever assembled. Over half of his starting eleven were players that everyone agreed were outstanding. Billy Hillenbrand would continue to demonstrate his football talents for years in the National Football League. Pete Pihos and Lou Saban are enshrined in the annals of Indiana football and professional football for their outstanding playing and coaching.

At Northwestern was the indomitable Otto Graham. Wherever he played, whether at Northwestern or with the Cleveland Browns, he brought his teams to greatness. One could make a strong argument that he was the greatest passer and quarterback in the history of all of football. When Paul Brown began to develop the personnel for the first Cleveland Brown team, it was Otto Graham who headed the list of players he wished to sign. As a young man, he was strikingly handsome, had intelligence, the passing arm and the field of vision that are almost unique in football history.

Purdue and Iowa were the only teams in the Big Ten who did not have the caliber of teams to compete effectively in the 1942 season. Nevertheless, Iowa would figure prominently in the choice of who would be National Champion.

Ohio State was the one team that the sports writers had difficulty with in predicting their performance in the coming season. The Massillon High School coach, Paul Brown, was now in his second year season. Moreover he was facing the likes of coaches whose national reputations were the best in the business. His one loss, one tie, first season was thought to be filled with good fortune except for the Michigan game in 1941. This Michigan powerhouse that had decimated Ohio State the year before 40-0, had to come from behind late in the last quarter even to gain a tie. The returning players for Ohio State were very reputable players and the additions from the freshman squad were outstanding. But still, they had the lightest line in the conference. Les Horvath and Paul Sarringhaus were equal to the backfield stars of other conference teams, but Gene Fekete, a sophomore, and George Lynn, the team's Captain were unknown factors. The best that could be said, before the season began, was that Ohio State was the dark horse of the Big Ten.

The sports writers had decided not to rank the Iowa Seahawks in the national rankings as they were a team whose line was formed from players from Minnesota and the Green Bay Packers. Their backfield and Ends featured Kutner, an All American End from Texas, Forest Evashevski, the great Michigan blocking back, and Dick Fischer and Jim Langhurst, star halfbacks from Ohio State.

Just before the season opened, Bob Zuppke would coach his last game, the College All Stars against the Chicago Bears, at Soldier's Field in Chicago. The Bears finally won the game against the spirited All Stars 21-0.

The predictions for the coming season were printed, the College All Star vs. Chicago Bears game was played, and now the actual season was to begin. Returning to Ohio State from the 1941 team were 11 lettermen. Of these, there were eight players from the starting 1941 team and three sophomores, Bill Willis, Gene Fekete, and Dante Lavelli. From all of the pre-season prognostications, unmeasured was the speed that Paul Brown emphasized in his concepts of football. Unmeasured was the physical conditioning, the physical talents, and the intelligence of the individual players that composed the 1942 Ohio State University football team. Most of the players had come from the rough and tumble Northern and Eastern parts of Ohio. They were molded into the finest team ever to represent a university in the entire history of football.

The first Saturday of the season was Sept. 27th. The already unquestionably formidable Iowa Seahawks were just able to squeak by Otto Graham and his Northwestern Wildcats 20-13. Notre Dame, the 1941 National Champions, were tied by Wisconsin 7-7. Minnesota, as expected, ran roughshod over the Pittsburgh Panthers 50-7 and Ohio State opened against a very poorly prepared Ft. Knox service team 59-0. The first team played only the first half, but Ft. Knox made no first downs, and were held to just 14 yards rushing against 440 yards rushing by Ohio State.

The next weekend was characteristic of the entire season. Minnesota lost to the Iowa Seahawks 7-6 by fumbling the ball on the one yard line in the last minute of the game. The highly vaunted Notre Dame team that was tied by Wisconsin the week before, lost to Georgia and Frankie Sinkwich 13-6. Northwestern beat Texas in an intersectional game, 3-0. Indiana kicked off to Ohio State who scored on their first possession. Scoring by Ohio State on our first possession was a characteristic of the team the entire season. Gene Fekete scored three touchdowns and two extra points to lead the Buckeyes to a 31-21 victory. Our total offense was 450 yards in this game, but, nevertheless, the winning margin was not achieved until the last quarter when conditioning and speed spelled the difference in the ninety degree weather.

The third weekend of the season featured Michigan and the Iowa Seahawks. Michigan was convincingly defeated by the Seahawks 24-16. Bierman continued to triumph over Crisler. Alex Agase, the All American guard from Illinois captured the newspaper headlines by scoring two touchdowns as a lineman against Minnesota and handed them their second loss 20-13. Agase recovered a fumble in the Minnesota end zone and also had actually stolen the ball out of the grasp of a Minnesota back and then ran the ball into the end-zone for a touchdown, his second of the day. Notre Dame with such football greats as Bertelli, Rymkus, Yonaker, Evans, and Crieghton Miller re-established their winning ways by defeating Stanford 27-0. Stanford's coach was the famous Marcie Swartz, the legendary Notre Dame halfback. Ohio State's opponent that weekend was Southern California. I had injured my shoulder against Indiana but by this time Dante Lavelli had recovered from his injuries that he sustained prior to the start of the season. California was out to avenge their defeat from the previous season but the offensive prowess of Ohio State was again in evidence with a total of 442 yards gained equally divided between running and passing. Bob Shaw and Dante Lavelli were among the best receivers in the country and Sarringhaus, Horvath, and Tommy James complimented the running ability of Gene Fekete. Our victory over Southern Cal 28-12 was marred by Dante's severe knee injury that would sideline him for the rest of the year. I can still visualize the play as Dante went high in the air on a crossing pattern on the Southern California's one yard line and was tackled by two defensive backs while he was still in the air. He held on to the ball in spite of his excruciating injury which tore the distal lateral epicondyle of his left femur. This would be the only serious injury that Dante would sustain through his outstanding professional career of ten years with the Cleveland Browns.

Ohio State had captured the imagination of the nation's sports writers. This previously unheralded team was now rated as the number one team in the nation. Of the first ten teams in the poll, four teams were from the Big Ten. Gene Fekete, as a fullback, was the leading rushing back in the country. The linemen were gaining more and more attention especially Lin Houston, Bill Willis, and Chuck Csuri. Bob Shaw had no equal in the conference and all were emerging as All Americans. Bill Vickroy, our Center, would be named All Conference and Hal Dean, who would have an outstanding career with the Los Angeles Rams, was the other guard with Lin Houston. Whoever was not injured at the other End completed a formidable line that exemplified Paul Brown's style of football—speed and execution.

The fourth week of the season featured Notre Dame against the Iowa Seahawks. Notre Dame routed the highly acclaimed Seahawks

28-0. Bernie Bierman was quoted as saying that the score was a fluke and it would not happen again. Ohio State had an easy time against Purdue winning 26-0. Purdue had 14 yards rushing and one first down against the Buckeyes 301 yards and 22 first downs.

Paul Brown's winning record as a coach was now being heralded. His coaching record through 1941 was 103 wins, 9 loses, and 4 ties. In his nine years as head coach at Massillon High School, he had only 7 loses and 6 of them occurred in his first three years. It was more and more evident that all of the accolades proclaimed by his supporters were actually true. Any uncomplimentary remarks by the press or other coaches were quickly dismissed.

The next weekend Ohio State faced Northwestern who had handed the Buckeyes their only defeat in 1941. Ohio State won easily 20-6. The offense was now averaging 431 yards per game. Minnesota continued their dominance over Michigan defeating them 16-14. Only Ohio State was undefeated which, in itself, was remarkable compared to the see-saw records of the other Big Ten teams. Throughout the rest of the country only Georgia and Alabama seemed to be on a par with these teams. Iowa Seahawks and Indiana played to a standoff until the fourth quarter when Indiana's defense crumbled and Iowa scored four touchdowns overwhelming Billy Hillenbrand, Pete Pihos and Lou Saban and company 26-6. Michigan returned to winning by defeating Illinois 28-14.

Tragedy struck Ohio State against Wisconsin. The night before the game in Madison and throughout the afternoon of the game, dysentery struck almost the entire team. Players were either too sick to play or had to leave the game repeatedly to relieve their discomfort. While Ohio State was laid low by illness, Wisconsin was at its best. Elroy Hirsch, Pat Harder, Dave Schriener, and company won convincingly 17-7. The coaches and sports writers dropped Ohio State to sixth and now featured Georgia as number one led by Frankie Sinkwich of Youngstown, Ohio.

That Monday's conference before the start of practice demonstrated Paul Brown's passion. It was inconceivable to him that his team should ever lose, no matter the circumstances. Then he proceeded to talk about November. "This is the month", he said, "that separates good football teams from truly great football teams. We will have cold days in which to practice, and we will have rain and snow. Regardless of the circumstances, the great teams show their "Blue Steel" in

November." He made several changes in the first string lineup for our game against Pittsburgh. Don McCafferty would start at one of the Tackle positions and I returned to one of the End positions. I don't know how much it mattered, but when we were returning on the train to Columbus from Wisconsin, I was sitting by myself in the coach car feeling a little unhappy when Paul sat down next to me. "What's the matter, Don?" he asked. "You know I could have played today", I answered. "Yes, I know, " he said, and then rose and returned to talk with his staff.

The Ohio State-Pittsburgh game was really no contest as the Buckeyes rolled up 507 yards of offense with the first team playing only the first half. Gene Fekete ran 84 yards for a touchdown from the line of scrimmage early in the first half and State went on to win 59-19. Wisconsin must have been still celebrating their win over Ohio State the previous week as they were beaten by Iowa 6-0.

There were only three more weeks in the season with Ohio State facing Illinois at the giant Cleveland Stadium. Michigan faced Notre Dame and Wisconsin played Northwestern. After losing to the University of Iowa the previous week, Wisconsin trailed Northwestern until the last minute of the game when they scored to win 20-19. The Michigan team devastated Notre Dame 32-20 and set the stage for the conference championship showdown against Ohio State the next week in Columbus. The stadium in Cleveland for the Ohio State-Illinois game was packed with every seat filled, 72,000 spectators. They had come from all over Northwestern Ohio to see their personal selection of Paul Brown, the coach of the Ohio State team. The game would fulfill every opinion that they had of Paul's genius. They were not disappointed. The first quarter began with Illinois kicking off to Ohio State. Tommy James received the kickoff and promptly ran the ball across the Illinois goal line for a touchdown. Then Ohio State kicked off to Illinois. After three plays they were forced to punt. Again, Tommy James received the punt and again ran the ball back across the Illinois goal line for another touchdown. Ohio State had two touchdowns in the first three minutes of the game. By the time the quarter was only five minutes old, the score was Ohio State 20 Illinois 0. Illinois was devastated, experiencing the worse defeat of their season 44-20. I remember the Illinois tackle who faced me on defense during the first quarter. He asked from across the line of scrimmage, "What are you guys doing?" "Just watch," I replied. Thus the stage was set for our coming encounter with Michigan for the conference championship.

The preparations for the game against Michigan were similar to the previous weeks except for a decided increase in intensity in almost every phase of our practices. On Monday, at 4 o'clock sharp, we gathered in the conference room. The assistant coaches handed out the Michigan scouting reports which were at least twice as detailed as any of the others. Paul went through the report and commented on their defensive alignments that they would probably use against us and also their offensive formations and plays. He listed our offensive plays that would be best to use against the defenses that were outlined. He also commented at length about the defenses we would use against the Michigan offense. As I would start at the left end position, I carefully studied the Michigan offense, and made special notes to myself to be prepared for the different offensive sets that Michigan would use. Paul particularly emphasized the "buck-lateral" series that was designed to take advantage of an overly adventurous End. As a play in this series would begin, it would appear that the back receiving the ball from the Center would be exposed to an onrushing End. This would be the undoing of such a penetrating move. A pulling guard or blocking back could throw a block on the End and expose the defensive Halfback to the entire interference coming around the end of the line leading the ball carrier. It was essential to be able to recognize this formation, and stay "in your own back yard". I still cherish this play book which we had started at the beginning of the season outlining the offensive plays and defensive alignments that Paul determined would be most successful against each team we opposed.

After the conference on Monday, and on each of the successive afternoons that week, there was a progressive increase in the intensity of practice with body contact drills and scrimmages through Thursday afternoon. It was essential that our play execution during practice be as close to game conditions as possible. It was highly improbable that Tommy James would be able to play against Michigan as he had injured his shoulder against Illinois. During this week, like all of the others, there were no distractions. Our one and only purpose was to beat Michigan on Saturday.

The Ohio State stadium was packed with spectators sitting in the aisles after all the seats were filled. With gas rationing at its strictest, thousands of people must have used all of their gas ration stamps for a month to go to the game. No one was disappointed for this game had everyone on the edge of his seat for almost the entire game. Bob Shaw demonstrated his All American caliber by taking a pass away from three Michigan defenders and then broke away from them and raced down the sideline to score a touchdown. This pass play covered sixty

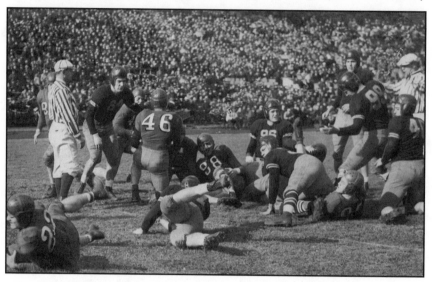

Ohio State vsIowa Seahawkss Horvath scoring a TD.

yards.Two other passes, one from Horvath to Sarringhaus, and, the other, from Sarringhaus to Horvath resulted in Ohio State's other two touchdowns. Michigan, on the other hand, fumbled twice in the fourth quarter to place the game out of the reach of the Wolverines. Ohio State was now the sole champion of the Big Ten Conference having played one more game than Wisconsin.

The weather for our last game of the season against the Iowa Seahawks was ideal, in contrast, to the weather for our game against Michigan that was rather cool, overcast and misty. Bierman had remarked that his team had not lost to a Big Ten team and was confident that it would not happen on Saturday. Lt. Trevor Rees, our Freshman coach under Paul, had entered the naval service and was now the assistant coach to Bernie Bierman. Coach Bierman was convinced that he could beat Ohio State if he could stop Gene Fekete from overwhelming his defensive line. Trevor tried to convince Coach

Bierman that it would be a mistake to try to control Ohio State's offense by stopping the running of Gene Fekete, but Bierman refused to consider Trevor's opinion. If Ohio State had played well against other opponents this season, the team was superb against the Seahawks. I vividly recall one end sweep that was recalled by the referee after it had gained thirty yards. Paul decided to run the same play again after the penalty was assessed. Exactly the same result occurred. The movie pictures of these two plays were so similar that one would assume that the play was run twice in the movie. Our blocking, tackling, and timing was absolutely perfect. After the game, Coach Bierman remarked that he had never seen such overall team speed in a collegiate football team before. Ohio State won by a convincing 42-10 score against a Seahawk team that had defeated every other team in the Big Ten.

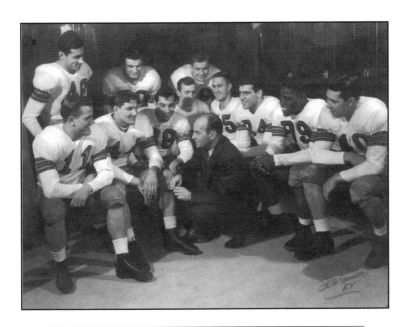

OHIO STATE UNIVERSITY
1942 National Champions
Don Steinberg, Chuck Csuri, Lin Houston, George Lynn, Gene Fekete, Paul Sarringhaus, Les Horvath, Bill Vickroy, Hal Dean, Bill WIllis, Bob Shaw and Paul Brown.

The season was now over and we had become a Paul Brown team in every respect. Paul, who rarely, if ever, made a flowery remark about any of his teams was quoted as saying this was a great and outstanding squad. We received numerous ovations of many kinds, but the outstanding crown of our efforts was being declared the 1942 National Champions for 1942 by all the coaches and newspaper polls. Every player on the starting team received recognition as an outstanding player in the Big Ten Conference. Lin Houston was voted a consensus All American by all of the polls. Bob Shaw and Chuck Csuri were also named to many All American teams. Gene Fekete was included as the first string Fullback on the All American team by radio announcer, Bill Stern. He was one of the top ten players considered for the Heisman Trophy. Bob Jabbusch was selected by the Chicago Tribune for its All Sophomore team.

The Freshman team that was coming up to the varsity the next year promised a continuation of our 1942 effort. Lou, "the Toe", Groza of the Cleveland Browns and Horace Gillam, the great punter for the Browns and a host of freshmen would be coming to challenge the varsity. We had only one starting senior on the 1942 team, but under Paul Brown's rules, the best player would be started in every position regardless of a players previous year's status. This growing dynasty was not to be for by spring most of the 1942 squad as well as many of the freshmen, would have enlisted or had been drafted into the various branches of the service to fight in World War II.

The reflection of this lost football dynasty persisted for many years in the choice of who would become the team captain for the coming year. The captain of the team was chosen by the squad for his distinctive qualities of leadership and football ability. From 1942 through 1947, the choice of Captain was a member of the 1942 team.

It is difficult to describe fully the admiration every player of the 1942 team had for George Lynn. Charles Csuri who is now the Emeritus Professor of Fine Arts at Ohio State was chosen to follow George in 1943. Chuck left for service before the beginning of the season and Jack Duggar replaced him. In 1944, Gordon Appleby led the Ohio State team through an unbeaten season and ranked as the number two team in the nation behind the Army team of Davis and Blanchard. Bill Hackett was to be the captain of the 1945 team but an auto accident, which resulted in a head injury, ended his athletic career. That year the captains were appointed for each individual game. I was the team captain for the Pittsburgh game. In 1946, Warren Amling, Martin's younger brother, was team captain and the first player who was not a member of the 42 squad. In 1947, Tommy James was to be the captain but left for the Detroit Lions before the season started and was replaced by Bob Jabbusch. Except for Warren Amling, we were all members of the 1942 team and still fondly remembered by Ohio State fans.

FOOTBALL GETS IN
YOUR BLOOD

Any way you look at it, we were nuts about football. With the separation of the members of the 1942 team from Ohio State to enter the service and being spread across the world fighting the war, one would assume that football would become a just a wonderful memory. Surprisingly, this was not the case. Almost every one of the players continued to play if they were offered the opportunity whether it be in service, or at Ohio State or other universities, or in the professional leagues after the war. Frequently, they would make coaching football their careers at the high school, university or professional levels. This thrust to continue to play football began with the College All Star game against the Chicago Bears in Chicago in 1944. The game was a reunion of the 1942 team with seven players from the OSU 1942 team on the squad of about 45 players among whom were many of the college stars who had competed against them in 1942.

I was, perhaps, one of the nuttier players on the team. After entering medical school, I declined taking my undergraduate degree as I still had one more year of eligibility. The medical students at Ohio State were part of the Army Student Training Program (ASTP) and were not allowed to participate in intercollegiate athletics. For the next two years I would practice in the Spring with the 1943 and 1944 teams hoping to be able to play another year. The war ended my senior year and although I was still in the ASTP, the Colonel who headed the program at OSU allowed me to play. The only stipulation he made was that I wear civilian clothes when we traveled out of town to play other universities. I joined the team my senior year in med school in 1945.

Since Ohio State was a "land grant" university, two years of military training were required of all male students in their freshman and sophomore years. The training in field artillery was superficial, at best. We trained in map reading and moving relics from the First World War called French 75's. With the advent of the draft, the Ohio State students were assigned to Ft. Bragg, North Carolina, a giant artillery training base. They formed a football team to play the other military bases and large universities in the area. The 1942 Ohio State

Championship team had now become the Ft. Bragg "Bombardiers". The playing coaches were Lin Houston and Don McCafferty. In addition, there were Hal Dean, Dante Lavelli, Paul Sarringhaus, Carmen Naples, Bob McCormick, John White and a few other players who stayed only a few weeks as they were passing through to other assignments. Since Carmen Naples and Don McCafferty were instructors at the camp, they were part of the Bombardiers for the entire duration of the War. It was here that Don McCafferty would start his coaching career that would culminate in being the first coach to win the NFL Super Bowl in his first year as head coach. Several other players from the team played with other service teams. Tom Antonnuci played with the Iowa Seahawks, Tom Taylor with Notre Dame, Jim Rees with the Bunker Hill Naval Air Station, and Cy Souders at Great Lakes. Hal Dean ended his service football with the 11th Airborne Div. in Japan and Ken Coleman with a service team in Europe.

Most of the team had not completed their educations prior to entering the service. When they returned to pursue their undergraduate and graduate degrees, many of them returned to the Ohio State football team or to the football teams of other universities. John White had been assigned to the V12 Program at the University of Michigan where he became an All Conference Center and Captain of the Michigan team. This team was declared National Champions that year and to my knowledge, he is the only collegiate who played on two National Championship teams from different universities. Jim Rees played two years at North Carolina State University while he pursued his degree in Agronomy . He concentrated his studies in soil analysis and land reclamation. As expected, a large number of the players returned to Ohio State to continue their educations. Chuck Csuri, our 1942 All American tackle, returned to his studies in the College of Fine Arts after his harrowing experiences in the war. He played football in 1946 before graduating and then joined the faculty at Ohio State in the College of Fine Arts. Paul Sarringhaus joined Robin Priday, Jack Roe and myself for the 1945 season. The media considered him the most promising returning player in the nation and featured Paul on the cover of Life magazine. After graduation, he joined the Detroit Lions and later returned to his home in Middletown, Ohio, to manage their land appraisal department. Hal Dean returned to collegiate football at Ohio State and received his undergraduate degree in geology. He furthered his education at Stanford University gaining a master's degree in oil geology while playing professional football for the Los Angeles Rams. Cy Souders returned from service to play two more years for Ohio State and then turned to professional football with the Detroit Lions. His university degree in commerce enabled him to reach a high level management position in the trucking industry after his ten year career in collegiate and professional football ended. Tommy James returned to play for Ohio State for two years before starting his illustrious career with the Cleveland Browns. With all of our players, education was our primary purpose for returning to the universities. Although football was our "passion", it ranked a distant second to education.

Bob Zuppke, the legendary coach of the University of Illinois, when he discussed football players whom he had coached, frequently remarked that many of his best players were just hitting their stride when it came time to graduate. Just after World War II, a major expansion occurred in professional football allowing the most outstanding players, who wished to do so, an outlet into professional football. In addition to the long revered National Football League, a new league was forming who called themselves the All American Football League. It was not particularly lucrative to play professional football, but it did offer continuing fame and recognition and a salary for doing something they loved to do. During the last year of the war, Paul was invited to become the Head Coach of the newly formed Cleveland Browns in the new league. The Cleveland Rams had moved to Los Angeles and with Carol Widdoes, Paul's previous assistant coach, so successful with the 1944 team at Ohio State, he felt his future belonged in professional football. Knowing Paul, I believe that he would never consider disturbing his relationship with Carol Widdoes by trying to return to Ohio State. Many of us had continued to write Paul at this disturbing time in Paul's life. He never failed to answer our inquiries and this letter to Robin Priday reaffirms our pride in our coach.

6 June 1945
Lt.P.R. Priday, 0-713967
A.P.O. 140, c/o Postmaster,
New York, New York

Dear Robin,

A lot has happened since you last heard from me. I presume that you have heard that I resigned at Ohio State to enter the professional football field. I have a part interest in the new club in Cleveland in the All-American Conference. My leaving Ohio State was a tough decision for me to make and I did not do so for financial reasons.

The man who said that wars are "hell" was certainly right. In my particular case it broke up the vast dreams I had for a dynasty at O.S.U. It is a long story and one that only time will bring to light.

I have had quite an education since leaving the University. I made every effort when I left to do so in good taste and with a friendly feeling with everybody. Apparently my departure caused some bitter feelings, because soon after I had signed my other contract, Jack Fullen, with St.John in the background, came out with a long article about what I had been offered to remain at Ohio State. It was a face saving type of thing which I truthfully denied when I read it. Saint never talked long term contract nor finance with me when we discussed my future at Ohio State. His discussions were very general because he did not think I was serious about leaving. In fact, he gave me the impression that he thought I was putting the wedge on him for more money. Finance has never determined the jobs which I have taken. In the Ohio State situation, I knew that it would be difficult for me to return there and work under the setup which was destined to be there. With this knowledge, plus the fact that Widdoes enjoyed good success last year and would probably be reluctant to step back in his old role, caused me to feel that it would be better for everyone if I got out.

The next step in their rather systematic effort to work on me came when St. John dropped Great Lakes from the Ohio State schedule. It was their way of punishing me for going into a different classification of ball.

Then the third step was the recent blast which Widdoes took at me because some of the Ohio State players have written to them and indicated that they planned to play professional ball for me if they were unable to compete this coming Fall. The thing that bothered me most was that Widdoes, who owes every opportunity he ever had to me, would take the first opportunity he could find to publicly take a shot at me. Insofar as the issue is concerned, I haven't changed my mind one bit about men going back to school and finishing their educations. I do know, as you know, from being in service, too, that many men are not going to be in position after three or four years in the service to return in the same manner in which they left. If they need and want the kind of *help we can give them to finish their educations, then I mean to do so. I plan to encourage them in the getting their degrees just as I have always done at Ohio State. Nevertheless, Widdoes would have everybody believe that I have suddenly become an entirely different person just because I am now in a different phase of football. The whole thing is quite a let down to me. It has been some time since this happened, but I have not yet had the first word from Widdoes about it. Ernie Godfrey called me on the phone and we had quite a discussion about the whole thing being a mistake, but I felt very free in the whole matter because I had said nothing throughout the controversy. The only thing that bothered me was that one of my own fellows would do this to me. I am sure that I wouldn't have done it to one of my friends.*

The last step in the whole thing has been the fact that St. John has written to my commanding officers in an effort to have me shipped out of Great Lakes or penalized me in some way because I have changed jobs. The men to whom he wrote feel as I do— that it is fighting below the belt. Nothing will come from his effort but it certainly was a letdown to me to know that he would go to such lengths to hurt a person in such a manner.

This just about gives you the story of the changes I have made. It is not an easy transition to make under the circumstances, but you can rest assured that I will get there before it is all over.

I enjoyed your letter and I hope that you will see fit to write again. I have given you this little discussion of my leaving Ohio State because I thought it would probably interest you, and I do want you to know the truth of the situation.

With my personal regards, and looking forward to seeing you after the War.

> *Sincerely,*
> *Paul E. Brown*
> *Lieut. j.g., USNR*
> *Football Officer.*

Paul accepted this new challenge, and the machinery was put in place for Paul to assemble a squad for the Cleveland Browns. Letters and contracts were sent to many of the 1942 players and several of the Freshmen while they were still in service. Typically, Lin Houston was fighting in the South Pacific when he received the Brown's offer with a bonus of several thousand dollars and a monthly pay of $200.00. For a soldier receiving $30.00 per month, it must have seemed like a fortune for doing something he loved to do.

During this era of professional football, most of the players were the stars from major universities in contrast to the frequency of small college players in the pro ranks today. The stars for the Cleveland Browns were the 1942 Buckeyes, service football players from Great Lakes, and players who demonstrated outstanding ability to Paul Brown when they played against Ohio State or Great Lakes. At the head of the class of these players who were opponents was Otto Graham from Northwestern, and Marion Motley who had played for Canton McKinley High School while Paul was coaching at Massillon.

The Cleveland Browns would dominate the All American Football League for the five years of the league's independent existence. After the merger of the two leagues, they continued to dominate the National Football League for five more years. Players from the 1942 team would contribute almost a quarter of the players. On offense were Dante Lavelli, Lin Houston, and Lou Groza. Dante was the most outstanding End in the league during the years he played. Paul liked to refer to him as "Mr.Clutch" for his remarkable play in critical situations, but he was better known as "Mr.Glue Fingers" to the public. Lin Houston was the keystone of the offensive line and certainly deserves to be in the NFL Hall of Fame. Lou "Toe" Groza was, not only a great Tackle, but was the Place Kicker "par excellence" of the NFL. Gene Fekete played one year as the Fullback alternating with Marion Motley, but the knee injury that he sustained in his first practice for the All Star game in 1944 prevented his continuing as a player. On the defensive team were Bill Willis, Tommy James, Les Horvath and Horace Gillam. Horace and Lou were members of Ohio State freshman teams. Bill Willis continued his athletic superiority as the premier nose guard in the National Football League and is now enshrined in the National Football League Hall of Fame along with Dante Lavelli and Lou Groza. His strength, agility and speed of response are legendary in the league. Tommy James, our outstanding halfback and safety man in 1942, became a fixture as a defensive halfback with the Browns. Although he was quite short, his football savvy and jumping ability made him a natural in this most exacting position. Les Horvath returned to Paul after two years with the Rams and then ended his football career to begin his practice of dentistry in Los Angeles. Several years ago, I was visiting Les in Los Angeles and had a problem with a tooth. As a dentist, he had the smoothest technique and gentlest hands of any dentist I have ever used. There were several other players who had played for Ohio State in 1941, 42, 43, and 44 who were to play with the Browns. Among them were Bob Cherokee, Bob Gaudio and Tony Adamle.

After leaving the University of Indiana, Bo McMillan became the Head Coach of the Detroit Lions. He must have been very impressed by the playing skills of the 1942 Buckeyes as he brought six players from the 42, 43 and 44 Ohio State teams to the Lions. Cy Souders who was an All Conference and Honorable Mention All American was signed by the Lions. Jack Dugger who was a reserve tackle in 1942 became an All American in 1944 was signed to a contract as were Tommy James and Paul Sarringhaus. The most talented football player that I have ever known was undoubtedly Bob Shaw. He had no peer in size, speed, and pass catching ability. After his discharge from the service, he joined the Los Angeles Rams and later played for the Chicago Cardinals and three Canadian League football teams. While he was with the Cardinals, he caught five touchdown passes in one game, a record which was not equalled until 1990. He also led the Canadian league one year in passes caught with the Roughriders. Don McCafferty played two years with the New York Giants before starting his coaching career. Hal Dean, who became a world renowned oil geologist, graduated from Ohio State and then joined the Los Angeles Rams with Bob Shaw and Les Horvath. He was the starting offensive guard for the Rams for three years during the years they were the National Football League champions despite being the smallest guard in the league. He always remembered Paul Brown's remark that with well hewn skills, speed and intelligence, a player could compete at any level. In all 17, players on the 1942 Ohio State team played professional football and in the majority of instances, it was with a championship team.

Gordon Appleby, George Lynn and I received offers to play professional football. Gordon Appleby was the number two draft choice of the New York Giants after the 1944 season but felt he was too small to play professional football and began his business career with the Lincoln Electric Corporation. George had a contract and bonus to sign with the New York Giants, but preferred to pursue his career in collegiate coaching at Kent State and later the University of Oklahoma and Stanford. For several months before my graduation from medical school, I was urged by the Head Coach of the newly formed Brooklyn Dodgers Professional Football Team of the All American League to join their team in Brooklyn, New York. I had already decided that it was time for me to end my football career and had accepted an internship in Detroit after my graduation from Ohio State. I declined his weekly entreaties but I might add that he made coming to Brooklyn very enticing which included a residency in surgery along with my football contract. At that time, a general surgical residency was the ultimate goal in post graduate medical training. And so I was left with only a dream of some day playing in at least one professional football game.

Many members of the squad turned to coaching at the high school, university, and professional level after their playing days were over. Coaching in high school were the players who dedicated their lives to the guidance of young men. Most of them became the principals of their respective high schools after many years in coaching and classroom teaching. Oftentimes their records of winning teams closely resembled the records set by Paul Brown at Massillon. Bill Durtschi, Robin Priday, Gene Fekete, after his many years with Woody Hayes, Bob McCormick, Bob Frye and Cy Lipaj spent many fruitful years in the development of high school students.

Bill Vickroy, John White, Gene Fekete and George Lynn spent many years as university football coaches. Bill Vickroy's contributions to the University of Wisconsin at La Cross as coach and athletic director were so well recognized that he became the president of the small college athletic association, the N.A.I.A. There are no athletic scholarships offered by these universities. Bill's success as a coach and athletic director was duly honored by the university by placing Bill in their Hall of Fame. George Lynn spent many years with Trevor Rees at Kent State, and with Bud Wilkinson at Oklahoma and later with Stanford. J.T. White coached at Michigan after graduation and spent seventeen years with Rip Engel and Joe Paterno at Penn State. Gene Fekete was the Backfield Coach for Woody Hayes at Ohio State for nine years before returning to coaching at the high school level.

Both Bob Shaw and Don McCafferty had outstanding coaching careers in professional football. Bob Shaw was the head coach for three Canadian Professional League teams and was named the Coach of the

Year in 1976. He had several years of coaching at the collegiate level in preparation for coaching at the professional level. As an assistant coach, he coached with the Colts, the Saints, the Bears and Bills. His coaching career spanned a period of 24 years. After Don McCafferty ended his playing years with the Giants, he joined Trevor Rees at Kent State and then moved on to the Baltimore Colts where he remained for 15 years as an assistant coach. He was promoted to head coach after Don Shula moved on to the Miami Dolphins. In his first year as Head Coach, he won the NFL Super Bowl. Unfortunately, Don had a fatal heart attack just before he started his second season as coach of the Detroit Lions.

I don't believe that summarizing the coaching careers of these men properly emphasizes their true contributions to the growth and educations of the young men they taught in high school and college. I believe it dramatically emphasizes our bonding to Paul Brown. This bonding was not an occasional relationship with some of the players. The bonding was and is felt among all of us. They carried on Paul Brown's attitude that education was their primary goal at every level of education. Paul Brown's approach to coaching and teaching filtered through to all of these fine athletes and later coaches. To quote Bob Shaw, "All we had to do was to recall and reemphasize Paul's directions." One can only applaud the teachings they emphasized by interjecting these valuable lessons for living to their students.

BOB SHAW

Football: Ohio State, 1941, 1942 – All American, 1942
Pro Football Career, 8 years
Los Angeles Rams & Chicago Cardinals
Record 5 touchdown passes in one NFL game
Canadian Football League, 3 teams

Education: B.A. and Masters in Education

Career: Professional Football Coach
Head Coach of Saskatchawan, Toronto & Hamilton
Coach of the Year in Hamilton, 1976
Assistant Coach with Four NFL Teams

Married: Mary – 46 years – Two children & two grandchildren

Service: World War II – 104th Infantry in Europe

BOB SHAW

Most athletes have only a passing relationship with sports as their lives eventually enter into other interests or professions. Very frequently, an athlete who majors in education will become a teacher or a coach in secondary education and primarily be involved in the progressive development of young men. A few may continue their sports affiliation with universities such as Gene Fekete at Ohio State or George Lynn at Oklahoma and Stanford. On our 1942 team, we had an unusually large number of players who played professional football after military service and two of us became both players and coaches in the professional leagues. Don McCafferty played for the New York Giants and later became the coach of the Colts and Lions. My professional life involved playing for several American and Canadian league teams and being the Head Coach or assistant coach on many more. My entire life has been totally devoted to athletics, football in particular.

Aside from assisting the coaching staff at nearby Otterbein College after my retirement, my career in playing and coaching football spanned a period of forty years. These years were filled with the joys and trials that accompany winning and losing. As a player or coach, your joys are your associations with usually kind and dedicated players and winning football games. Your trials involve doing your best, but your team may still not win. Frequently, after losing a single important game or a championship, there is the problem of withstanding the statements and opinions of many people who may or may not have a direct relationship with the team. I have had a full and exciting life in football which I really believe is our national sport. In football, I feel that I had an important place while I played and coached.

I was born and raised as an only child in Fremont, Ohio. Both my father and mother were employed in industry as workers in automotive plants. While I attended high school, the pattern for my future was forming. I was endowed with all of the physical assets anyone could dream of. I had size, speed, strength, agility, and a heart set on physical excellence. By my senior year in high school, I was 6'3" tall, and weighed well over 200 pounds. I had lettered in every major sport every year in high school. In track, I held the Ohio State Shot Putt record. In basketball, I was selected to the first string basketball Ohio All-Star football team. In football, I co-captained the team, and was selected as an End on the All-Ohio Class A first team.

All of these athletic honors precipitated dozens of scholarship offers from universities across the country. There were all kinds of inducements offered to me to attend any of these schools. All of them included a completely financed education. I did visit one university in North Carolina. My Dad and I drove to the university whose athletic inducement even included a job for my Dad in addition to a completely financed education. While we were driving back to Fremont, my father said, "Son, after listening to all of those attractive offers, I believe it would be best for you to go to Ohio State. This is your home state and where you will probably live after your graduation." His sage-like advice, along with the friendly and honest approach of Ernie Godfrey, induced me to attend Ohio State in 1940. I enrolled in the College of Education my freshman year, and joined a freshman football team that was so filled with talented athletes that our annual game against the Varsity was one of the most difficult games they had all year. We would power Paul Brown's first two years at Ohio State. I believe that Paul looks back on these years, as we do, as an outstanding period in our lives.

Both of our years with Paul, particularly in 1942, demonstrated the results of Paul's coaching genius. All of our memories of these years are happy ones that culminated in our National Championship recognition in 1942. One had only to pay attention to his organizational skills, to his ability to bring out the maximum efforts from his players, and to understand his approach to football. He devoted hours with his assistant coaches to develop the necessary progression in his practice sessions. He evaluated the assets that each of his players possessed and how to best refine them and incorporate them into a team. It was not difficult to see and understand the advantages of lower body strength, speed and intelligence that he insisted upon. These were the basics for any future professional player or coach.

While I attended Ohio State, my athletic achievements continued. In football, I was All-Conference for two years, and an All American in 1942. In addition, I also lettered in basketball and track. My collegiate career stopped abruptly with the onset of the World War I. When I entered service, I was shipped to Ft. Bragg. I was not stationed at Ft. Bragg long enough to play with the "Bombardiers" as I was sent to Engineering School at Northwestern. The program was suddenly disbanded before the year of schooling ended. I was supposed to return to the artillery, but my papers were mixed up with another soldier named Shaw. I found myself in the 104th Infantry fighting across Europe until we met up with the Russians at the end of the war in Europe. As part of my service with the 104th, I was the bodyguard for the general.

After I was discharged, I was drafted by the then Cleveland Rams which began my professional playing career that lasted eight years. My first year with the Rams, we were the National Football League Champions. The team moved to Los Angeles where I played through 1949 with Hal Dean and Les Horvath from our 42 team. I was traded to the Chicago Cardinals the following year. It was with the Cardinals that I established the record of catching five touchdown passes in one game. This record was not tied until 1990, a record that lasted individually for 40 years. The following year, I joined the Calgary Stampeders in the Canadian League where I set the scoring record for the league in 1951. My playing career ended with the Toronto Argonauts in 1953.

That same year, I returned to college at Otterbein and Southern Mississippi, to complete my Master's degree in Education with a minor in Physical Education. My first coaching job was running the entire athletic program at Washington Court House, Ohio. The next year I moved to Cuyahoga Falls High School near Cleveland where I was the Head Coach in football. It was time to return to professional football.

I returned to professional football coaching as one of the assistant coaches, along with Don McCafferty, of the Baltimore Colts under Web Eubank. By the end of the season in 1958, we were the champions of the National Football League . In 1959, I joined the coaching staff of the San Francisco 49ers as the offensive End coach. I interrupted my professional coaching by returning to the college level at New Mexico Junior College. Here I remained for two years developing my skills as a Head Coach. In 1963, I was appointed the Head Coach of the Saskatchewan Rough Riders in the Canadian Professional Football League. After two years, I became the Head Coach of the Toronto Argonauts. After three years, I returned to the NFL as an assistant coach for the New Orleans Saints, Chicago Bears, and Buffalo Bills. In 1976, I became the General Manager and Head Coach of the Hamilton

Tiger Cats and was named the Coach of the Year in the Canadian Football League. My professional football career ended in 1979. Forty years had passed since I left Fremont High School to attend The Ohio State University.

Associated with my career as a coach were numerous other related experiences. There were innumerable speaking engagements along with radio and television programs. I have organized many coaching clinics as a well as being the guest speaker at other football clinics. Several years were spent organizing and directing high school football camps, recruiting, and evaluating players for both college and professional football.

My wife, Mary, and I have been married since 1944. We have two children and two grandchildren. My son, Webb, graduated from Northwestern University and is now an executive for the Eaton Manufacturing Co. Our daughter, Amy, is a schoolteacher in Hollywood, Florida.

A lifetime of athletics has been very gratifying, as well as, challenging. Aside from football, there were three years as a professional basketball player in the old National Basketball League with Cleveland and Toledo. Later, I was also a scout for the New York Yankees. However, there is one event that I frequently had to miss because of my tight fall schedule, our five year reunions of our 1942 National Championship team. I don't believe that any collegiate team had so many renowned athletes during their playing and coaching days, or so many men who have made outstanding contributions after football and after leaving Ohio State. It is always a warm feeling to be remembered. When Ross High in Fremont initiated its Hall of Fame this past year, I was one of their first selectees.

GENE FEKETE

Football:	Ohio State, 1942
	Bill Stern's All American Team
	Top 10 Players considered for Heisman Trophy, 1942
	Cleveland Browns, 1 year
Education:	B.A. and Master's Degrees
Career:	Coach at Northern Illinois University
	Assistant Coach at Ohio State
	Wes Fesler, 3 years
	Woody Hayes, 8 years
	Head Coach for Columbus Pro Football, 2 years
	Principal at Briggs High School, 13 years
Married:	Dottie – 46 years – Two sons & three grandchildren
Service:	World War II – Army

GENE FEKETE

Just South of Budapest, Hungary, three families, the Feketes, the Csuri's and the Horvaths would leave their small villages to migrate to America and settle in Northeastern Ohio.

My dad had left Hungary to avoid military conscription into the Austria-Hungarian army when hostilities were imminent just prior the First World War. He first settled in Akron, Ohio, and was employed by the Goodrich Rubber Co. With the onset of the Great Depression, the plant was closed and the only jobs available were in the coal mines near Athens, Ohio. He worked in this backbreaking job until the coal dust threatened to destroy his vision. Friends of our family who lived in Findlay, Ohio, urged him to settle in Findlay where he could find employment with the Cooper Rubber Co. Mom and dad, with my oldest brother, Alex, packed their meager belongings and moved to Findlay. The rest of the family, my sister, my brother, John, and I were born and raised in Findlay.

All the boys in the Fekete family were outstanding athletes. Alex, who was much older than John or me, ended his education after high school to help support the family. John and I attended Findlay High School where we were involved in every seasonal sport: football in the fall, basketball in the winter, and track in the spring. John accepted an athletic scholarship to Ohio University in Athens, Ohio, where he starred as a Halfback. In his senior year, he was named to the first string Little All American Team whose players were selected from all of the small colleges and universities in the country. When someone is so proud of his brother, it isn't hard to idolize him.

While John was excelling at Ohio University, I was attracting more and more attention. In addition to being selected to the All Ohio teams in both football and basketball, I held the record in football as the second leading scoring back and the leading ground gaining back of all the major high schools in Ohio. It may have been that the coach at Ohio University assumed that I would naturally follow my brother John's footsteps as no one from the Ohio University coaching staff made any effort to contact me. During this time, I was actively recruited by Notre Dame, Ohio State, Michigan and many other universities across the country. Michigan alumni filled the corporate offices of the Ohio Oil Company in Findlay which was the largest and most influential company in the area. The Ohio Oil Company would become the Marathon Oil Corporation as we know it today. These Michigan alumni frequently displayed an aura of grandeur and wealth in contrast to the Ohio State recruiters from whom one felt warm, "homey" approach. Ernie Godfrey's sincerity and friendliness convinced me to attend Ohio State University.

As I recall, I don't believe my father ever saw John or me play any high school sports until he read of our accomplishments in the newspapers. Surprisingly, this was very common among the fathers who had migrated from Europe to America. Perhaps, they left the rearing of the family to their wives and their interests centered around their men friends. However, after reading of his sons' accomplishments in the sports pages, he became an avid sports fan.

My freshman year at Ohio State involved attending classes, playing Freshman football, and becoming accustomed to being away from home. The friendships that I quickly made in the fraternity house and in football practice helped immeasurably. This freshman football squad was the first team that Paul Brown and his assistant coaches had recruited. He was looking for specific types of players to fit the type of team he wished to develop. Primarily, he wanted a young man who could learn and understand what he wished to teach them. For example, in the timing of an offensive play, he might instruct a backfield man to take three steps to the left and then cut sharply into the line. Taking three steps was crucial to the success of the play so he meant three steps, not one, two, or four. Secondly, he wanted speed in every position. Bill Willis, as a Tackle, could match any backfield man in speed. In our game against Illinois in 1944, he caught Buddy Young, who had an almost clear field to a touchdown, from behind. Buddy Young was a world class sprinter. And lastly, he was seeking players with exceptional lower body muscular development. One has only to compare the size of Les Horvath's legs to the rest of his body to understand the significance of lower body development. Of course, a player who did not have the temperament to follow his guidance and very exacting instructions would be of no value to Coach Brown regardless of his athletic ability.

We spent the fall season learning the fundamentals of his offenses and defenses. Paul and Trevor Rees continually emphasized intelligence, speed and execution in our drills and intrasquad scrimmages. But education was foremost in their minds. We were constantly asked about our performance in the classrooms. If assistance were needed in certain subjects, tutoring was made available. Many times I believe Paul paid for these tutors himself. Occasionally, one of the other players who was a good student, was asked by Paul to help another player having difficulty with a subject to assist him. Thus, by the time we were ready for Varsity football, the ground work for the real reasons for being in college were laid.

About half way through the freshman year, we were about to start a major revolt, but Hugh McGranahan, Paul's assistant line coach talked us out of it. Dante Lavelli, John White and I had become close friends. There were over a hundred young men on the freshman squad and we were unhappy about being relegated to the fourth and fifth teams. There were about a half dozen boys who had followed Paul from Massillon and it was very difficult to be selected to scrimmage. Scrimmaging was the only way to demonstrate our individual talents. My brother, John, was starring at Ohio University and we decided that, perhaps we would transfer to Ohio University. This was the week that the Varsity was in Los Angeles playing Southern California. As a group, we confronted Hugh expressing our concern about our lack of scrimmaging and we were thinking of leaving Ohio State. Hugh asked us to wait until Paul returned. Things changed dramatically after Paul came back from Los Angeles.

The fall of 1942 stands out among my fondest memories. Paul constantly reminded us that we were different from other young men. We were "Blue Steel" as the finest grade of steel made in the mills of Massillon. The actual season began with Fort Knox service team and ended with the Iowa Seahawks. The Fort Knox team was big and slow and ill prepared to play the caliber of football expected from Big Ten universities. In contrast, the Iowa Seahawks were "loaded" with All Americans, professional players and were coached by Bernie Bierman. Bierman was the legendary coach from the University of Minnesota who had just completed five years of unbeaten football and two National Championships.

Paul had developed a method to increase my motivation as a player. Just before we would be going down to the playing field from our conference room in the stadium to play the game, we had our pre-game session with Paul with the starting eleven players. At the end of the session, as the other players started down the steel staircase, he would take me aside and remark, "Gene, you are going to have the greatest game you have ever had." This remark, in addition to his being able to "psyche you up" just by looking at you, made me feel like taking on the world let alone a rival football team.

This was the era of football when each player played both offense and defense while he was still in the game. Compared to today's two platoon players, there is a wide contrast between the type of players who had to play " both ways" and today's players. Nevertheless, when you compare the statistics of all of the Ohio State teams through the years, except for one team, the 1942 team was foremost in scoring per game and yards gained per game. This team averaged 33 points per game against their opponent teams almost all of whom were vying for national recognition as the best teams in the nation. For most of the year, I was the leading ground gaining back in the country in spite of the fact that I played only a part of the game, and the other fullbacks would play as soon as the outcome of the game was assured. Coach Brown was never really concerned with promoting the popularity of any individual player. He was truly always concerned with safety, so that a first string player would not be injured uselessly. His primary concern was the team's overall cohesiveness. Second and third string players frequently participated in most of the games. It really did not make much difference as Cy Lipaj and Dick Palmer were great fullbacks in their own right and would have been the first team fullbacks on most other teams.

After the season was over, we had been chosen as the National Championship Team. Bill Stern, the famous radio announcer, had compiled his own selections for an All American team. As one of the leading ground gaining backs in the country and the leading scorer, he chose me as his All American Fullback. As a sophomore, I was named the first string Big Ten Fullback and was among the top ten players considered for the Heisman Trophy.

During my sophomore year at Ohio State, I worked part time at the Lazarus Department Store in downtown Columbus to earn money for my expenses in school. Here, I developed a wonderful friendship with Si Lazarus, the owner of this hugh department store. He was an extremely wealthy man devoted to assisting hundreds of young people who needed financial aid to complete their educations. I was never required to report to work at a particular time, but I always put in as many hours as possible working in the store. I knew how much he appreciated my efforts and just before I was to leave for military service, he came into the shipping department. He wished me good bye and said, "Gene, when you return from service, there is a job as an assistant buyer in our store for you. I think that you will have a fine future in retailing." Then he handed me a large box filled with clothing to use while I was in service. Every year, thereafter, I received a Christmas gift and a letter from Si and later his son, Ralph.

In 1943, I entered the Army and was sent to Ft. Bragg and then to the Pratt Institute in Brooklyn, New York to be trained in engineering. I was not at Ft. Bragg long enough to play with Lin Houston and Don McCafferty's "Bombardiers", the 1942 team who were stationed at Ft. Bragg. Later, I was transferred to the Manhattan Induction Center as an assistant psychologist. The College All Star game against the Chicago Bears was coming up in 1944, and I was chosen to participate. The proceeds from this game were to be given to the various service organizations to entertain the service men away from home. My immediate superior officer refused to grant me leave to join the team in Chicago. A loud roar was heard all the way from Army Headquarters directed at my superior officer. "Private Gene Fekete is to participate in the College All Star Game in Chicago!" Due to the delay, I was ten days late reporting for practice. I really was in poor condition as I had little physical exercise for a year. The first day of practice, I took a hand off from Otto Graham, the Quarterback, and started to cut up the field. The ligaments in my left knee snapped spontaneously and heralded the end of my athletic career.

After my discharge from service, I returned to Ohio State to complete my education. I was asked by Colonel Potter of the Air Force to write a service manual for the Air Force Conditioning Program. This manual formed the thesis for my master's degree in Physical Education. By the end of the war, my knee had healed sufficiently for me to join the Cleveland Browns with the rest of the 42 team and other players who had impressed Paul Brown when they played against us. I alternated with Marion Motley that year until it was obvious that my knee could not sustain the punishment of professional football. After winning the championship playoff game, I received $833.00 after taxes, my share of the split to each player.

In 1946, Dottie and I were married. It was a wonderful occasion for us as some our best friends in football came to the wedding. Our wedding picture with Don McCafferty, Dante Lavelli, and Lou Groza was featured in newspapers across the country as far away as Honolulu.

Football and coaching were my first priorities. I accepted the coaching position at Northern Illinois University and then returned to Ohio State as an assistant coach to Wes Fessler for two years and Woody Hayes for eight years. Coaching under Woody took almost all of my time and I felt that my family was now growing and needed more of my attention. Woody was so devoted to football that I don't really believe he could understand how I could ever leave football. My wife and I discussed my situation many times and we both agreed that our two sons should have much more of my time. I decided to try the insurance business but found it was not for me. After receiving my Master's degree in Administrative Education, I returned to teach at the high school level. I became the West High School coach where I remained four years. At this time, a professional football team was organized in Columbus to compete in a league with New Jersey, Grand Rapids, Pittsburgh and Massillon. I was hired as the Head Coach of this team and was able to handle both positions. The league lasted two years and the last year we played for the league championship against New Jersey, a team coached by Steve Van Buren. Like the rest of our 1942 players, football really gets into your blood.

When Briggs High School was opened in Columbus, I was appointed the principal of the school. As the chief administrator, I developed all of the school programs for our 1000 students. Fond memories are often unexpectedly renewed as Hal Dean's daughter came to Briggs High School to do her student teaching. I was principal for thirteen years and retired in 1975.

Dottie and I will be married 46 years soon. We have two sons and three grandchildren. One son is the head of an investment banking firm and the other is in the wholesale jewelry business. As I look back on my life, I am filled with pride in my relationships with Paul Brown, Wes Fessler, and Woody Hayes. All of these men made significant contributions to the development of my educational goals for my high school students.

TOMMY JAMES

Football: Ohio State, 1941, 1942, 1946
Captain-elect, 1947
Detroit Lions, 1947
Cleveland Browns, 1948-1955
Baltimore Colts, 1956

Education: B.A. in Education

Career: Professional Football then Sales
Active in civic groups in Canton-Massillon area

Married: Rosemarie – Three sons

Service: Surgical Technician in South Pacific

TOMMY JAMES

As I recall the events in my life that standout as significant to me, I would mention our last reunion of our 1942 Ohio State team. This may seem strange, but this reunion mended an uncomfortable feeling that I had been carrying for a number of years. It was similar to a misunderstanding one might have with a close relative. It proved once again the correctness of Paul Brown's convictions. One must understand that Paul and I had been together for so many years that a father-son relationship was firmly established. I had really played for only one coach, Paul Brown, through high school, college and professional teams. The only other years I did not play under Paul were one with Ohio State when I returned after the war and one year with the Colts after being the defensive cornerback for the Browns for eight years.

Paul had always maintained a social distance from his players. The newspapers often chided him for being rather "antisocial" with the members of his teams. In spite of their opinions, he continued to maintain this rule of not being overly friendly with any of his players. In this respect, he considered us only as a team. There would be nothing to praise from one player over another. With all of the great players lauded by the newspapers such as Dante Lavelli, Otto Graham, Lou Groza, and so many others through the years, he never deviated from his perspective that each squad was a team of players and not a group of individual stars.

At our last reunion in 1987, almost every surviving player attended. Forty-five years had passed since we had played at Ohio State. Paul Brown was there with his wife, Mary, as we greeted one another as if all the past years had shed away. We were back together again as a team with an emotional closeness that few people ever experience. Of course, Paul was the principal speaker at our dinner. He began by repeating as he had in his book, "P.B. The Paul Brown Story", that we were his favorite coaching experience as well as one of his fondest memories. Then he took the time to single out one event in his life that was especially difficult for him. Since Paul and I had been together for some eighteen years, he had always carried some misgivings as to how to tell me that the time had come for me to give up my football career. These situations are always difficult for coaches and players but, in this situation, we had developed an almost family relationship. He said at this reunion, "Tommy, I did not know what to say to you, so I said very little." Once, again, his convictions were correct. I could only imagine what a heartache I would have carried if Paul had been overly friendly because of the many years we had been together.

I was reared in a small community equidistant between Canton and Massillon. Because of its location, I had the choice of attending high school either at Canton McKinley or Massillon. I chose Massillon and became the first string halfback under Paul Brown. Throughout my high school years, we had never lost a football game. I played on his last team before he left Massillon for Ohio State. Our last game was against Canton McKinley, our traditional rival. They were an outstanding team with Jack Dugger who would later become an All American with Ohio State, Marion Motley, our great Cleveland Brown fullback and NFL Hall of Fame selection, as well as other fine football players.

I enrolled at Ohio State and majored in Social Sciences with a minor in Physical Education. Prior to the War, I played on both the 1941 and 1942 teams. Perhaps my most memorable college game was against the University of Illinois in Cleveland in 1942. I ran the opening kickoff for a touchdown. On the first set of Illinois plays they were unsuccessful in making a first down and were forced to punt. I caught the punt and again ran the ball back for a second touchdown. These two touchdowns along with another scored by Les Horvath had given us a 20 point lead before the first quarter was five or six minutes old. The game was not against a mediocre team as Illinois was ranked among the twenty best teams in the country. The game must have been particularly frustrating to Alex Agase, their All-American Guard. On one play, later in the game, I injured my shoulder and while I was lying on the ground, he came over and said, "And how do you like that, you " Blankety Blank". This season was exceptional with almost every team we played vying for national recognition.

Following the 1942 season, I enlisted in the Army and spent the next thirty months in the South Pacific. I was assigned to an Army hospital unit as a medical corpsman for most of this time. I became a surgical tech in the station hospital. We were preparing for the invasion of Japan when the war ended. While I was still in service, I received a

letter from Paul Brown offering me a contract with the new Cleveland
Browns in the All American League. I had decided to return to Ohio
State to complete my degree instead of playing professional football. In
my senior year, I had been elected the Captain for the 1947 team at
Ohio State. There was so much turmoil in the Athletic Department of
the university with the departure of Paul Bixler, the last of Paul Brown's
staff as Head Coach, that I decided to accept an offer to play for the
Detroit Lions and Gus Dorais. Gus Dorais had gained his football fame
with Knute Rockne in popularizing the forward pass. Unfortunately, in
the second game with the Lions, I broke my arm which required a
surgical repair and almost ended my football career. My arm healed by
the next year when I rejoined Paul with the Cleveland Browns. We
were the perennial champions of the All American Conference and
also, after the merger, with the National Football League. I played the
defense halfback position for most of these years despite my short
stature. The defensive cornerback is a highly skilled position that
requires speed, agility, and the football "smarts" which are much more
acutely defined than being an offensive halfback. It is interesting that
both Les Horvath and I who had gained so much recognition as
offensive halfbacks would play professional football as defensive backs.
We were both well schooled by Paul in all aspects of football. My career
lasted seven years with the Cleveland Browns. I found it very difficult to
realize at the time that my athletic career was coming to an end, and I
would have to return to the life of an average citizen after so many years
in the public limelight. Both Lin Houston and I had similar adjustment
problems at the end of our careers. He made his point by returning to
Paul's office the next year with his football shoes hanging around his
neck as he entered the office. I accepted an offer to play for the
Baltimore Colts, and this, too, lasted only one more year.

     During one of my seasons with the Browns, I suffered a severely
broken nose. I asked Paul if I could wear a face mask to protect my nose
but he thought it would impair my vision. However, by the next year,
Paul had changed his mind. He advocated and insisted that all players
should wear face masks to prevent facial injuries. My football career
ended in 1956, the same year that John Unitas came to Baltimore. My
football life spanned almost twenty years, all but two with my coach,
Paul Brown.

     I was the eldest of four boys and the first member of all of our relatives to attend college. Football was to become a heritage in our family as it had in so many of the players on the 1942 team. My brother, Art is on the Perry High School Board along with my brother, John. Both attended universities and received their degrees. Our youngest brother, Don, quarterbacked the University of Miami Hurricanes and is now the Head Coach for the University of Washington. He has had an outstanding career both as a player and a coach.

My wife, Rosemarie, and I have reared three sons, all of whom are college graduates. Tommy III is an executive with the Sara Lee Corporation in Grand Rapids, Micheal teaches and coaches at Massillon, and Bobby is in management training for Roadway Express. Since my retirement, I have remained closely involved in many civic and athletic activities in the Canton-Massillon area.

LIFE

OHIO STATE'S
STAR HALFBACK

OCTOBER 22, 1945 **10** CENTS
BY SUBSCRIPTION: TWO YEARS $8.50

PAUL SARRINGHAUS

PUBLIC ACCLAIM

In the days before professional football teams became as sophisticated as they are today, the football seasons in the fall were heralded by the playing of the College All-Star team against the winner of the National Football League Championship of the previous year. From the time of the end of the baseball World Series until this game was played, the newspapers across the country were filled columns about the up coming All-Star game. Frequently, prognostications of who would win were made by sports columnists and coaches. Since the star college players were much more publicized than the professional players, there were often lopsided predictions that favored the All-Stars. The game in the fall of 1944 was played before a sellout crowd at Northwestern's Dyche Stadium in Chicago, the last week in August. The 1944 All Star game was dedicated to the servicemen of our country and the proceeds were to go to the U.S.O. for the benefit of our soldiers, sailors, and airmen. This enabled the sports staff of the Chicago Tribune to seek out all of the football players from the Bears as well as the university players, who were still stateside. The game had the good graces of the War Department. Ensign Sid Luckman was given leave to return to play for the Chicago Bears who were the National Football Champions of the previous year as well as some of their other players in service. This was a fairly depleted professional team as most of their players were overseas. Otto Graham, the All-American Quarterback for Northwestern, returned to his alma mater along with about 45 players in stateside service or in university programs. This game was like a reunion of the Ohio State 1942 team. Three players, Bill Willis, Gordon Appleby, and Jack Duggar were recruited from Ohio State. Lin Houston, Bob Jabbusch, Gene Fekete and Paul Sarringhaus were given special leave to report to Chicago to train for the game. It was necessary for Lin Houston to play the entire game as the Guard who was to have substituted for him in the second half was injured on the first play. The game ended with the Bears winning 24-21. Three players on the starting team for the All-Stars were from the Ohio State 1942 team.

Each week during the football season, the coaches, sports writers, and the public are polled by a variety of methods to determine who is presently the best team, how are the teams ranked among the top ten or twenty in the nation. Each week the newspapers laud the emerging stars and praise the coaches who deserve recognition. Each week the lists change, but, by the end of the season, the All Conference players are chosen and the All-American selections are made. One player is awarded the Heisman Trophy as the most outstanding player in the country. In 1944, the Heisman award went to Les Horvath, our outstanding right halfback on the 1942 team. There are several polls that choose All Americans each year. They all vary a little because there are so many star players and with so many football teams that is difficult to choose the same eleven players in each poll. Nevertheless, Lin Houston was the consensus All American Guard in 1942 in all of the polls. Bob Shaw, our outstanding right End, was chosen as an All American as was Chuch Csuri at Tackle. Bob proved his great talent as a professional for many years and, until this year, he, individually, has held the record of five touchdown passes caught in one game in the National Football League. He has had a long career as an outstanding professional league coach after his playing days were over. Gene Fekete was the favorite fullback in the country as he held the rushing record most of the season in 1942. He was considered for the Heisman Trophy in 1942 and was selected to Bill Stern's All American team. 1944 was another cardinal year for Ohio State Football as the team went undefeated and ranked second in the country behind the great Army team with Davis and Blanchard. Besides Les Horvath, there were three other All American selections on the team, Bill Willis, Jack Duggar and Bill Hackett. All of these players were also on the 1942 team. Bob Jabbusch was a Sophomore in 1942 and was selected by the Chicago Tribune for their All American Sophomore team. Cy Souders has received numerous national awards during his collegiate career as well as the Chicago Tribune Silver Football Award.

There is one medal coveted by athletes who were outstanding students as well as athletes. To receive this honor in the Big Ten from among the hundreds of Ohio State athletes is particularly desirable as only one athlete in the entire university is selected each year. In the eyes of the scholar-athletes, it ranks just below being selected as an All American. For four years, a member of the 1942 team received this award. Bill Vickroy received this Medal in 1942, Jack Duggar in 1943, Don Steinberg in 1945 and Bob Jabbusch in 1947.

Many years after our athletic careers have ended the most outstanding players in the colleges are chosen for the Intercollegiate Hall of Fame. Two players have received this coveted award, Bill Willis and Les Horvath. The National Football League Hall of Fame recalls the star players who have finished their careers after ten years or more. Hundreds and hundreds of players in the National Football League have finished their careers and only six or seven of them are selected each year. Two of these players from our 1942 Varsity team and one from our 1942 Freshman team have been selected to this very select group of players. Dante Lavelli, "Mr. Glue Fingers", was All-Pro for seven of his ten years with the Cleveland Browns and is in the National Football Hall of Fame. The two greatest football players I have ever know were Bill Willis and Lin Houston. Bill had an outstanding career as the Nose Guard on defense for the Cleveland Browns during their most illustrious years. He is enshrined in the Pro Hall of Fame. Lin had a similarly outstanding career with the Browns and certainly deserves to be the Hall of Fame. Lou, "The Toe", Groza was a freshman in 1942. He has held a singularly admired position in the hearts of the American public is also in the Pro Hall of Fame.

In the spring of each year there are sports banquets held across the country. Many, many communities honor local sports heros of yesteryears along with the recognition of the efforts of graduating scholar athletes from the area high schools. In cities such as Toledo, my home, one athlete from each decade is recognized after his sports career is at least twenty years past. This is the selection process used in most of the local Hall of Fame Awards. Hall of Fame awards are made from high schools, local communities, universities and coaching associations. For athletes with greying hair and balding heads, it is a particularly pleasant feeling to know that you, in particular, have been remembered of the thousands of athletes that have passed through your communities. Of the 39 players who survived the war, 18 have been recognized in local halls of fame. The latest of whom is Bob Frye. Mansfield St. Peter's High School has named their gymnasium in his honor for his outstanding career as a high school coach. The following members of Ohio State National Championship team in 1942 have received such an award.

Cy Lipaj, Lakewood High School Cleveland, Ohio

Gene Fekete, Findlay High School, Findlay, Ohio

Robert Jabbusch, Elyria High School, Elyria, Ohio

Hal Dean, Wooster High School, Wooster, Ohio

Don Steinberg, Scott High School, Toledo, Ohio and Lucas County Hall of Fame, Toledo, Ohio

William Durtschi, Galion High School, Galion, Ohio

Lin Houston, Summitt County, Massillon, Ohio and The Ohio State University Hall of Fame

Bob Shaw, Ross High School, Fremont, Ohio

Bill Vickroy, University of Wisconsin, LaCross, Wisconsin and N.A.I.A Hall of Fame

Ken Eichwald, Lakewood High School, Lakewood, Ohio

Bill Hackett, Ohio State University, Columbus, Ohio

Les Horvath, Cleveland, Ohio and Ohio State University

Jack Duggar, Ohio State University, Columbus, Ohio

Bill Willis, Ohio State University, Columbus, Ohio

Robin Priday, West Jefferson High School, West Jefferson, Ohio

Dante Lavelli, Cleveland, Ohio Hall of Fame

Bob Frye, Ohio High School Coaches Hall of Fame

Wib Schneider, Gahanna High School Hall of Fame

Paul Selby, The Selby Scholarship Fund, University of West Virginia College of Law

There have been approximately 55 football players who have been awarded places in The Ohio State University Hall of Fame. The list of players goes back to the early 1990s when football was first played at Ohio State. From the 1942 Ohio State team, five players are now in the Ohio State Hall of Fame, as well as our coach, Paul Brown.

BILL WILLIS

Football: Ohio State, 1942, 1943, 1944
All American, 1944
Intercollegiate Hall of Fame
Cleveland Browns, 8 years – All Pro
NFL Hall of Fame

Education: B.A. in Education and Masters

Career: College Coach, 1 year
Professional Football, 8 years
Director of Ohio Youth Commission, 24 years
William K. Willis High School

Married: Odessa – Three children & three grandchildren

Service: Medical Disability

BILL WILLIS

I am sure in everyone's life, there are "ruts" in the road to success and happiness. However, not to be self-defeating in one's quest is to relish the joys and subdue the humiliations along the way. I could always visualize, through my own efforts, that light of achievement as I had to deal with never-ending incidents of discrimination. During these years, we gave leadership and strength to the struggle against those biased people who prevented Black athletes from fully expressing their talents in university and professional sports. Jackie Robinson and Kenny Washington in baseball and Marion Motley and myself in football were the pioneers in opening the way for other Black athletes to follow.

God had endowed me with physical attributes that most people only dream about along with a quiet nature and intelligence to overcome all adversity. My personal "ruts in the road" were poverty, the early death of my father, and fighting not to surrender my future to the social problems of my youth. My father died when I was only four years old. This tragedy left my mother to rear two sons, Clyde and myself, in dire poverty during the Depression of the Thirties. She did housework in homes in Columbus to support her children and was ever mindful of the necessity to educate her sons. My older brother, Clyde, was an outstanding athlete at Columbus East High School. Nicknamed "Deacon Willis", he was selected as the All State Fullback and was the pride of entire Black community. One day, some of my friends and I were playing in the park throwing a ball back and forth when one of the people watching shouted, "Let's see if you are as good as your brother!" The ball came sailing through the air, I jumped to catch it, and I dropped it. "Well, you ain't no Deacon Willis, that's for sure." I survived this comment and went on to East High the next year.

One of the first "incidents" that I remember occurred my junior year in high school. The Columbus East football team traveled to Toledo to play Toledo Devilbiss. After the game, Coach Webster gave each of us fifty cents to buy dinner before climbing into the bus for the trip back to Columbus. Two of my Black friends and I went into a restaurant nearby and ordered sandwiches. The proprietor made the sandwiches which we paid for, and then he said, "We don't allow you boys to eat in the restaurant." We sat at one of the tables discussing what to do. First we thought we would just leave the sandwiches uneaten, but then decided to open the sandwiches and throw them on the floor as we left the restaurant. This we did, and then raced back to the bus and hid under the seats until it was time to leave for home.

My athletic career in high school, both in football and track, was outstanding. I played Tackle and End in football and ran the dashes and threw the shot putt in track. Coach Webster, our football coach, wrote Paul Brown at Ohio State about my high school record. He felt that I should be recruited by Ohio State as I was well suited to his type of football. He emphasized my size as well as my speed. During my Freshman year at Ohio State, one of the physical education departments was gauging the physical performances of entering freshmen. To the amazement of the examiners, most of my performance tests were off the chart compared to the other students. The Freshman year in football further improved my techniques and speed of response. These two improvements in performance are essential in players of Big Ten caliber. In the spring, Paul would start the practices by designating a first team. I was to be one of the starting tackles along with Chuck Csuri. We had plenty of competition from Don McCafferty, the future coach of the Baltimore Colts, Jim Rees, a hard working high school fullback who Paul converted to a tackle, and Jack Dugger who would be chosen as an All American tackle in 1944.

There was so much talent on our line along with the intensity of training under Paul Brown that the players who formed the line of the 42 team were almost to a man either to be selected as All Americans or would have outstanding careers in playing or coaching in universities or the professional leagues. By mid-season we were judged the best team in the country. The entire season was marred only by our loss to Wisconsin when most of the team was stricken with diarrhea. The remainder of the year we were unbeaten and untied. We ended the season by beating both an outstanding Michigan team and the highly vaunted Iowa Seahawks. Our last game against the Seahawks was a masterpiece of offense and defense.

In the spring, the Penn Relays were held in Philadelphia. We traveled by train to Philadelphia and were checking into the hotel the day before the track meet was to begin. As I came to the front desk to check in, I was told that the hotel did not allow Black people to register.

Other arrangements were made for me to stay with a Black family in the city. After the Penn Relays were over, I went back to the hotel to join the team for our train trip back to Columbus. I was told the track team from Ohio State had already left. Stranded in Philadelphia, I called Paul Brown who arranged for the money and a ticket to get me back home.

I was drafted into the service in the late summer of 1943. Expecting to be sent to basic training camp from Ft. Hayes in Columbus, I put my toothbrush in my pocket and reported to the induction center. To my surprise, I was declared 4-F because of severe varicose veins. The induction officer told me that the Army had no provisions to correct this type of disability in inductees and to return after I had surgery. I had no money to have the surgery, so I returned to the university and fall practice for the 1943 season.

Ohio State had only Army training programs which prohibited any trainees from playing intercollegiate sports in contrast to the other Big Ten schools with Navy programs that allowed participation. We became known as the "Baby Bucks" for the war had shattered Paul's dream of a football dynasty. The enlistments and draft left few players with Big Ten experience to face other schools well-entrenched with experienced collegiate or professional football players. With the material available to him, Paul built a very respectable team. I was the only first string player from the previous season along with Jack Dugger, Bill Hackett, and Cecil Souders who were on our 42 roster. Les Horvath was in dental school and Don Steinberg in medical school. But all of them were part of the Army training program at Ohio State and not allowed to play. I am sure that this was Paul's only losing season but one in which he can take great pride. Soon after Paul himself enlisted and was sent to the Great Lakes Training Center to be the Head Coach of their football team. He left Carol Widdoes to coach the team in 1944. These "Baby Bucks" had grown up. Les Horvath was released from Army service and now had another year of eligibility due to a change in the collegiate rules to four years instead of three. Now with an experienced line and the addition of three outstanding freshmen, the 1944 team remained unbeaten the entire season and were the champions of the Big Ten and ranked second only to Army in the polls. Les's play was so outstanding that he was selected for the Heisman Trophy. Jack Dugger, Bill Hackett and I were picked on All American teams. Carol Widdoes was named the Coach of the Year.

After graduation, I was appointed the Head Coach at Kentucky State University. This was Kentucky's "separate but equal" policy to educate Black students. We were a small school and played similar Black schools in the area. We had a small stadium and cheerleaders who would admonish us with the usual plea, "We want a touchdown! We want a touchdown!" When the team was finally able to score, the girl students would respond, "We're Satisfied, We're Satisfied" in their sexiest voices. My heart was not really in coaching. The war was over and the papers were filled with the news that Paul Brown was organizing a professional team to play in Cleveland. I called Paul and wanted to try out for the team. Paul told me he would get back to me in the near future. In the meantime, the Montreal Argonauts were trying to sign me to play in the Canadian League. I was just about resigned that I would not hear from Paul and was packing my bags to go to Canada and away from the discrimination still rampant in the United States. Unbeknown to me, Paul was trying figure a way to circumvent the unwritten code against Black athletes in the new conference. One of Paul's best friends was Paul Hornung, the sportswriter for the Columbus Dispatch. I was on my way to Canada when Paul Hornung called, "Why don't you go to Bowling Green University where the Browns are training and try out for the team? "Well," I answered, "I called Paul and he never called me back. Anyway, I'm going to Montreal tomorrow to try out for the Argonauts in the Canadian League." Paul insisted, "I really think you should stop in Bowling Green." Hornung was never known to me to be a very insistent person, so I assume that Coach Brown had solved his dilemma in this manner.

I arrived at Bowling Green University about 11:00 the following morning in the middle of their practice. Paul merely said, "Bill, get your uniform from the equipment manager and I will meet you at the other end of the field with the Center, two Guards and Otto Graham. The Center was Mo Scarry who had many years of professional experience. I had developed a technique of watching the Center and charging as soon as I saw his hands tighten on the ball. My reaction time was so fast that I was in the backfield before the Quarterback could receive the ball and pivot to start the play. In two hours, I had arrived at the Browns' training camp, practiced and signed my contract. This little ploy with Paul Horning had accomplished Paul's goal to sign me and Marion Motley.

The Cleveland Browns were a formidable team for ten years, the last five in the National Football League after the merger with the All American League. Our Ohio State 1942 team was the nucleus of this team. During my pro career of eight years we were the champions or contenders for the championship every year. After an appropriate number of years, I was inducted into the Professional Football Hall of Fame. Shortly thereafter, I was also inducted into the Intercollegiate Hall of Fame. Very few players have been so honored.

The same discrimination that I had had in high school and college was still present in the professional leagues. Oftentimes, Marian and I had to stay with friends in the Southern cities when we played in the All American League. After a lifetime of slanted social overtones of racial bias, the acceptance of Black people into the social fabric of our country was beginning. This first acceptance was through Paul Brown's unwavering attitude that the best players should play on his team regardless of any other factors. Marian Motley and I led the way for Jackie Robinson and Kenny Washington from UCLA to be given the opportunity to participate in professional athletics. I always maintained my self respect without surrendering to the injustices I felt so often in high school, at the Penn Relays in Philadelphia, or in the early years of professional football. We had led the way and had broken the barriers against Black athletes in America. I feel that I had made the right choices and I was truly able to lead the way and help my people.

One afternoon in 1947, Marion Motley and I were having lunch in a restaurant in downtown Cleveland. There were a group of girls sitting together at a nearby table. One was a lovely girl named Odessa. I was sure she was smiling at me, but to this day, she claims she was smiling at the man at the table behind me. This beautiful girl with the lovely smile was more than I could resist. I went over to her table and introduced myself. It was the beginning of a beautiful courtship and we were married the following year.

Odessa and I did not turn out any super athletes like their father, but we were blessed with three sons whom we are very proud. One son has his A.B.and master's degrees in public administration and is employed at the state level of human services. Another son specializes in career planning and counseling for the state and federal government. Our third son has already achieved two master's degrees in mathematics and Business after receiving his undergraduate engineering degree. Of course, our greatest joys are our three grandchildren.

After my retirement from professional football, I was appointed by the Governor of Ohio to be the head of the Ohio Youth Commission. My Master's degree in Education was extremely important as we were dealing with hundreds of boy and girls with social problems who were unable to function in normal society. I retained this position for twenty-five years and through three governors. A grand ceremony was held in my honor to celebrate my retirement. A high school which was built near Columbus to assist in the rehabilitation of these youngsters was named in my honor, the William K. Willis High School.

PAUL SARRINGHAUS

Football:	Ohio State, 1941, 1942, 1945
	Ft. Bragg Bombardiers, 1943
	Detroit Lions, 1946
	Chicago Cardinals, 1947
	Second Team All American
Education:	B.A. in Education
Career:	Teaching Secondary Education
	Land and Building Appraisal
Married:	Lillian – 41 years
	Two children & three grandchildren
Service:	Ft. Bragg and Ft. Campbell
	Artillery and Supply Co.

PAUL SARRINGHAUS

I n every football season there are particular football games that
standout in your memory. This is also true of events in games that
you remember as lasting mementos. Their importance may not even
be of great significance but there they are. During the 1941 season,
which preceded the use of face masks, I was struck in the nose. My nose
was bleeding so profusely that we had to call a time out. I went over to
the bench expecting to be replaced in the line up when Paul asked, "Do
you think it is broken?" "I don't know whether it is or not," I replied.
"Well, we need you in the game and we'll fix your nose later." I guess
Paul didn't consider a broken nose of much importance, and I returned
to the game as soon as the bleeding stopped. Another time, I was
playing safety man on defense, when a halfback ran past me for a
touchdown. I don't really believe that I saw him. Mistakes like that were
intolerable to Paul Brown. He immediately replaced me in the game and
asked, "Why didn't you tackle him?" In my best bravado, I answered,
"Where I come from, they never got that far." Recognizing that my
nearsightedness was a problem, by the next game, I had contact lens and
I entered a new world. I could see what was going on without my glasses.
I am fairly certain that I was the first player to be fitted with contact
lens to correct my nearsightedness.

Coming to Ohio State was an ambition that started well back in
my childhood. My heart was set on attending Ohio State primarily to
avenge the defeat by Notre Dame late in the fourth quarter after it
appeared that Ohio State would win the game. I was eleven or twelve
years old and I hadn't the foggiest idea how the scheduling of games
were arranged.

My grandparents had come from Germany at the turn of the
century and had settled in Hamilton, Ohio, a small city close to
Cincinnati. Mom and dad were living in Indiana when I was born. We
were very poor but my dad had a thorough love for baseball. My mother
often told the story of dad buying a pair of baseball shoes despite our
poverty. But more important was the death of my father in the post
World War I flu epidemic when I was only two years old. Mom struggled
to keep us together working as a seamstress in a department store. I was

enrolled in a grade school where I spent three years in the first and second grade. It was accidentally discovered that I was not mentally retarded, but that I was unable to see the blackboard. I was fitted with eyeglasses and soon I could read, write, and learn as well as the other children. Our life in Indiana was a continual hardship. The only financial asset my mother had was the family home in Hamilton that her parents had left her in their wills. We returned to Hamilton where I continued my grade school and high school education. Hamilton High School was the only high school in the city. The number of students in the high school was as large as any in the state, and Hamilton High was a football powerhouse, particularly my senior year. I played in all of the team sports but football was my game. As Captain of the team, I was the leading scorer in the state and named All State halfback in 1939. I was heavily recruited by over forty universities across the country, but my only consideration was Ohio State. My childhood ambition to beat Notre Dame continued still not knowing that university schedules are arranged years in advance. Most of the university alumni in Hamilton were from Ohio State and meeting Ernie Godfrey convinced me to attend Ohio State.

There were no athletic scholarships as we know them today. The athletic department had part time state jobs for us or part time jobs in private companies in Columbus whose owners were devoted Ohio State alumni. Besides waiting on tables at the fraternity house to earn my keep, I worked at the David Davies Baby Beef Co. along with Les Horvath and several other football players. The only thing "Baby" about the sides of beef were on the company labels. The evenings were spent throwing 200-300 pound sides of beef to be loaded or unloaded.

Ernie Godfrey had recruited an outstanding freshman team in 1940. When Paul Brown came to coach his first year at Ohio State there were still many outstanding athletes from the 1940 Varsity team who were still eligible to play. Nevertheless, over half of the 1941 starting team were 1940 freshmen. By the end of the 1942 season, these 1940 Freshmen were All Americans or first team All Conference. From the first two teams of the 1942 squad, all of the players were at least Honorable Mention All Conference or would be All Americans during their collegiate years. Gene Fekete was a contending athlete for the Heisman Trophy as a sophomore. Les Horvath won the Heisman Trophy in 1944.

I continue to look back with intense pride to our 1942 National

Championship team. I am sure the success was due to Paul Brown. His absolute demands for discipline and his relentless pursuit of victory are characteristics which were singularly Paul Brown. I was the power halfback, the safety man, and occasionally the punter. During the season, I scored 13 touchdowns and was named All Big Ten and second string All American. Our game against Michigan was the most memorable to me as we beat Michigan with three touchdown passes, Horvath to Sarringhaus, Sarringhaus to Horvath and Sarringhaus to Bob Shaw.

I was majoring in education at Ohio State when everything was interrupted by the war. My first permanent assignment was to Ft. Bragg where our displaced Buckeyes were now the Ft. Bragg "Bombardiers". I only played one game with Lin Houston and Don McCafferty and all the others before I was reassigned to Ft. Campbell, Kentucky. While in Service I played in the Chicago Tribune All Star Game against the Chicago Bears who had a tough time winning 20-17. Unfortunately, I fractured my ankle in this game. I was never sent overseas and spent the next two and a half years in artillery and supply companies in the states.

After my discharge, I returned to Ohio State to complete my education in 1945. My return to football was heralded across the nation with my picture on the cover of Life magazine as the most promising player of the coming season. We had outstanding personnel returning to this team but things were not the same without Paul Brown. We remained unbeaten until well into the season when we lost to Purdue. I separated my shoulder and that ended my playing career for the season and my selection as an All American.

Following my graduation in education, I was drafted by the Detroit Lions and played one year for them and the next year for the Chicago Cardinals. Pro football lacked much of the spirit that pervades college ball and I returned to use my degree in teaching the next year. After several years in teaching, I entered the real estate appraisal business which has remained my profession. Much of my work over the past 30 years has been as a consultant to Hamilton County on appraisals.

Lillian and I have been married for 41 years and have two children and three grandchildren. Both of our children are college graduates and one son is an attorney.

Sitting here in my living room recovering from hip replacement surgery and recalling our college years, we were an outstanding group of people brought together by Ernie Godfrey and Paul Brown.

PUPPY LOVE AND ENDURING MARRIAGES

Miriam Roberts had just left the school cafeteria and was slowly walking down the long hall of Elyria High School with thoughts of her classroom work the farthest thing from her mind. Here she was beginning her senior year in high school and she had not been asked to be a member of the Aeros. This was the problem that was occuping all of her thoughts. The girls in the Aeros were her best friends and still they excluded her from their club with all of the social events and parties that filled the Aero's social calendar. Today was particularly troubling as she had just finished her lunch with these girls. Vivian, who was vice-president of the senior class, explained to Marian that the criteria for being in the Aeros was to have a boy friend. It was fine for her, as her boy friend was the president of the class, and Marian, now in her Senior year, didn't have even a prospect for a boy friend and she was missing all of the fun. Nancy, one of the Aeros and a close friend to Marian caught up with her in the hall and said, "Isn't there someone who you like and might ask you out for a date? Perhaps we could put a bug in his ear." "Well, there is one boy, Bob Jabbusch, who is the smartest boy in the science class and is going to be the Captain of the football team. But he is so shy I doubt that he even goes out with girls." The wheels soon began to turn as "by chance" Bob Jabbusch was discretely told by an Aero member that he really should ask Marian Roberts out for a date. Within a few weeks, Marian and Bob were seen holding hands as they walked through the halls to their classes and Marian was now a full fledged member of the Aeros. Marian and Bob graduated from Elyria High and went off to Ohio State. Bob was sent overseas to fight with the infantry in Europe and when the war ended, in story book fashion, Marian was waiting and they were married in Texas where Bob was discharged. Together they returned to Ohio State University so Bob could complete his education in engineering. During the next year, Marian and Bob's son, Mark, was born on Dad's Day while Bob, now the Captain of the Ohio State football team, was playing in Ohio State's football game against Iowa. This marriage is now in its 47th year and has been blessed with three children and seven grandchildren.

Jack Roe and Mildred had been sweethearts all through high school. Jack was the all-state Center for Youngstown High School and was the personal choice of Paul Brown's who had remarked to Jack that if he were ever to be a college coach he would like to have Jack on his team. By coincidence, Paul followed Jack to Ohio State. Paul's interests in his players was just as intense as his desire to develop winning football teams. This included knowing important facts about each of his players. Marriage was almost unknown among college athletes and when Jack introduced Mildred to Paul at one of our team's social gatherings, he said, "Coach Brown, I would like you to meet my wife." Paul Brown almost fell out of his chair, and Jack found himself relegated to the fourth string instead of competing with Bill Vickroy for the starting Center position. Times have changed but this marriage has endured through fifty one years. The early days of surviving on a part time salary and the kindnesses of their landlady left two dimes each week for Mildred and Jack to go to the movies.

Cy Souders, who has had one of the more illustrious lives among the members of the team, was married, had a children and ran a boarding house while he was still a freshman in college. While Cy was a freshman, he and Jean eloped to Kentucky soon after her nineteenth birthday. When their little girl was born, Cy quit school to work in a steel mill to support his new family. When Paul Brown became coach, he was induced to return to school and return to the football team. So he was still a freshman, a husband, a father, and the manager of a boarding house while he played freshman football.

The sociology of the 40's was markedly different from our situation today with its frequent divorces, broken homes, and no separation of teenage and adult social patterns. Almost every player who had a high school girl friend maintained this relationship even after being separated by years in the service. When the boys returned, they invariably married their high school or college girl friends. It was almost as if it were a "fait accompli". The girls waited until they returned from service and soon they were married. And all of these marriages have lasted through the years unless they were separated by an untimely death. If one of the players were then to marry again, the second marriages were also successful.

The prize for the most children goes to the Antonnuci family of eight children. The Antonnuci Engineering Co. provided the means for 15 professional degrees from Harvard, Ohio State and many other universities where undergraduate, masters and doctorate degrees were achieved by each of the children. The prize for the largest number of grandchildren goes to Carmen Naples. He had to leave college just before he earned his degree in chemistry to manage the family restaurant in Youngstown upon the death of his father. If you visit Youngstown and eat at the " Golden Dawn", I am sure you will meet at least one of his 25 grandchildren.

I am sure the people of our country would like to return to these years of stability created by the unswerving commitment of married life. There is no greater pride and happiness in this world than succeeding generations of families of parents, children and grandchildren.

Fraternity Christmas Formal

CECIL SOUDERS

Football:	Ohio State, 1942, 1943, 1944, 1946
	Great Lakes Naval Training, 1944
	Bainbridge Naval Training, 1945
	Detroit Lions, 3 years
Education:	B.A. in Business Administration
Career:	Vice President
	Suburban Motor Freight Company
Married:	Jean – 51 years
	Two children
Service:	U.S. Navy

CECIL SOUDERS

In the merry-go-round of life, one would be hard put to predict a smoothly running course toward success when a boy falls in love, marries, and has a child by the time he is 21 years old. Following these "events", he would play collegiate football for five years, service football for two years and professional football for three years. From a distance, one might say, I should have grown up sometime. For a short period of time I quit college, as I felt it was the proper thing to do when our baby was born. Nevertheless, looking back, I had a wonderful education at Ohio State. Jean and I have been married for over 50 years, and my sports career was filled with some unique experiences and memorable occasions. I wouldn't trade my "merry-go-round" for the experiences of any other man.

All of this began in the small town of Bucyrus near the center of Ohio. We lived on the edge of town where my parents were in the business of hatching chicks which were then sold to the poultry farmers. The wide open spaces and the forests nearby were perfect for all of our outdoor activities like chasing rabbits, playing "kick the can", and refusing to show up for piano lessons. As a boy we had a cow in town for milk, all kinds of domestic animals and a pony cart for me to check out the countryside. I rode in several of the county fairs racing my pony cart as a sulky and was nicknamed Cecil, the Jockey.

In the spring, the local Y.M.C.A. organized baseball teams in the sandlots around town. I played first base admirably but my athletic eye was on football. I couldn't wait until I was old enough to play football. Organized football was played only in the high school until I organized a league among the boys in the elementary schools. The number of players each team would have for a game was determined by the fewest players who would show up at each game for one of the two teams. For a football field, we stacked out the yard markers in a cow pasture. I was ten years old at the time, and my football "self image" was firmly implanted and never discarded.

In high school, I played with the freshman football team and then three years with the Varsity. We had unremarkable seasons but I do clearly remember our game against Galion, my senior year. Bill Durtschi was one of Galion's star backs, and man, were they big! They beat us up unmercifully. My senior year in 1938, I was six ft. one in. and weighed about 170. I played fullback, end, linebacker and also did the punting. I was selected to join the All Central Ohio team to play in the Kumquat Bowl in St Petersburg, Florida against an All Florida team on Christmas Day 1938. It was a great experience meeting a number of young aspiring football players. It was here that I was recruited by Louisiana State University.

I was convinced that I would accept the scholarship to Louisiana State when a young lady, Jean Hoover, and Mr. Ohio State, Ernie Godfrey, entered my life. Jean had moved from Chicago to Bucyrus the year before and was the prettiest cheerleader in the school. Ernie used every guile he could muster to convince me to come to Ohio State. He found out that Jean was my girl friend and wasted no time in convincing her that she should keep me in Ohio and not in Louisiana with all those Southern gals. I am sure that this had much to do with my staying in Ohio as I didn't want to leave my love behind.

Ernie had invited me to Columbus several times. On one trip I met the then great Francis Schmidt, the Head Coach at Ohio State. What a character he was and what a driver! Ernie and I were sitting next to Coach Schmidt as he drove his roadster through the streets from downtown Columbus to the campus. The car was careening wildly in his favorite sport of passing streetcars on the wrong side of the street and disregarding all of the oncoming automobiles. All the while he was screaming, "Come to Ohio State! Come to Ohio State!" In later years, I related this "death defying" stunt to Paul Hornung, the reporter for the Columbus Dispatch. He said that Schmidt was once an Army major and used this stunt to demonstrate "courage" and this was one of his trademarks. I was only one of 150 young men who joined the freshman team in 1939. I made the first string and one of our duties was to play offense and defense against the Varsity. I always had a great deal of fun anytime I played football and on one particular afternoon I was playing End on defense and driving Schmidt crazy after tackling the ball carrier for losses on nine consecutive plays. His profanity was merciless, and soon he started shouting, "Get this kid out of here, I don't want to see anymore of him"!

Shortly before Thanksgiving, Jean and I decided that we wanted to spend the rest of our lives together. On Nov.18th we ran away to

Kentucky and were married. The following year, after our baby was born, I dropped out of school and went to work in a steel foundry. I returned to Ohio State in 1941 with a wife and child and still a freshman. Jean was 19 and I was almost 21. It may be hard to believe, but we ran a boarding house to help pay the bills. We were a little family struggling to exist, working full time jobs, going to school and playing football. Since there was not grant-in-aid I don't think we could have made it without some help from our parents. Our marriage is now past its 50th year.

I went out for football in the fall, after Ernie had introduced me to Paul Brown. During the season I was the second string to Bob Shaw but still played in most of the games. It was a wonderful experience to have played under Paul as well as winning the National Championship. I returned the next year, the year of the "Baby Bucks" as we were called in 1943. We had to play against teams who were loaded with professional players and outstanding college players. They were in the various military programs carried out on the college campuses. Almost all or our players were freshmen with little football experience, but we were a happy group and as the season progressed we got better and better. I think this team was an excellent example of the wonderful coaching ability of Paul Brown. I caught the eye of the national wire services that year. It was unusual to find a married man with a child playing Big Ten football. At the time, I am sure there were a lot of people who were wondering what was the world coming to, seeing my picture and descriptions of our family life on the sports pages of newspapers across the country.

Before the 1944 season, Paul had left for the Navy, but he had established his will to win with the remaining players along with Les Horvath, and three great freshman backs. It was a repetition of the 1942 season, but this time we were undefeated. Les would win the Heisman Trophy and we were named second in the nation as the most outstanding team behind Army with Davis and Blanchard. During the middle of the season, just after the Wisconsin game, I was drafted into the Navy and sent to Great Lakes Training Center in Chicago. My first Saturday at Great Lakes we were scheduled to play Wisconsin. For the second time in two weeks, I was again facing the same Wisconsin tackle. I am sure he was surprised to see me facing him again. "Do you have a twin brother playing for Ohio State," he asked? "Nope," I answered,"I just wanted to play against you again.". I really don't think he believed me. This was one of the many, many funny happenings in my life.

At the end of my 1944 Ohio State–Great Lakes season, I was transferred to Bainbridge, Maryland Naval Base. We were the sports headquarters for the Navy and played other Navy service teams including the Annapolis Naval Academy. It was here that I had my only sea duty. It was an overnight ferryboat ride from Baltimore to Norfolk to play the Norfolk Base team. I tell everyone that I got seasick. While I was at Bainbridge, I was drafted by the Washington Redskins who wanted me to play on Sundays after our Naval base games on Saturdays. I didn't think this was a good idea.

I returned to Ohio State after my discharge in 1946 to finish my senior year and get my degree. The Detroit Lions had traded for me and wanted me to sign with them for the fall of 1946. Paul Bixler was now the coach at Ohio State. He and my wife wanted me to stay in school, and I had to decide between school and the pros. There would have been no question about this except that I was now 25 years old. I decided to stay in school. I have received a multitude of honors in collegiate football during the years. I played in four post season All Star games, made All Big Ten several times, was twice honorable mention All American, and voted the most valuable player on the Ohio State squad in 1946. My collegiate honors were topped off by being awarded the Chicago Tribune Silver-Diamond Football Award.

Football continued in our lives as we moved on to the Detroit Lions after graduation. I joined the Lions in 1947 along with several other players from our 1942-46 teams. There were Tommy James, Paul Sarringhaus, and myself from the 1942 team and Russ Thomas and Dick Flanagan. I answered an ad for a position with the Suburban Motor Freight Co. who had offices in Detroit and Columbus during my second year with the Lions. I played football for two more years while I was also working for Suburban Motor Freight. After three years, I decided it was time to leave football and concentrate fully on my job with Suburban.

My years in football had given me numerous wonderful experiences as well as meeting outstanding and prominent people. Once while I was in California, I was staying at Don Ameche's beach house in Malibu. I met many of the famous movie stars of the day—Bette Davis, Lauren Bucall, Humphrey Bogart, Sam Snead and Bob Hope. Don gave me a personal tour of Hollywood and it was really something to remember. My football career was guided by many coaches—Frank Leahy, Wally Butts, Bernie Bierman, Andy Kerr, Moose Krause, Bo McMillan, Gus Dorais, and George Wilson. I had spent two years with Paul Brown and he was the best of all the coaches. In 1947, after graduation, he told me, "Cecil, I would like to have you on the Cleveland Browns but your're getting a little old for helping to start a new team in a new league." Good man, that Brown.

I started out as a salesman for Suburban Motor Freight and after two years I was made the Detroit Terminal Manager. A few years later, I was also put in charge of our terminals in all of Michigan and Indiana. We later moved back to Columbus and I was promoted to vice-president of the Company. During my 37 years with Suburban, I had hired many famous Ohio State grads like All American Jack Dugger, Jack Lininger, Rick Hoyt, and many others.

During my life, so filled with football, business and memorable experiences, none have been more important than our married life and two children. I remember, well, going off hand in hand with my little daughter and dropping her at the first grade of school before going to my classes in 1946. She also was an Ohio State grad and her son, Randy, is also now at Ohio State. There were some trying times, but, by golly, we made it thanks to my wife, Jean.

JACK ROE

Football:	Ohio State, 1941, 1942, 1945
Education:	B.A. in Education
Career:	Wholesale Food Brokerage
Married:	Mildred – 50 years Two children & one grandchild
Service:	World War II – Bomber Pilot Thirty-five Misisons over Germany

JACK ROE

World War II in Europe was drawing to a close, and I had been grounded after sustaining a shrapnel injury near my knee joint. A fragment of flak had pierced the fuselage as I was piloting our B-17 on my last bombing run into Germany. One weekend, as the war was winding down, my friend and co-pilot decided to take leave and fly into Scotland to a small city named Bellshill. Here my father and his family had lived before coming to America. I had often wondered why my father seemed to be constantly encouraging me to become a fine athlete. At times his encouragement was more like insistence. We arrived in the town on Sunday morning and, by chance, I introduced myself to many of the townspeople. As soon as they realized who I was, they recalled, with almost a frenzied enthusiasm, many of the past athletic exploits of my dad, their star soccer player. We marched down to the center of the town and opened the Beer Pub so they could properly express their happiness that I had taken the trouble to return to the town of my ancestors.

The steel mills in the Ohio valley were built around Stubenville, Ohio and Wheeling, West Virginia. In order to find experienced steel workers for the mills, the companies went to Scotland to find men with experience and encouraged my dad to come to America. Dad left Scotland for Stubenville and, later, brought over his father and three brothers. He was a quiet man, and I had no inkling when I was a young boy that he had been a star soccer player. However, he did urge me over and over to play football. Stubenville High School was frequently one of the powerhouse centers of football in northeastern Ohio. Our last game of my senior year was against Canton McKinley, the arch rival of Massillon High School. We had lost to Massillon the week before 6-0 in a driving rain storm. After the game with Canton McKinley, Paul Brown came into our dressing room. He had come to the game to scout the Canton Bulldogs who would be playing Massillon the next weekend. He introduced himself to me and said, "Jack, if I ever have a chance to coach a college team, I would like to have you on my squad". I did not realize how important this meeting would be at the time. At the end of the season I was selected as the All Ohio Center. In the spring of 1939, an annual banquet of all the All Ohio players was held in Columbus. Here I met Frances Schmidt, the Head Coach of Ohio State and Ernie Godfrey one of his assistant coaches. They had been alerted to recruit me to came to Ohio State by Dr. Cox, a dentist, from Stubenville. It didn't take much persuasion for them to fulfill my dreams of playing collegiate football with a national football power like Ohio State. I have always felt that I was the personal choice of Paul Brown's to the All Ohio team as he headed the selection board. By the spring of 1941, Paul had been appointed the new Head Coach at Ohio State University. I now felt that good fortune and hard work often go hand in hand. I remembered my meeting with Paul in our dressing room at Stubenville, being named All Ohio, enrolling at Ohio State and finally Paul Brown being named the Head Coach. Assuredly, this was a combination of fates.

During the 1941 and 1942 seasons at Ohio State, Bill Vickroy and I were the most experienced and able Centers and we competed for the starting position until one day when I found myself relegated to the third and fourth string. Paul, at that time, was intensely interested in all of our activities and liked to know as much about his players as possible. We were at some social gathering one evening when I introduced the young lady I was with to Paul. "I would like you to meet my wife", and Paul almost fell out of his chair. I suspect that this was more than he could handle since it was so rare that a college athlete would be married. I am sure he did not appreciate not knowing important matters about his players, such as being married. Mildred and I had been dating since she was thirteen years old, and she was the only sweetheart that I ever had. My first year at Ohio State was an academic disaster. After we were married in 1940 when Mildred was eighteen years old, there was a remarkable academic reversal. I was doing very well in the College of Education. Well, be that as it may, Mildred and I are celebrating fifty years of very happy married life this year.

I have always felt very proud to have played on our 1942 team as all of the young men and coaches were quality people. This feeling is repeatedly reinforced at each of our five year reunions. I am sure each of us has saved memorabilia of these wonderful years and the close friendships we made have lasted a lifetime. I often wonder how in the world we got along going to college, playing football, working part time in the Ohio Bureau of the Aged, and being married. We had a small apartment rented from the mother of one of the college professors. She was more than kind to us, and at the end of each week, we saved two dimes to take us to the movies. Of course, after the war, when I returned to finish my degree at Ohio State, I was still being paid by the Air Force while I was playing football for Ohio State in 1945. My wife was succeeding very well as the private secretary to Columbus's shopping mall magnet and later working for the owner of the White Tower Hamburger Chain. But, these were later years and could never compare to the happy week-ends when we had only two dimes left to go to the movies.

After the 1942 season, everything changed rapidly with us and the rest of the team. I enlisted in the Air Force at the beginning of the war. I attended cadet training school with Dick Palmer. He had been the star halfback with Cleveland Shaw High School and our 1942 team. Through high school he had been friends with Dorthey Parker, who later would become a noted movie actress. We were often together and at our cadet school graduation, our class was featured in the movie, "Winged Victory".

I was a pilot of a B-17 Bomber throughout my service with the Air Force in Europe. I recall my first mission flying into the heartland of Germany. I thought there were thunder clouds forming over our target area. My senior pilot explained that this was not a cloud formation but enemy flak filling the sky. To this day, I have always felt I had a "Protector" looking after my safety. During my 35 missions into enemy territory our B-17 bomber was shot down three times. Each time, I miraculously survived and was able to make my way back to friendly territory. It is very difficult to describe in words how one feels in any battle. Everyone is totally frightened that he may not survive. A strange thing happened to me that assured me that I no longer needed to be afraid. We were on a mission over Germany when the cloud formations often obscured the positions of our planes in the flying formation. While I was flying thorough one of these clouds, I thought I heard the command, "turn right" although the battle plan at this point was to turn left. I asked the other pilot if he heard this command and he stated he heard nothing. I "heard" this command again and decided to turn right instead of left. Almost instantaneously, we avoided a B-17 who most certainly would have crashed into our plane if I had turned to the left. From then on, I was convinced that I no longer need be afraid and I would survive the war.

It was a standing rule that pilots would have 25 missions into enemy territory, but by the end of my flying service I had 35 missions. The first mission was on Christmas Day 1944 and the last on my birthday in 1945. The only injury that I sustained was a piece of flak that lodged in the area of my knee. It was never very troublesome to me until later on in life. Our squadron was also involved in breaking the stranglehold on our forces in the Battle of the Bulge. Our squadron was unable to fly due to the inclement weather, but as soon as the skies cleared, we were in the battle to relieve the pressure on Bastogne and defeat the German offensive.

Being unable to fly because of my shrapnel injury, I was made the Physical Education Director for our unit while we were still in Europe. Shortly after returning to the States, I became a flight instructor at Lockbourne Air Base just outside of Columbus. After my discharge at the end of the war, I returned to Ohio State to complete my education in the College of Education and rejoined to football team for the 1945 season. I graduated with my A.B. degree in 1946. I received an inquiry from the Los Angeles Rams about my interest in professional football but decided not to pursue it as I intended to enter dental school. My desire to finally support my family changed my mind about dental school as this would mean four more years at the university. I received an offer to be the sales manager for a local automobile agency in Columbus and this ended my scholastic years. My association with the auto agency lasted two years. I went to work for the Abbott Food Co. where I remained for twenty-five years until my retirement. We were a small food brokerage firm which grossed about $10,000.00 per week when I started with the company. By the time I retired we had grown steadily and now grossed $250,000.00 per week. I had the good fortune to participate in the company's profit sharing plan which has made my retirement financially sound.

As I look back, I have a deep pride in my enduring marriage to Mildred, my high school sweetheart. We have two adopted sons and one grandchild. My years of participation in football both in high school and at Ohio State fulfilled my father's aspirations for me although I am sure he was much more renowned than I. As for my military service, I really feel that there was a Divine protector for me as I was able to survive so many harrowing war experiences with only a minor injury. There are several other members of our team who had similar war experiences with miraculous survival. I am really looking forward to 1992.

GEORGE SLUSSER
U.S. Air Force

THE VALIENT AMERICANS

All men pray for peace, but, strangely, it is not always possible. The citizens of all nations are often called to the defense of their countries to defend against aggression or possible subjugation. The citizens of America responded to these threats in a manner that made the decade of the 1940's the proudest hours of our nation's existence.

Wars are not fought by generals who plan or direct. A War is fought by the foot soldiers, sailors, and airmen in actual combat. Men would die in these battles as did George Slusser, Tom Cleary, and Warren McDonald. Tom and Warren were substitue players on the 42 team but both were hard-working faithful cogs in this championship team. George Slusser, although he was not a first string player, was a vital part of our playing team. He was a Massillon High star halfback for Paul and recieved an athletic scholarship to Dartmouth University. When Paul came to be the Head Coach at Ohio State, George left Dartmouth to join Paul's team at Ohio State. Like Lin Houston and Tommy James, George had a close personal relationship with Paul Brown like members of a common family. George had a wonsderful flair for living. He was handsome, gregarious, and fun loving. It seemed only natural that he would become an Air Force fighter pilot as one visualizes fighting heros in the movies. But his life would end tragically when his plane crashed on the last day of the war.

Playing service football games were only minor episodes in the military lives of the 1942 team. Most of them would join their fellow Americans who fought the war across the globe. Dante Lavelli fought with the 28th Division, "The Bloody Buckets" Division. This division fought it way across Europe against the best of the German Army. Almost one in five of the 75, 000 soldiers who fought with this division during the course of the war would not be returning home. Bob Shaw fought with the 105th Division. At one time he was the personal body guard to the general of the division. In Europe, "The Battle of the Bulge" was the turning point in the war when Germany planned and almost successfully destroyed the Allied lines in the west. Among the soldiers who were called upon to hold fast were Dante Lavelli, Ken

THOMAS CLEARY
U.S. Navy

Coleman and Martin Amling. Martin Amling's artillery regiment was on the outskirts of Bastogne that wintery December. For 175 days they fought the Germans and slept in foxholes. Only one night was he able to find cover in a barn. To survive in this terrible weather, he said they had to adapt like animals. Ken Coleman's military career began with the British at Cherbourg where he was decorated by Winston Churchill. With numerous battle ribbons and Medals of Honor from England, France, Belgium and Holland, he too was surround at Bastogne. In order to break the hold that the Germens had on Bastogne, General Patton's army with Bob Jabbusch and Bob McCormick was pushing North to destroy the German effort. For days the weather over the Battle of the Bulge was so poor that the American Air Force with Paul Matus, Robin Priday, and Jack Roe were unable to fly. When the weather finally cleared on December 23, 1944, they were finally able to attack the Germans from the air. When Paul Matus's squadron took to the air, their battle plans were already known to the Germans. This sabatoge cost the lives of all the members of his crew except himself and his co-pilot. Paul related the events of his capture by the Germans and extent of the knowledge the Germans knew about him personnally. They knew everything about Paul from the time he was in grade school. This accounting, that he contributed for this book, is a masterpiece of history as he related the events of fifty Luftwaffe fighters attacking his squadron and his eventaul internement in Germany. Robin Priday's service career as well as Jack Roe's adds to our appreciation of the wonderful qualities of America. In this most important battle, eight members of our 1942 team were directly involved. Chuck Csuri's regiment had moved so fast in the last months of the war that they lost contact with the American lines and were surrounded. Chuck volunteered to try to re-establish contact with the American lines by working his way through the German positions. He went through the most harrowing hours of his life and recieved the Bronze Medal of Honor for his bravery.

Our Captain, George Lynn, had much different duties during the war. He was the commander of a large landing craft that had to be sailed across the Atlantic. Several times they would lose contact with their convoy which added to the problems of a flat bottomed ship in the North Atlantic. At the time of the invasion of Europe, his landing craft went into action bringing the soldiers to the European shore under the

WARREN McDONALD

U.S. Army

relentless fire power of the Germans. As soon as they disembarked one contingent, it was back to England for another regiment of soldiers.

Many of the Fort Bragg "Bombardiers" were transferred to the South Pacific after their training in artillery was "completed". Lin Houston fought with his unit from island to island as they worked their way back to the Phillappines fighting almost continuously for five months. Hal Dean was rather bored with the field artillery and volunteered for the parachute service. He, too, was sent to the south Pacific where they fought to retake the islands. Hal ended the war as a commander in the 9th Airbourne Division. Being a forward observer for the artilley is one of the more dangerous jobs in the service with a strong possibility one would not survive. Bill Vickroy was commissioned as a Lt. upon leaveing Ohio State where he spent four years in the R.O.T.C. Since Ohio State was a Field Artillery Reserve Officer unit, he remained a forward observer in the South Pacific. Bob Frye was also a forward observer in the South Pacific. All of these members of our 42 team were in combat units in the Second World War.

But service life was not without its humor. Cy Souders continued his admirable lifestlye as an ensign in the Navy. During his time in the service, his only sea voyage was a ferry boat ride from the Bainbridge Naval Station in Maryland to play football in Norfolk, Virginia. Of course, he got seasick.

KEN COLEMAN

Football: Ohio State, 1942
101st Airbourne Division – Europe, 1945

Education: B.A. in Business Administration

Career: Eastern United States Sales Director
Miror Corporation

Married: Judy – 45 years
Two children

Service: Infantry Commissioned – Officer in the Field
Fourteen Battle Ribbons
British, French, Belgium and Dutch Medals of Honor
Three Purple Hearts

KEN COLEMAN

Growing up in Brooklyn, New York, when someone spoke about sports it invariably involved baseball and the Brooklyn Dodgers. As a young boy and a teenager through high school, I ate, drank and dreamed about baseball. One day a notice was placed on the high school bulletin board that the Brooklyn Dodgers were planning a week long camp on baseball at Ebbetts Field for all interested high school athletes. With my glove and bat in hand, I attended these sessions religiously where we pitched, batted and fielded under the guidance and observation of our heroes, the World Champion Dodgers. After the week was over, day dreams about baseball filled my waking hours. About three weeks later, a letter arrived addressed to me from the Brooklyn Dodger Baseball Organization.

Dear Ken,

We were so impressed with your high school records and your hitting skills at our baseball school at Ebbetts Field, that we have chosen you as one of five young men whom we feel are excellent prospects for a career in the Dodger Baseball Organization. After your graduation from Madison High, we will offer you a bonus of $2800.00 to sign a professional baseball contract with the Dodger organization. Please consider this as a firm commitment on our part.

Sincerely Yours,
Office of Player Recruitment

Ma! Ma!, I shouted racing through the apartment looking for my Mother. "The Brooklyn Dodgers want to give me $2800.00 to sign a baseball contract! Think of it, I could be a star baseball player playing for the Dodgers." My mother turned around and looked me straight in the eye. "This is not for you. My son should have a college education and become someone we will always be proud of. You must go to college, you must go to college," she repeated over and over again.

My dream was buried, and in December the following year, at the age of sixteen, I graduated from Madison High School and was off for The Ohio State University. Ohio State was the educational conduit for hundreds of boys and girls who had graduated from high schools in New York City. Spring quarter, in 1940, revolved around attending classes, moving old French 75's in ROTC, and fulfilling my freshman obligation in physical education. Besides baseball, handball was my game. So I enrolled in handball classes to fulfil my phys. ed. requirement with none other than Ernie Godfrey, Mr. Ohio State, as my instructor. Ernie had quite a reputation in handball having been the National Champion in his youth. Ernie had two loves, his wife and Ohio State. He would volunteer to coach any sport requested of him. At that time he was an assistant coach in football and the Head Coach in baseball as well as his duties as an instructor in physical education. After he had demolished all the other students enrolled in hand ball to cover their phys ed requirement, he met up with me. In our first game, I won, and then the second, and then the third. Ernie was well into his middle years, but he must have taken these games to heart—he would not accept this smart aleck kid on the baseball team that spring. I must have rubbed him the wrong way.

Undaunted, if I couldn't play baseball, I would try out for the football team. My only association with football was my older brother who had been a star fullback for Syracuse. I became a "walk on" in a sport where Ohio State was often a national contender with a football recruiting system to match. Paul Brown had just become the Head Coach after Frances Schmidt had been dismissed. With "hat in hand" I went to the athletic offices to see Paul Brown having never practiced football or played in a football game. Paul must have recognized something in my determination. After analyzing my speed, agility, and intelligence, I was place with the Ends.

During the 1942 season, I was a reserve End and Center. The daily practices learning the "art" of football against the experienced players who actually played in the Saturday games, had many satisfactions in spite the pain and frequent periods of exhaustion. One day Paul approached me and said, "I see from your scholastic records that you received a K credit in Spanish." K credits were given to those freshmen who the university felt were so proficient that beginning Spanish was unnecessary. "Dante Lavelli is having difficulty with his Spanish, and I wonder if you would tutor him?" I agreed and tutored Dante successfully so he could remain eligible to continue to play football. The university made no amends to athletes as you were expected to achieve as well in the classrooms as any other student. This type of camaraderie enabled our team to fulfil the ambitions that Paul Brown had for us.

The dynasty that Paul was building at Ohio State in 1942 was soon to fall with the onset of World War II. I enlisted in the infantry. Infantry training was child's play compared to the rigors of football training under Paul Brown. I rose to become a sergeant in the Airborne Infantry. We shipped out for Europe to continue our training for the invasion of Europe. Just before the invasion, I was assigned to a British intelligence unit and I was with the British when they landed in Europe. We captured the Port of Cherbourg on the north coast of France. There was a German naval bunker built deep in the ground in the harbor area. They had sufficient supplies to last for many years in spite of being surrounded by British forces. I dropped a telephone down one of the ventilator shafts and found a British soldier fluent in German. The soldier spoke with the Germans below in the bunker and after several minutes, he informed me that the admiral in the bunker refused to surrender to any one but a Panzer general. Surveying the situation maps, I could not locate any tanks in our area. Instead, we brought up a number of personnel half-tracks and drove them up and down in front of the telephone. The Germans surrendered and about a month later Winston Churchill landed at Cherbourg. He personally awarded me the highest British medal for non-British soldiers.

Soon after, I returned to join my infantry unit as we fought across Europe. I was commissioned in the field and rose to become a captain by the end of the war. In all, I received 14 medals and three Purple Hearts for wounds I received in battle. Among these medals were the Croix de Guerre from France and Belgium, and the Dutch Order of William besides my decoration from Winston Churchill. Towards the end of the War, our unit was surrounded in the Battle of the Bulge in Bastogne waiting for the weather to clear so the German encirclement could be broken. The number of our 1942 team members who were involved in the Battle of the Bulge was amazing.

As the war was winding down, there was more time for diversions and football once again came into my life. We were still stationed in Europe when I joined the 101st Airborne Division's football team both as a player and a coach. We had quite a team with many former professional and prominent college football players.

After the war ended, I returned home to New York. After all of this time, my sweetheart, Judy, was still waiting for me. Our romance started at Ohio State during my sophomore year and now it was time to continue our lives together. We decided to get married not withstanding the fact that I was penniless. The favorite spot for honeymoons for people from New York with very limited assets was Atlantic City. We drove to Atlantic City and registered in a hotel that coincidentally was having a reunion of soldiers who had been wounded in the war. One afternoon, I was standing at the hotel bar, along with several of the veterans among whom was a paraplegic. This unfortunate man was in his wheel chair close by the bar. Surprisingly, he was blatantly blaming the Jews for his paralysis that had resulted from his war injuries. This diatribe continued until I walked up to him. "Say," I said, "Don't I know you?" The man showed no sign of recognition. "Weren't you hit by a mortar shell that tore open both of your legs?" "Yes," answered the veteran. "Was that on the day in Bastogne in the late afternoon when the snow was almost three feet high?" "How did you know," questioned the man? "Do you remember the soldier who carried you through the snow to the aid station that saved your life?" "No", he answered. " Well, I would like you to know that it was me, and, incidentally, I'm Jewish."

After our honeymoon, Judy and I returned to New York to our little apartment in Manhattan. I started my commercial career as a salesman for the Miror Corporation, one of the leading manufacturers of kitchen utensils, pots, and pans. I have stayed with this one company through the years. For the past fifteen years, I have been their sales director for the eastern United States. I direct their large sales force and fulfill their marketing objectives. I am gradually slowing down but still maintain an office in New York for the company. Judy and I have two children. Our son is an attorney in Charleston, West Virginia. I am told he is one of the outstanding attorneys in the city. Our daughter is married and lives in Georgia.

As I look back, I have had wonderful associations with our teammates in football. I have had perhaps unbelievable experiences in the service of our country. And, lastly, I have a wonderful wife, career and family.

PAUL MATUS

Football: Ohio State, 1942

Education: B.S. in Agricultural Sciences

Career: Supervisor in Plumbing Tool
             Company. Assisted in invention
             of pipe tool extractor.

Married: Eleanor – 45 years
             Two sons & four daughters

Service: Bomber Pilot in Europe

PAUL MATUS

One can make a very convincing argument that the years of 1941-1945 represented the most glorious period in American history. As a young man, these years were my most memorable. They were my formative years when dedication to noble purposes were fulfilled in spite of the World War that interrupted my education and athletic career. I fortunately survived my harrowing experiences in the defeat of Nazi Germany.

My father immigrated from Slovakia to America early in the 1900's. Soon after, he was able to send for his brothers and sisters. Life in Czechoslovakia was devoid of any future for them. He had come to America finding employment only as a coal miner in Western Pennsylvania. My mother, whose parents had also come Eastern Europe, insisted that dad leave the mines and move to the Cleveland area where my cousin, Cy Lipaj, and his family had settled. Like Lin Houston's Father's friend, dad was at the entrance of a mine shaft when an explosion ripped through the mine. The force of the explosion carried my dad through the air into an adjoining field. Certain that he had been killed, the rescue squad was more than startled to find my father, with extensive burns, walking back towards the mine. This miracle of survival paralleled my experiences as a B-26 bomber pilot over Germany during the Second World War.

Our family moved to Lakewood, Ohio where my father was employed as a Foreman at the Cleveland Welding Co. until the company closed due to the Great Depression. With a family of five boys and being unemployed for over two years, we moved to a farm of ninety acres near Wakeman, Ohio. Here we all pitched in to care for the farm animals, planting grain and vegetables, and harvesting.

My cousin, Cy Lipaj, being a high school football star, was actively recruited by Ohio State. Together we enrolled at Ohio State in the College of Agricultural Engineering. My primary interest in sports was baseball, but baseball was only played in the Spring. A notice was placed in the gym recruiting players for the Freshman football team. This induced me to try out for the team without any previous football experience. There were about 125 "walk ons" who met under the stadium with Paul Brown and Trevor Rees, the legendary All American

End who was now the Freshman football coach. Information cards were passed out to identify our previous football experience which I left entirely blank. When my name was called, Coach Rees asked why I had not filled out the card. I could only reply that I had never played football. In fact, I didn't even know how to wear the components of the uniform that was assigned the following Monday. Knowing nothing about football, the next two weeks of practice were the most miserable of my life. I was knocked about unmercifully. However, Coach Rees was most interested in players who had courageous hearts and speed as these were the basic ingredients necessary to teach football. Without heart, any talent is wasted.

Much to my surprise, I received an invitation from Paul Brown to join Spring practice with the Varsity. A total of 100 players received these invitations, and 10 would be cut each week until a squad of 50 players was reached. I fully expected to be cut each week, but each week I survived the cut. One day, Paul walked up to me with Coach Rees. "Teach Matus to play football. Listen and learn what Coach Rees tells you." I was overwhelmed to learn that Paul Brown thought enough of me to have Trevor Rees personally instruct me. Perhaps my participation in the Freshman intersquad game had convinced Paul to keep me on the squad. I caught several passes, one for a touchdown. This game had been broadcasted back to my hometown where my friends ribbed me about not using our little 250 person community of Kipton as my home town rather than Wakeman, a town of 600.

It is difficult to fully describe how I felt being a part of the 1942 Ohio State University National Championship team as a third string End or Guard. My father had never seen a football game until he was invited with the other team fathers to sit behind the bench the Saturday afternoon of our game against Pittsburgh. The first half was a veritable rout and the second half was played by the Ohio State third and fourth string players who also continued the rout trying to impress their fathers. When I entered the game, I made the next three tackles. It was like a dream come true to hear the announcer sound my name at the end of each play before over 60,000 spectators. I am sure it made my father very proud.

Soon after the end of the season, I decided to enlist in the Air Force. Paul Brown had become my inspiration. I was convinced of one of his ideals. There should never be a deviation in one's purposes. It was deeply instilled in me. When I went to visit with him just before leaving for the Service, he emphasized again to fulfill my job and he had no doubts that I would do my best.

When I was entering the Shreveport Air Force Base, I walked into Robin Priday who was about to ship out for overseas. With the millions of men in service, it was very unusual to meet one of my 1942 teammates.

I was assigned to pilot a B-26 Marauder Bomber for the 9th Air Force. With Dante Lavelli, Martin Amling, and Ken Coleman on the ground in the Battle of the Bulge, I was flying with my squadron over the battlefield. Unfortunately we were grounded by extremely bad weather during a critical time of the fighting. We had to wait for four or five days before the weather had cleared enough to resume our air strikes and bring relief to our troops. When the weather cleared, we were intercepted by 60 German fighter planes. They had been fully informed of our take off and battle plans. We lost almost our entire squadron, and, like my father, I survived by bailing out of our completely crippled plane. We lost five of our seven crewmen to gun fire. I was taken a prisoner of war until the end of the fighting in Europe. My life as a prisoner of war paralleled the harrowing and demeaning experiences of our fellow soldiers. In one way or another, the Germans knew everything about me and the other prisoners. They even knew the details of my life in the United States prior to the War. In spite of the extent of this sabotage of our war effort, the soldiers and civilians of the United States can be justly proud of our fighting forces.

After the War, Eleanor and I were married. We continued to live on my parent's farm with my other brothers and their families. I retired after 37 years as a Supervisor for the Ridge Tool Co., the manufacturer of plumbing tools in Elyria. I participated in the development of a pipe extracting tool as well as installing an efficient record keeping system for the company. We have two sons and four daughters. Our elder son is a Physician and the younger son has a very successful Business Forms company. He was also an outstanding high school football player. Three of our four daughters have college degrees from Ohio State and Kent State Universities. Our youngest daughter married soon after high school to a 1000 acre farm and a successful floral arranging business while helping her husband on the farm.

In the last paragraph of the letter that Paul Brown sent us before fall practice in 1942 there is one of the many impressions of Paul Brown that has lasted a lifetime. This letter is still one of my prized possessions.

MARTIN AMLING

Football: Ohio State, 1942

Army Division Football, 1945

Education: Agricultural Degree in Horticultural Science

Career: Commercial Growing and Hybridization of Roses
President of Pana Federal Savings Bank
County Board of Commissioners

Married: Jean – 46 years
Three children & six grandchildren

Service: Field Artillery in Europe

MARTIN AMLING

I was one of the few players on the 1942 Ohio State football team who was not from Ohio. I enrolled at Ohio State knowing that Ohio State University had a world-renowned agricultural college where I would major in horticulture. My family, in Illinois, was a major producer of hot house grown Roses for the florists throughout the mid-west. Several years prior to coming to Columbus, my father and his brothers had moved the greenhouses from the Chicago area to Pana, Illinois. It was here that my dad had hybridized a new variety of rose named "Happy Days" which remained a favorite hybrid for over ten years, in contrast to other Hybrids that retain their outstanding characteristics for only a few years. I would return to Pana after college and Army service to manage the greenhouse operations and raise my family. Pana is a small town in the center of Illinois where the Amlings have a major influence in the operations and politics of the town and the surrounding county.

Going out for football was the one desire that I wished to fulfill during my college days. It seemed to me a natural course of events, and I had a wonderful experience being part of the 1942 National Championship Ohio State team. I was physically much smaller and less experienced than the first and second string players, but even as only a reserve lineman, I look back with pride on being a member of the squad. My brother, Warren, was an All-American Guard whose team brought Ohio State an undefeated season in 1944. I really feel that the 1942 and 1944 football teams at Ohio State gave the university its grand reputation as a major football power in the nation through the years.

The war interrupted my education after two years at Ohio State. I spent three years in service before returning to complete my education after my discharge. I received my basic training at Fort Bragg and was stationed there with Hal Dean and J.T. White. I wasn't at the base long enough to play with the "Bombardiers". We shipped out for Europe and our artillery unit fought the Germans across France and Germany after the invasion. During the last winter of the war we never slept a night indoors. The only comfortable sleep I had was one night in a hayloft of a barn. Otherwise, we had only foxholes. As I think back, it was amazing how we adjusted to the extremely cold weather with its howling winds and wet penetrating snow. The best comparison one could make is the adjustments animals make to survive. Oftentimes, we would find an old mattress to drag into the foxhole and we would improvise light with small flashlight batteries to read by at night. These 150 days and nights lasted through the Battle of the Bulge where we had a position just outside of Bastogne to defend against the German divisions.

After the fighting stopped, like the rest of our team, I joined the division football team in Europe where we played football against other division teams. After discharge, I remained in the Army Reserve and was called up for service in the Korean War. Fortunately, I remained stateside during this war.

I returned to Ohio State to complete my education and received my degree in horticultural science. During my last quarter in college, my wife, Jean, and I were married. Jean is a university trained dietician, but following our marriage, and settling back in Pana, her career is confined to feeding me and our three children. The management of the greenhouse is still continuing after twenty-nine years. We supply the major cities in the mid-west with freshly cut roses. Like so many of our members of our 1942 team, I have participated in a number of civic organizations. At various times I have been on the local hospital board, the county board of commissioners, and in the last election I ran for this board uncontested. Along with my other activities, I am the president of the Pana Federal Savings Bank and am happy to report that in these times of tumultuous financing of small banks, we are still solvent. Besides Warren, my other three brothers had college educations in Illinois and Indiana. My eldest brother is an attorney and is now the mayor of Pana. Another brother is a school teacher and the other is a cartographer for the Air Force.

Pana is a small town of 6500 people. We now have a lovely home just south of the city on Possum Creek where our three children and our six grandchildren come to visit their grandparents. I have recently retired from raising roses to a 338 acre ranch. We raise grain and cattle so my days and nights are filled with plenty of activity. Sportswise, my pleasures have been golf and hunting. Two of our children attended the University of Illinois where we rarely miss a home game. Every morning, my pals and I meet for coffee at the local "Liar's Club" to discuss politics, farming, the events of the Rotary Club, the Lions Club, and the Lutheran church.

Small town living has always been a satisfying experience. Here Jean and I reared our children and helped bring happiness to our grandchildren. Our memories of Ohio State and the 1942 team give us a great deal of pleasure. I thank God for surviving through the horrible dangers on the Second World War. I think my football years impressed upon me the importance of constant participation in the needs of our community and to do so sincerely and honestly. We all need one another's help.

AFTER FOOTBALL,
AFTER MILITARY SERVICE,
AFTERWARDS

T he years of playing intercollegiate and professional football had ended. The war had been won and our citizens across the country returned home from every spot on the globe. One question has always been asked by the men of America, "Whatever happened to yesterday's All Americans?"

There are three sports that are prominent in our lives today. Baseball which has always been regarded as a professional sport. Basketball has emerged as an important sport both on a collegiate and professional level. Football was primarily an amateur sport until after World War II when there was major expansion of professional leagues. Now there was a financial side to be considered that, in some ways, has been "hard to digest". Collegiate football has always offered an education toward a higher level of expectation for success than would be possible for men and women who have not had a college education. Professional football offers a great deal of money for a few number of years. However, professional football may often interfere with the completion of a college education. It may also make a college education secondary to the dream that one may be selected to play for a professional team. With so few players selected and even fewer who will win a position each year on a professional team, the odds resemble a state lottery.

This is the reason I have endeavored to bring the Ohio State University 1942 Championship team to the attention of the public. Everyone has a right to know what happened to these athletes afterwards. What happened afterwards is in many ways more interesting and certainly more important than playing football. Following this chapter are the results of Paul Brown's values that he stressed while coaching football. We would be imbued with these qualities for the rest of our lives. Each life, of course, is different. Success in every field of endeavor was achieved. Almost every player completed his college courses and received his undergraduate degree. Their educations were further rewarded by fourteen master's degrees in engineering, education, science, and commerce. Furthermore, there were four doctorate degrees among the 40 players who survived the war. Each family has had long and enduring marriages. Their children's collegiate educations have led them into highly specialized fields that have carried forward the attitudes of their parents.

Each autobiography relates conquering poverty in the families of most of the members of the team. Each autobiography graphically demonstrates that football was the pathway to a higher education. Many thousands of young people who would follow have had the good fortune to be "touched" by one of our players from the 1942 team.

I have related the quality of innovation that Paul Brown had displayed in his coaching. As a group, we changed this innovation to creativity in our professional or commercial fields. Chuck Csuri is not just the Professor of Fine Arts at Ohio State, Chuck is the pioneer in the development of the visual graphic displays you see on your television screens at the beginning of almost every program or sports event. His work in using computer capability as a medium of serious artistic expression is a field of art that is only in its infancy. However, to view his work is an experience that cannot be forgotten. An entire chapter of a recently published book, "An Ohio State Profile" written by Jane Ware, is devoted to Charles Csuri. The author describes him as a living example of a Renaissance man.

Bill Willis's football career was phenomenal, but his contributions to the development of schooling for disturbed young people in Ohio is equally or more important. We had great satisfaction watching his play on the football field for fifteen years. We can take more satisfaction knowing of his contributions to young people that has covered twenty five years. Paul Selby, as dean of the West Virginia University Law School, expanded and developed the teaching of labor law in this state that was often the center of controversy between the needs and safety of the miners against the companies that owned and operated the mines. His methods of arbitration has set a pattern that is frequently used in many controversies to bring peaceful settlement to many similar national controversies. When he was honored by the West Virginia University at the completion of his tenure as dean, he made known the appreciation and pride he has always carried by his association with Paul Brown and the 1942 OSU team.

Loran Staker, after graduation, became a member of the faculty in the College of Engineering in Architecture. He had an illustrious career in the designs of hospitals and shopping centers. Loran won a special award for designing inexpensive small homes that featured a variety of alterable uses of space depending on the needs of each family who would live in one of his homes.

After his All American honors in football in 1944, Dr. Bill Hackett completed his doctorate in veterinary medicine. After graduation, he specialized in the care of cattle being fed in large feed lots. He was able to solve many of the health problems confronting the grouping together of large numbers of animals in confined areas. His creativity in the science of recycling animal wastes both as fertilizer and as useful feed for other animals has made a monumental contribution to supplying the protein needs of an ever growing world population. In addition, he has accomplished all of these advancements in a non-chemical pollution free environment. Bill has received many national awards for his work and he was also instrumental in bringing Paul Brown back into coaching after his unfortunate disassociation with the Cleveland Browns, the team Paul had founded and nurtured.

During my career as a general surgeon, I have always participated in laboratory and clinical investigations in medicine. In 1981, my paper on the treatment of generalized infections of the abdominal cavity was considered a major contribution at the International College of Surgeons meeting in Paris, France. As time passes and other investigators publish their results using this approach, it appears that this technique is becoming the standard of treatment for this frequently fatal complication. I have also had articles published on the efficacy of community surveillance programs in the detection of early and still curable cancer as well as other articles on surgical techniques and the chemotherapy of cancer.

Dante Lavelli made several interesting innovations in offensive football during his career with the Cleveland Browns which were soon adopted by other professional and collegiate teams. One of the most significant was "breaking the pass pattern". When it appeared that defensive pass coverage prevented the successful completion of a pass, he would turn back along the sideline toward the line of scrimmage so the pass could be successfully completed. Another innovation was to break his pass pattern and race toward the opposite side line and a certain touchdown if Otto could be protected by his offensive line long enough. Fans still smile about the grasping of the goal posts on wintery icy days to make a 180 degree turn and a certain touchdown. All of these techniques were carefully worked out with exact timing by Dante, Otto Graham, Mac Speedie and Paul Brown.

Bob McCormick and Bob Jabbusch have made significant contributions in developing industrial processes. Bob McCormick has eight U.S. patents in the field of packaging. One of his patents describes an important contribution to the transport of military wounded. He developed a light-weight collapsible stretcher. Hundreds of thousands of these stretchers have been in use to fulfill the needs in both military and civilian life to transport the sick and wounded. Bob Jabbusch, the first member of his family to ever receive a higher education, was an outstanding student as well as being chosen by the Chicago Tribune as a member of its Sophomore All American team in 1942. For many years Bob was the director of research and development for the FMC Corporation. He has traveled extensively for the corporation all over the world supervising the construction of large industrial facilities and developing the equipment needed to process large quantities of food and to manufacture oil drilling equipment. All of his achievements, which include three U.S. patents, followed his engineering degree at Ohio State and his master's degree in business administration from the University of Indiana. Martin Amling is the older brother of Warren Amling, an All-American Guard in 1944. Martin returned home after service and assumed the management of the family business of supplying roses to the florists across the mid-west. Among his many local and civic responsibilities is the presidency of the local bank that is still solvent in the present tumult of farm financing.

Hal Dean is a leader in the modern methods of oil and gas exploration. At the same time that he was ending his career in professional football with the Los Angeles Rams, he was attaining his master's degree in oil geology at Stanford University. His discoveries of oil in Mexico and off the shores of the Yucatan Peninsula were major strides in opening the Mexican petroleum industry. In addition, his work led to the discovery of major oil and gas deposits in Texas, Canada and Central America.

Oftentimes I have claimed that the Ohio State University team of 1942 was the most outstanding team to play collegiate football. I am quite sure this is true, but they can also be admired for their service to their country in the time of war, and in their individual accomplishments in their chosen professions after their athletic careers.. A truer appreciation of each of their lives, as examples for other young people, can only be gained by reading their autobiographies.

Autobiographies offer a much deeper insight into motivation than can be culled out of trying to analyze the "greatness" of an athlete from record breaking statistics. Statistics are cold and records will always be broken by up and coming "stars". Physical prowess is always an asset to a football player as is agility, speed and determination. But a better determinant as to a "star's" greatness is what were the factors that brought him to, in this case, Ohio State, and how did he use his education? His moral and ethical values are often the true rewards of his coach's efforts. There are always little nuances that spring forth in an autobiography that can give instruction to young men who will follow. If you are a young man or woman, to follow in the paths of these men is to find the sources of success and happiness in your lives.

CHARLES CSURI

Football:	Ohio State, 1941, 1942, 1946 All American, 1942
Education:	B.A. and Masters in Fine Arts
Career:	Professor of Fine Arts Director of Super Computer Center at OSU Pioneer in Computer Graphics World authority in use of computer graphics as a medium for serious art expression.
Married:	Lee – 42 years Two children
Service:	Infantry – European Theater Bronze Medal for Bravery in Action

CHARLES CSURI

Sometime in 1920, my father and mother left our little town in Hungary with my two older brothers. Like so many of the villages in Europe, this town was one without hope. There was rarely any possibility of ever changing any of its citizens' poor fortune. These destitute people joined in the mass migrations from their homelands to America like so many other Europeans. They came to America seeking a better life for themselves and their children. Along with the other immigrants from middle Europe, my father found employment only in the "back breaking" coal mines of eastern Ohio. I was born shortly afterwards. To add to the despair of trying to fed, house and raise a family, one day an explosion occurred in the mine shaft and seriously injured my dad. At the age of 27, he had to have his leg amputated above the knee to save his life. Being crippled, along with being penniless, led to a deep emotional depression. His only salvation was the close relationships he had maintained with his friends from Hungary who were living in Cleveland. They urged him to come to Cleveland where we moved when I was still a small boy. Any change in life compared to the meager existence from mining coal could only be an improvement in our family's affairs.

After we moved to Cleveland, my father decided to become a shoemaker. He first began his new occupation by setting up a small shop in our home. Of course, the equipment and tools he needed had to be altered to compensate for his disability. This ingenuity, which had always been characteristic of Hungarian people, allowed him the wherewithal to support his family. I really believe that living in the oppressive atmosphere of European village life prevented any expressions of ingenuity that life in America allowed and nurtured. The millions of destitute new Americans who would blossomed into successful citizens is a true testament to the greatness of our country. My two older brothers were able to finish high school and then they went to work as was the custom of our families as higher education was still beyond their reach. Nevertheless, many years later, one of my older brothers attained a university degree. We lived in the Hungarian enclave on the West side of Cleveland, and I attended West Tech High

School. I was rather small as a freshman, but before the beginning of my sophomore year, I had a sudden increase in growth. I decided to join the football team having little experience in this sport. West Tech was a football power in Cleveland making football the most popular game to be played. One afternoon, during a scrimmage, I came to the sudden realization that I could compete successfully against any of the other players regardless of their size or strength. On our coaching staff was Ed Brickles, a close friend of Paul Brown's who had just become the Head Coach at Ohio State. Coach Brickles felt that I had become good enough to play at Ohio State and, after graduation, I enrolled in the College of Fine Arts at Ohio State.

I began spring practice during my freshman year as the second string tackle behind Jack Stevenson. He had been elected the Captain of the football team for the coming year. Jack was a large and affable young man and was well liked by everyone on the squad. It soon became apparent that Paul was only interested in bringing his best players to each position and no other factors, such as being the Captain of the team, made any difference. Jack started the first game in the fall of 1941 but I was sent into the game shortly afterwards to substitute in his position with Jim Daniels at the other tackle. I was among the lightest and smallest tackles in the conference and Jim was one of the largest and heaviest. As I look back upon my relationship with Paul, he was one of the fairest men I have ever known and would serve as a role model for me for the rest of my life.

The fall of 1942 was my third year in the College of Fine Arts and I was becoming more and more convinced that this would be the path of life I would follow. The football season was an overwhelming success. I was chosen for All American recognition along with Lin Houston and Bob Shaw. The athletic talent on this team was remarkable from player to player, not only on the starting team but on second and third teams as well. I don't believe anyone could have improved on the quality of our backfield or our line. In addition, there was a freshman team coming up to the varsity for the 1943 season who would have challenged us for almost every position despite the loss of only three seniors through graduation on the entire team. A dynasty was building, but it was not to be, as by spring of 1943 almost the entire team had enlisted or had been drafted into service. I had been elected to be the Captain of the team for the coming year of 1943 but my army service began early in the spring.

The first weeks in service were spent in basic training, a particularly boring period. I noticed a memorandum on one of the bulletin boards recruiting soldiers interested in the medical corps. This could only be an improvement over my present circumstances. I made the necessary application to be transferred to the medical corps and, after a short wait, my papers came through assigning me to an engineering program in New Jersey. The Army was proceeding in its inexplicable way once again. For the next year, I was enrolled in an extremely fast paced engineering program that was able to complete two years of engineering courses in one year. One day the program was suddenly discontinued. I found myself suddenly back in the ranks of the infantry ready for assignment to the European theater where the Battle of the Bulge was in progress around Bastogne. I was assigned to a First Army unit of engineers who were among the advanced battalions for the division. For the next nine months, we were in almost continuous action. Our losses through death and injury were tremendous. At one point, we had advanced so far forward through the German lines that we were cut off and surrounded by the German Army units. I volunteered to attempt to re-establish contact with our division by working my way back through the German lines under continuous bombardment and small arms fire. It was the most harrowing experience of my life and how I survived was beyond my comprehension. My helmet was shot away and even my leather belt. I was finally able to contact our American lines. I received the Bronze Medal for Bravery in Action.

After my discharge, I returned to complete my education at Ohio State in the College of Fine Arts. My experiences in the war had completely altered my attitude toward football. Now football seemed infantile compared to the savagery that I had witnessed and encountered during my Army service in Europe. However, due to the social pressure of my presence as an undergraduate and my renown as an athlete, I did return for the 1946 season. It was a far different experience than 1941 and 1942. Nonetheless, it may have been influential in bringing me into the faculty of the College of Fine Arts after my graduation in the spring of 1947.

During my third year on the faculty, a young lady, Lee Echols enrolled in one of my classes. She was intelligent, perceptive and beautiful. She had been reared as an adopted daughter of a deeply religious, albeit just as prejudiced Baptist family in Alabama. Her intellectual emancipation fit perfectly with my perceptions of beauty and art. Our enduring marriage has continued with the same love and warmth for over 40 years. Lee's artistry is displayed in her mystical and mythological wood carvings that penetrate one's psyche the more one views her work.

During the decade of the 50's, my painting followed the precepts of modern art as I conceived them. In 1957, my work received critical acclaim at an exhibition in New York. Continuing in this mode, would have necessitated moving to New York. This was impossible as we were now raising a family, a boy and a girl, as well as continuing on the faculty at Ohio State for my livelihood. When my daughter, Carolyn, was six years old she found my Bronze Medal for Bravery in my drawer. "Daddy, what is this? " she asked. I replied, "This is the medal I received for defeating the enemy with my sword". This was all she had to hear, and, on the very next day, the medal was displayed at school for "show and tell" with equal billing with the sword story.

In the early Sixties, my career made a dramatic change. I was introduced to the power of computers by one of my friends. The ability of computers to achieve both linear as well as perceptions of third dimensional depth brought together in my mind the mathematics of my Army engineering courses with the infinite colors and artistry of modern art. In addition to my personal excitement in the use of a computer as the medium for artistic expression, the powers of the computer could be used in a multiplicity of practical areas. This form could be useful in structural model making, tool and machinery design, advertizing, science and health. Almost every field of endeavor could benefit from computer technology. Since almost all of the university departments required outside funding to allow the development of new concepts of science, humanities or art, we applied for a grant from the National Science Foundation to enable us to advance our work. Our first biannual acceptance was for $100, 000 to relate our work to science. Each year, thereafter, brought additional funding into the department for an accumulation of grant funds of over $8,000,000. Our department in the Fine Arts College rapidly expanded as students with computer backgrounds and interests in Art forms joined our artistic fields of endeavor.

Several business men began to recognize the value of our work in advertizing as we had made several projects for the Armed Services.

Some programs would enable a pilot or a tank officer to actually see, in the most minute detail, a military objective without actual combat. I was approached to form a private company that could utilize our work and put it on a profitable footing. We first began making video displays for television and movie companies to introduce sports events such as football games, basketball games and surrealistic moving objects. I felt that selling the computer softwear was the proper approach to this type of marketing, but the business men felt otherwise. What had started out as almost assured success, fell rapidly into a decline. They misunderstood that the profit from selling a video display to a company, such as a national broadcasting company, was limited as they could use the same programs over and over again once the program was paid for. In addition, these men created chaos in the lives of our artistic people as they could not comprehend the freedom of time and expression that these men and women needed to express their talents.

This episode in my life was a rather bitter pill, but it was only a rut in the road toward my personal desires to develop serious computerized art. My efforts were rewarded by the art critic's acclaimed of a series of computerized faces of a woman showing the aging changes from her youthful beauty to her appearance as an elderly woman. One of my computer images called "The Hummingbird" has been purchased by The Museum of Modern Art. Each year our efforts are enhanced by the development of more and more powerful computers that enable deeper artistic expression as well as an infinite varieties of colors and combinations of colors. At present, the possibilities are limited only by the extent of one's artistic imagination.

In the area of computerized art, world wide attention in the use of this medium is developing by leaps and bounds. Recently, at an art festival in Rome, Italy, the works of thousands of artists, working with the medium of computers, were displayed. It was at this festival that one of my computer pictures was awarded the second prize. Dr. Maurizio Calvesi who is in charge of the International Arts Festival and who is a world famous art critic and art historian has often expressed the opinion that the future of art forms may well lie in this new field of art expression. These innumerable colors and perceptions are only available through computer graphics. Recently he wrote an extensive and very complimentary history of my work and the progress of this new art form in the magazine, "Art", that is published in Italy. Our initial pioneering effort at The Ohio State University to its present sophisticated development has all occurred during my active life as an artist. Many of our students at Ohio State have spread out across the country working in computerized graphic art or in artistic expression. My position as chairman of the Computer Art Department and my many duties as editor of Art magazines and other mundane duties will probably give way to my total dedication to serious computerized art.

I wrote the following paragraph about my present artistic persuasion, utilizing the mechanics of the computer, much as a traditional painter would use the medium of the canvas and the various pigments:

"My view of the world tends to be humanistic but, in certain respects, I am a hopeless romantic with a love affair with the art of the Past. Since I understand computers graphics, I have a natural inclination to play with Physics, Mathematics, and Realism. I am interested in conceptual contradictions and incongruities about an idea. I construct, in the computer, the physically impossible, and I pursue notions about paradox and the nature of the Universe. Multiple layers of meaning are important. An emphasis on visual organization is essential as I am interested in creating ambiguity between the perceptions of two and three dimensional space. The illusion of surface properties of paint and texture are symbolic of human beings with their imperfections. A synthesis of art and science, through the use of computers, makes possible a holistic concept of artistic expression: The Spirit of the Renaissance is alive and well!"

PAUL SELBY

Football: Ohio State, 1942

Education: Doctor of Jurisprudence
Multiple Scholastic Awards and Honor Societies

Career: OSU College of Law
Dean of West Virginia University College of Law
Chief U.S. Arbitrator for National Coal Mining
  Review Board

Married: Jeannie – 45 years
Three sons & five grandchildren

Service: Medical Disability

PAUL SELBY

From my association with the Ohio State Championship team, I have had a constant reminder that experiences, no matter how one judges their importance at the time, can be lasting and rewarding. Paul Brown set the pattern for my efforts during the 1942 season when he insisted that every member of the team "go all out all of the time". Your position on the team, in my case being on the third string, made no difference. I recall clearly the day that the great halfback, Tommy James, and I were paired off for tackling exercises. We were just warming up, and I put little effort into this calisthenic. Being much larger than Tommy, I made no attempt to tackle him as hard as possible. When it was his turn to tackle me, I still recall the pain. He was imbued by Paul to "go all out all the time". Then he stood up and said, "We never let anyone off easily. Never do that to me again." I recall another occasion when Lin Houston had set me on my "can" for the umpteenth time while the coaches were trying me out as a Center and I was making a real mess of it. He pulled me up and said, "That time you really made me work at it". Tommy and Lin's remarks have stayed with me all of these years. They encouraged me and helped me feel that I was a part of this team of marvelous athletes. There were many similar recollections of the first and second string players who would teach, encourage and "pull us slow ones up" so we would feel we were true members of this team. They were, and are, really something more than just successes— they are true teachers. Through the years, times have changed dramatically, but this team was the outstanding example for the true "raison d'etre" for intercollegiate athletics and football in particular.

Jack Graf and Pete Herschberger were my high school heros. They had attended Upper Arlington High School, in Columbus, and then went on to Ohio State. Pete became one of the starting players on the 1941 team, and Jack would be awarded the honor of being the outstanding player in the Big Ten that year. I was several years behind them in school and would frequently walk across the Olentangy River to watch them practice. The Olentangy River separates the Ohio State campus from Upper Arlington with the stadium at the edge of the river. It was my dream from boyhood to some day play football for Ohio State.

My father had other plans for me. He was a prominent attorney in Columbus and felt I should have an eastern education at Dartmouth College. During the spring of my senior year in high school, I participated in a swimming meet where Fritz Mackey, one of Paul's assistant coaches, was officiating. I knew him rather well as he was a member of our church. Just after I finished my event, Fritz said, "Son, you could play football for Ohio State". I didn't know whether he was joking or not, but it was all I had to hear. My boyhood dreams would be fulfilled. That night I spoke with my dad that Ohio State was the university that I wished to attend. Surprisingly, he did not resist the idea. He really did his best to make my university years as productive as possible. I became a "walk on" during my freshman year. I may have been just "cannon fodder" for the 1942 team, but the experience has always filled me with pride.

I enrolled in the Arts and Science College at Ohio State with the intention of becoming a physician. My major was in social science, but for one reason or another, I also acquired 42 hours in accounting. I received my admission to the medical school in 1944 to begin as a Freshman medical student in the fall. During the summer, I changed my mind and decided that I really wanted to be an attorney. I continued my education having been declared 4-F as I had a chronic ear perforation and infection that was effecting my equilibrium. The honors I received as a member of the football team for my scholarship, continued through my college years. Like other players on the team, I achieved my pin in Phi Eta Sigma, the Freshman Honor Society, Romphos, the most coveted sophomore honor, and Sphinx, my senior year in undergraduate school.

I entered the law school at Ohio State following the pathway of education already laid down by my maternal grandfather, Edward L. Hopkins (OSU 1893-95), and my Father who graduated from the Ohio State Law School in 1922. During my freshman year in law school, Jeanne and I were married and she has continued as my constant companion both at home and at the office ever since. During my years in Law School, I received many honors, but the most rewarding was my "Cum laude" by graduating second in my class. Among my other activities, I continued my affiliation with sports by being the student member of the University's Board of Intercollegiate Athletics. Both my father and I were awarded the Law Honorary, "Order of the Coif" twenty-five years apart.

Following my graduation and passing the bar, I practiced with a Columbus firm involved with litigation and tax problems both in the state and federal courts. In 1957, I was invited to join the faculty of the law school at Ohio State. I remained at Ohio State until 1964 rising to the level of Assistant Dean and Professor of Law. In 1964, I was appointed the Professor and Dean of the Law School at West Virginia University at Morgantown, West Virginia. Since learning and teaching go hand in hand, my interest turned to labor arbitration. Problems involved in coal mining in West Virginia were so common that settling disputes between the miners, their unions and mine owners were of national importance. I took leave from the university for three years to go to Washington D.C. as the chief umpire on the Arbitration Review Board. This board was the "supreme appellate" body to settle disputes between the United Mine Workers Union and the Bituminous Coal Operators Association. We had 120 field operators associated with this board covered by the National Bituminous Coal Wage Agreement of 1978.

I returned to West Virginia University where we expanded our Labor Law to four courses where there had only one prior to my experiences in Washington. I continued as the Professor of Law until May of 1989. My retirement from the university has had little resemblance to the freedom of action that retirement usually is perceived. The entire gambit of industry requires arbitration from mining to medicine and all the other industries as well.

My family from my grandparents to my grandchildren has demonstrated a deep dedication to education and achievement. We are now four generations showing a deep involvement in the practice and teaching of law. Jeannie and I have three sons. Not only has Jeannie been my constant companion, she has provided the wherewithal for a beautiful family life as well. My eldest son is an attorney, my middle son is the production manager for the Miller Brewing Company and my youngest son is a certified public accountant. Like my mother who was a soprano with the Columbus Opera Association, one daughter-in-law is a recognized artist whose works are displayed in the Milwaukee Art Museum. Another daughter in-law is a practicing attorney in West Virginia. Several of our grandchildren are very competitive in sports and all of them are fine students with fine futures.

After I retired from active teaching, I was named Emeritus
Professor of Law at West Virginia University. As dean, I was hoping to
have a photograph hanging in the law school along with the other
deans going back to the turn of the century. However, this was only the
beginning of the recognition the University had planned. The Paul
Selby Scholarship was founded and significantly endowed by my friends
and colleagues who represented not only the university but both sides of
arbitration, the industries and labor unions. The following is the
biography written for the recognition dinner given in my honor which
also recognized the importance of my years playing football at Ohio
State. I like to feel that all of this is true.

*Paul Selby came to West Virginia University College of Law as
Dean in 1964 fresh from the Directorship of Clinical Programs at Ohio
State. Dean Selby's stewardship of the College of Law forged a faculty
strong in theory as well as practice and set the stage for the future
growth of the Law School. He oversaw the creation of one of the finest
law school buildings of its time in the country. He enhanced the name of
West Virginia on the national map of Law Schools. Most important he
emphasized that the quality of a law school is measured by the quality of
its students and its faculty who populate the school and the quality of its
graduates. He broadened and deepened the faculty. He sought out
promising students diverse in background and vision. He forged strong
ties to our alumni and cared for the quality of practice in West Virginia.*

*Paul's commitment came early in life. He exemplified a great
generation of student athletes. (He was a member of the Ohio State
National Championship football team of 1942.) He has helped
innumerable students and colleagues to honor high aspirations. He
inspires all of us with his leadership and never compromising his kindness
his uncommon good sense and his extraordinary generosity.*

*Because Paul is an uncommonly quiet and modest man, much of
what he has given this school and his adopted state is known only to a
few. But this much is known: Many of us were able to get through law
school only because he bought our law books when we could not. Others
of us attended and finished law school because of Paul's munificent
contributions—personal and financial—to our scholarship programs.
Some of us have had Paul as arbitrator or counsel. Whether we won or
lost, we knew that Paul had attended our matters with rare expertise
and compassion. Most of us can remember a quiet conversation,*

academic or personal, when Paul offered us wisdom, giving us insight, and encouragement when we needed it at the moment. And all of us remember those times when Paul said, "Bunk" when it was needed to be said. We hope we never forget how. The College of Law is pleased to report that Paul will maintain an important teaching appointment this coming academic year. He has been voted the Professor of the Year by the Class of 1989."

I have the temerity to give you that quote to make a point. Although at the time, I was not so proud of being a "bench warmer" and the "cannon fodder" running opposing teams plays and defenses in practice, the "real team" made me think I was making a contribution. The point that I had learned from that experience were the habits and traits insisted upon by Paul Brown as well as the members of the team. "To go all out, all the time". Tommy James imprinted this on my backside and my mind and it has lasted a lifetime.

HAL DEAN

Football: Ohio State, 1941, 1942, 1946
Ft. Bragg Bombardiers
11th Airbourne Divison – Japan
Los Angeles Rams, 3 years – NFL Champions

Education: B.S. in Geology
Masters in Oil Geology from Stanford

Career: Pioneer in modern methods of oil exploration.
Principal geologist in opening Mexican oil industry.

Married: Estelle – 41 years – Passed away – Four children
Nancy Bartling

Service: Company Commander and Captain
11th Airbourne Parachute Division

HAL DEAN

My profession as an oil geologist, began many years ago at Ohio State where I majored in geology. It may seem far fetched for an Ohio State football Guard to have progressed in his education to reach my present level of achievement, but it was similar to many of our teammates. All of us started our undergraduate education while playing collegiate football, and then we served for several years in the armed forces. After the war, we returned to the universities to complete our degrees while playing either collegiate football or professional football. Oftentimes this education has became so highly specialized, that people are frequently surprised to hear about the many areas of accomplishment of our players. Their success was notable in almost every field of endeavor. A good term one can use to describe the members of this team could well be that we were multifaceted people. We were great student athletes who were molded by Paul Brown into a formidable collegiate football team. During the war, we served with notable distinction. After the war ended, we returned to complete our educations and make major contributions in each of our chosen professions or dedicated our lives to the advancement of other young people.

Both my father's and mother's families settled in Ohio very early in the 1800's. In the early years, they were farmers who tilled the very fertile soil of central Ohio. My mother graduated from Ohio University and then taught school near Athens, Ohio. My father was in graduate school at Ohio State and came to Southeastern Ohio as part of his scientific investigations for his doctorate degree in forestry. Here he met and courted my mother and they were married just before he departed for France in the First World War. When he returned from service, they moved to Wooster, Ohio. Wooster was the center for agricultural research for the State of Ohio. He held the position as the extension forester at the Ohio Agricultural Experimental Station. While he worked at the Center, he received many professional awards for his outstanding contributions to agriculture in Ohio.

I started school in a small one-room country school house and then entered Wooster High School. While in high school, I participated in all of the major sports and graduated with the eighth highest academic record of our 175 seniors. I had planned to attend Dennison University, but one of my dad's best friends, Ernie Godfrey, Mr. Ohio State Football, challenged me to enter Ohio State and play Big Ten football. Ernie's persuasion, Baker Hall, the just completed men's dormitory, and the dream of Big Ten football laid the pattern my future.

The Guards are the "guardians" of every football team. On every successful running play, one of the guards will be leading the interference around the Defensive Ends or between the Defensive End and the Defensive Tackle. Besides being among the strongest players on the team, the Guards must also be extremely agile. At the start of a play, one of the guards must "pull out of the line" in a fraction of a second to lead the ball carrier through the hole in the defensive line. He must do all of this without "telegraphing" his intentions to the Defense before the ball is snapped. Paul Brown had taught us that speed, agility, and a mistake-free performance would be sufficient to play football at any level. Our 1941 and 1942 teams set this pattern of achievement for my professional football carer. In later years, I would become the first string offensive Guard of the Los Angeles Rams being, perhaps, the smallest Guard in the entire NFL. In 1949, we played the Philadelphia Eagles for the Professional Football Championship. Like so many of our teammates, my football career extended over a period of ten years. Paul had instilled in us an affection for football that was not to be denied.

After the 1942 season, I returned to Wooster for a happy holiday vacation in my hometown. This was short lived as I was called into active duty in the U.S. Army being a member of the advanced R.O.T.C. unit at Ohio State. We shipped out from Ft.Hayes in Columbus for our basic training at Ft. Bragg, North Carolina. At the end of 1943, I was transferred to Officer's Candidate School at Ft. Sill, Oklahoma. After receiving my commission I was sent back to Ft. Bragg as a 2nd Lt. in Field Artillery. Things were rather dull at Ft. Bragg except for the "The Bombardiers". Lin Houston and Don McCafferty had organized this football team with members who were largely from our 1942 Ohio State team. More than half of the playing team were 1942 Ohio State players. After our football season was over, I volunteered for the parachute infantry at Ft. Benning, Georgia. I became the platoon leader of the 541st. Parachute Regiment and soon, thereafter, we were sent to the Philippines to fight in the Far East. I finished the war in Japan as a company commander in the 11th Airborne Division. I also played with our division football team which won the Pacific Service Football Championship in Japan.

After my discharge as a captain in the parachute division, I returned to Ohio State to continue my education in geology. I played football for Ohio State in 1946 but our season was a disappointing one. There were few members from our 1942 team on this squad, and I felt like an elder statesman. I was invited to play in the Shriner East-West Game in San Francisco and received a contract from the Los Angeles Rams shortly afterwards. Estelle and I were married in 1947 and we headed west to play football with the Rams and further concentrate my studies in geology at the Oil Geology Graduate School at Stanford University. Our Los Angeles Rams team was a spirited squad coached by some of the great legends of football. Our Head Coach was Clark Shaugnessy whose personal contributions to American football were without peer. His assistant coaches were equally outstanding with Danny Fortmann, the famous Chicago Bear guard and orthopedic surgeon, as well as, Hall of Famers George Trafton and Joe Stydahar. The personnel on this team were the most notable in Ram history with Bob Waterfield, Elroy Hirsch, Tom Fears and many others.

After three years with the Rams, professional football was becoming less enjoyable. I had received my master's degree in oil geology at Stanford and was anxious to start my career. Estelle and I headed for San Antonio, Texas, for my first oil geology position with the Magnolia Petroleum Corp., in January of 1950. It was a great experience for me learning about the oil industry and living in this strange land, Texas. Soon, Texas was becoming more and more like home, and our family was growing rapidly with the birth of our son, Hal Jr. and three daughters, Ann, Amy, and Nancy.

The scientific advancements in oil exploration were rapidly replacing the "hit and miss" approaches of former years. My training at Stanford and with the Magnolia Oil Corp. led to major advances in the technology of seismographic testing and evaluations of geological strata. We became very proficient in predicting the presence of oil or gas on land or under the sea floor. I left Magnolia Petroleum after five years to join an oil exploration company owned by Ed Pauley, the owner of the Los Angeles Rams. My new job was very exciting as we were looking for oil over the entire western hemisphere. Exploration is much like a

football team with several men who specialized in different fields
bringing together their technological knowledge to make our efforts
successful. Our units traveled extensively over South and Central
America and Canada, Texas, and Oklahoma. A major part of my time
was spent in Mexico where we mapped the oil bearing potential off the
shore of the Yucatan Peninsula in the Gulf of Mexico. We were the first
to use shallow water seismographic techniques to map the salt domes
east of Vera Cruz, Mexico. We had laid the groundwork for the
extensive Mexican petroleum production. After my long stay in
Mexico, I returned to the United States to explore for gas and oil in
Texas. My work led to the discovery of the Piedra Limbre Wilcox gas
field in Duval County, Texas. It was while I was living in San Antonio,
that I became acquainted with George Bush who, at the time was the
CEO of the Zapata Corporation, an offshore drilling company. It is a
warm feeling to have a continuing friendship with the President of the
United States.

As the lead geologist for many companies, I always seemed to be
headed toward executive administrative positions in management.
However, my basic desires continued to be in the area of exploration. I
decided to become an independent explorer in partnership with J.
Howard Marshall and Bill Mass. Mr. Marshall is a nationally acclaimed
executive and Bill Mass has recently been appointed by President Bush
as the head of the overlook civilian group for U. S. drug policy. We had
a great time for over fifteen years putting trades together, drilling deep
and shallow oil wells, and competing for the best drilling prospects
against the major oil companies-Exxon, Shell, Amoco, etc. We were
very successful and that was a great satisfaction.

One of my side line ventures involved the ranching business in the
Lower Pecos River Valley in Terrell County, Texas. This beautiful,
lonesome country with its deep canyons and flat divides has given me
many days of enjoyment. The ranch covers about a square mile of land.
My son, Hal, Jr. manages the ranching operations where we raise
Angora goats for their mohair and Brangus calves for the feed-lot
market.

After a very busy and satisfying career as an oil geologist, my wife
and I decided to gradually retire to California. It was in California
where we began our wonderfully happy married life. We built a home in
Rancho Santa Fe, just north of San Diego in 1985. Unfortunately, a

rapidly growing malignancy was discovered at this time and Estelle passed away in March of 1987 at Rancho Santa Fe. I have continued to live in Rancho Santa Fe and, at the same time, I have retained my residence and offices in Midland, Texas. Being married was a wonderful experience and, a year later, I remarried Nancy Bartling.

My experiences in athletics, oil exploration and ranching have all been built on the solid foundations established on the practice fields south of the Ohio State stadium. I have associated in business with some of the most successful men in the nation. My friendship with President Bush has been very satisfying. However, in the list of accomplishments in my life, I have always placed being part of the 1942 Ohio State National Championship team as number one.

ROBERT JABBUSCH

Football: Ohio State, 1942, 1946, 1947
               Chicago Tribune All Sophomore Team, 1942
               Big 10 Western Conference Scholar-Athlete Medal, 1947

Education: B.S. in Engineering
               Pi Eta Sigma Freshman Honor Society
               Two Engineering Honor Societies
               Masters in Business Administration from Indiana

Career: Director of Research and Development at FMC Corp.
               Supervised world wide expansion of FMC Corp.
               Three U.S. Patents

Married: Marian – 46 years
               Three children & seven grandchildren

Service: World War II – Infantry in Europe

BOB JABBUSCH

I would like everyone to know about Foxy Fabian. For Foxy was my football mentor and taskmaster who introduced me to the rudiments of football. He was my mother's brother, John, and lived with us during the late 1920's and early 1930's. Foxy had been a star football player at Lorain High School and my hero. Later, he played for a semi-pro team in Cleveland called the Panthers. This name in later years would prevent the new Cleveland professional football team under Paul Brown from using the Panthers as their nickname.

My father had settled in Elyria, Ohio, having migrated from East Prussia. My mother was born on Ellis Island while her parents were waiting to be allowed into the country coming from Austria. Dad worked in the steel mills in Elyria along with other family men who were striving to house and feed their growing families. Higher education for these families was only a dream. Even Foxy, who finished high school, had to go to the mills to support the family. Despite the ever present specter of poverty, my parents did know that education was the way out of the "steel worker's syndrome". By the time I was a senior in high school, they had saved a small sum of money for me to go to college.

Tragedy struck our family in 1940 during my senior year in high school in the form of a malignant melanoma discovered on my dad's leg. Dad had to take a routine physical examination in order to operate a large crane at the mill. This black lesion on his leg was discovered in a man who had no symptoms of illness. Dad was 47 years old. He was seen at the Cleveland Clinic where the doctors recommended a high amputation of his leg and thigh. There were no job benefits, no medical insurance, and, from the doctors, only a faint hope that he might be one of the lucky ones with this disease who would have a long term survival. My father decided to go ahead with the operation if I would promise him that I would go on to college. The money my parents had saved for me had to go to pay for his operation. After the surgery, the surgeons were confident that if dad could survive five years without a recurrence, he would have a long survival. The recurrence occurred shortly after the five years had passed and Dad passed away a year later. With no money, my high school coach, Roy Clymer, assured me that I could go to Ohio State and live in the Tower Club, the low cost housing on the campus that provided board and room for needy but good students. In fact, he further assured me that if I could make the freshman football squad, I would have a part time job while I was attending school to help pay for my expenses.

Now that Paul Brown had replaced Francis Schmidt as Head Coach at Ohio State, Coach Clymer was very, perhaps overly, optimistic about the chances of his team's captain playing for Ohio State. The high school coaches throughout Ohio had promised that their best players would be sent to Ohio State if the university appointed Paul Brown as their head coach. I was part of the fulfillment of that promise. I was 17 years old, a good student with three varsity letters from Elyria High and who, in later years, would be awarded a place in the high school Hall of Fame. If you were poor, but wanted a college education, the Stadium Club or the Tower Club at Ohio State was the answer. These clubs had been built under the vast expanses of the football stadium in large dormitory styles. This is the way Jim Rees and I were able to go to college—living Spartan lives in these dormitories.

I believe that my dad's adversity gave me that extra incentive to make good in football. Football offered me the opportunity for a college education. I was the first person in our family to go to college. I made the freshman team and Ernie Godfrey fulfilled my high school coach's promise. I was given a part time job in the State office building. I was even able to save enough money (not much) to send my folks some help during their trying years of 1941 and 1942 when dad was not working.

At Ohio State I was enrolled in the College of Engineering. Engineering would be my field as I had devised a system of clutch, brake, and accelerator devices so my dad could drive his 1935 Dodge stick shift with his remaining left leg. Thus he was able to return to work in the tool crib in the steel mill, and he was even able to drive to Columbus for Dad's Day in 1942 for our game against Pittsburgh. Down deep in my heart, I felt that this arrangement in the old Dodge was the most outstanding contribution I have made in engineering. The fact that I became the director of engineering and research and development for the FMC Corporation that made FMC the world leader in the packaging machinery industry for over fifteen years never equalled this feat of my teenaged years.

Football practice made it soon apparent that dedication to do one's best at all times, and having the ability to learn would be the keys to my survival both as a student and a football player. It was not difficult to appreciate the fatherly advice from our freshman coach, Ernie Godfrey. He often remarked, "You had better study hard, because you can't eat footballs." Encouraged by my Stadium Club buddies, I made the Freshman Honor Society, Phi Eta Sigma. Good grades and $90.00 a quarter for board and room were the prerequisites for living in the Stadium Club.

Paul was convinced that fierce competition makes better players and consequently better teams. By the spring practice in 1942 I had increased my weight to 190 pounds and had greatly increased my skills as a Guard, rapidly overcoming the ever-present problem of severely bowed legs. Much of my improvement was gained through the coaching of Fritz Mackey. He assisted me in sharpening my defensive charge and improving my reaction times in offensive techniques. Our practices that spring were rough and tough as Paul demanded each of us to battle it out for the starting positions. By the end of the spring practice, both Jim Rees, as a tackle, and myself, as a guard, had made the second string. Hal Dean, who was the starting Guard along with Lin Houston, was a close friend of mine but, by fall, I was able to compete for the position so that there would be little or no loss of effectiveness in the event of injury.

Culminating our team effort, under Paul's system of coaching, brought Ohio State the conference championship and its first national championship. It proved to me that without question goals can be set and accomplished through "true blue" effort. This was so ingrained in me at the age of nineteen, that I truly believe it was the key to any future successes I would have.

As the second string guard, I participated in many of the games during the 1942 season. After all of these years, two of them stand out in my memory. Against Northwestern, with Otto Graham, Hal was injured and I felt I had made a significant contribution to our victory. This was also true in our conference championship game against Michigan. In the last quarter of this game, I recovered a fumble after making a jarring tackle on the Michigan halfback. On the very next play, Les Horvath threw a touchdown pass to Paul Sarringhaus to make the score 21-7. Paul had remarked that great football teams win in

November, and, in this last quarter, there was no way for Michigan to recover. My play in these two games was so convincing to Wilber Smith of the Chicago Tribune, that he named me to his All Sophomore team. Later, I received an invitation to play in the 1944 College All Star Game against the Chicago Bears just before I went overseas. There was quite a reunion of our 1942 team for this game—Lin Houston, Bill Willis, Gene Fekete, Paul Sarringhaus, Jack Duggar, Gordon Appleby and myself.

While I was still in school, I volunteered for the Army Student Training Program (ASTP) which would give me the opportunity to continue my engineering studies and also to gain a commission in the engineering branch of the Army. Prior to starting the ASTP Program, we were sent for 120 days of basic training. During the last week of training, I fell over a wall in the obstacle course and badly injured my right leg. I was unable to straighten out my leg and was transferred to Percy Jones General Hospital where orthopedic surgery was necessary to correct the disability. There was no physical rehabilitation following the surgery, as we have today.

After my discharge from the hospital, I was transferred back to the ASTP program. In the spring of 1944, when planning began for the European invasion, our ASTP program was disbanded and I was transferred to the infantry with the 76th Division at Camp McCoy, Wisconsin. Just before going overseas I received my invitation to play in the 1944 All Star Game in Chicago from Wilbur Smith. During our practices for this game, I knew my right leg was not the same. I had lost some of my quickness in getting off the ball on defense, and lacked the strength in my legs that I had in 1942.

Our division was attached to Patton's Third Army. By January, 1945, we fought through Luxembourg to clean up the remains of the Battle of the Bulge, the last Nazi offensive in the West. We then dropped back to Luxembourg and made a frontal attack on the Siegfried Line at Echernach. We had to open a corridor for Patton's armor to roll into Germany. These three weeks of fighting could only be described as Hell. We fought from one German held pill box to another. We often carried flame throwers to destroy the enemy. After breaching the Siegfried Line, our fighting continued against German units who were led by fanatical SS officers still in charge. The worst fighting was at Usingen, where, on Good Friday, my best friend in the Army was killed next to me. My three battle star campaigns ended at Chemnitz,

Germany, where we met the Russians. Since I was not married and did not have enough points for discharge, I was transferred to the 45th Division in France to prepare for the invasion of Japan. Thank God, the bomb was dropped and we were saved from making this bloody invasion. If the Japs had fought to the end on Okinawa, just think how they would have fought to protect their mainland.

The 45th Division was deactivated in Texas in the fall of 1945. My high school sweetheart, Marian Roberts, and I were married. I was discharged and we headed back to Ohio State to continue my education. I was strongly motivated to obtain my engineering degree with the highest possible grades. Despite my motivation, it took a lot of reviewing of my past classes just to get back to my expected class level in the Engineering College. I also returned to the football team for spring practice. Despite the rehabilitation efforts by our fine trainer, Ernie Biggs, my right leg was still not back to its former strength. My severely bowed legs further complicated my situation. Although I started the 1946 season as the first string guard, I eventually lost the position to Bob Guadio who would later star with the Cleveland Browns and become an All Pro Guard. Overall we had a pretty good season but we lost to Illinois and then very badly to Michigan. Memories of the 1942 team were still fresh in the minds of Ohio State fans and soon chaos overtook the football program as several of our key players left school for the pros—Tony Adamlee, Bob Gaudio, Tommy James, etc. Paul Bixler, the last of Paul Brown's staff was fired as Head Coach and he was replaced by Wes Fessler, the legendary All American End from Ohio State. I was elected to be the Captain for the 1947 season, but we had little talent or speed on the team, and freshmen could not yet play. I have great respect for Wes Fessler both as a coach and a man. He did an outstanding job with our limited talent. We ended the season on a strong note, holding the number one team in the country, our arch rival Michigan to a 7-0 half time score. The depth of their talented football players took their toll in the second half. If there is a lesson to be learned from losses, I had learned that giving one's best efforts, even in a losing season, should not make one remorseful. I read these same sentiments in Paul's book, "P.B.'s Story" commenting on the 1943 "Baby Bucks" even though he had some great spot players in Bill Willis, Jack Duggar, Gordon Appleby, and Cy Sauders.

My years in Ohio State football and my desire to be an outstanding student, brought great rewards the year of my graduation in

1948 with a Bachelor of Science degree in mechanical engineering. I graduated with honors, selected to the Tau Beta Pi and Pi Tau Sigma Engineering Honor Societies, and was awarded the first Chick Harley Medal for my athletic career. I also received, perhaps, the greatest honor a student-athlete could hope for aside from being declared an All American. I was awarded the Western Conference Medal as the outstanding scholar-athlete in 1948. It may be only Ohio State football trivia, but in 1987, the year of our 45th reunion of our National Championship team, the giant scoreboard recorded the magnificent scholarly records of the 1942 team. Bill Vickroy received the Western Conference Medal as the outstanding scholar-athlete in 1943, Jack Duggar in 1944, Don Steinberg in 1945, and myself in 1947. There was never a question of the academic achievements of this 1942 team with its advanced master's and doctorate degrees in education, business, agriculture, economics, law, fine arts, architecture, geology, dentistry and medicine and athletic coaching. Notwithstanding these great honors, my proudest moment in my senior year occurred the Tuesday before Dad's Day playing Iowa at home. My first child, Mark, was born.

After graduation, I accepted a position as an industrial engineer with the Lincoln Electric Corporation in Cleveland. My two-year stay with the company was an excellent education in "hands on" experience in manufacturing systems, methods and goal setting. Since there were no openings available at that time for mechanical engineers at Lincoln Electric, I became employed with the FMC Corporation as a mechanical engineer in Illinois. I worked in the area of research and development and was later promoted to plant superintendent which was largely due to the experience I had gained a Lincoln Electric. In order to further my career, I spent the summers of 1954 and 1955 at the University of Indiana's business school for my master's in business administration. Shortly thereafter, the FMC Corp., purchased a packaging machinery operation in Green Bay, Wisconsin. Here, I spent the next seventeen years as plant manager. It was most interesting to me to be living in Green Bay during Vince Lombardi's coaching era with the Green Bay Packers. I soon realized what a great contribution Paul Brown had made in upgrading the quality of professional football which Lombardi essentially copied. Prior to Vince Lombardi's coming to Green Bay, there was little organized training evaluations or goals such as Paul had developed at Massillon, Ohio State or with the Browns. In prior years, the College All Stars were able to challenge the Championship Pro team in the pre-season opening game, but, no longer, as professional football had matured along the lines that Paul Brown had initiated and developed.

In 1973, the FMC Corporation reorganized and moved their corporate offices to Chicago. I accepted a position as senior project manager to introduce FMC products to foreign countries as well as to build manufacturing and assembly plants overseas. During the next eight years, I was responsible for new plant construction in Scotland where we built well head equipment. Then we were transferred from Scotland to France where we manufactured oil drilling equipment for Europe and the Middle East. We moved on to Belgium to manufacture canning equipment and to Italy to make packaging machinery and then to England where we manufactured harvester combines. After Europe, we were off to Argentina and Brazil to manufacture agricultural equipment and citrus fruit processing machinery. I returned to the United State in the late 70's when the company moved several operations to Riverside and Madera, California. In 1982, I was given early retirement with a consultant's contract. I remained active until the end of 1987 when we fully retired to sunny California.

The family that Marian and I had started at Ohio State, largely a Green Bay operation, has grown to three children and as of now, seven grandchildren. Of our three children, Lynn attended the University of Wisconsin. Our son, Mark, is a physician. Our daughter, Laura received her master's degree in business administration at Northwestern. After Lynn had received her nursing degree at Wisconsin, she enrolled in San Diego State University and earned a mechanical engineering degree. She is now employed in research and development with the Meditronic Corp. in Minneapolis that specializes in sophisticated cardiac pacemakers and other exotic medical products.

My retirement has been very gratifying now that I know my surgeries to correct my bow legs has been successful. They were causing me almost constant agonizing pain, but that is all behind me now. First my left leg was corrected by a surgical procedure called a double osteotomy to straighten a six inch deviation from normal. During my course of rehabilitation, after the surgery, the pain in my right leg began to subside. Instead of replacing the knee joint as the surgeon had anticipated, he was able to perform the same procedure on the right leg.

When our 42 team gathers for our 50th reunion in 1992, I'll have to wear a name tag as my old trademark, "Bows" will have long gone.

All of our activities as young men centered around football. For the most part, we came from first generation, poor families struggling through the Depression. Football provided the vehicle to carry us through the paths of higher education. Our Ohio State University 1942 team stands out as a unique squad with the most outstanding personality in all of the history of football to lead us and teach us the ideals to be cherished in the future as we wound our way through the years, raised our families, and reached the pinnacles of success in all of our endeavors.

DON STEINBERG

Football: Ohio State, 1941, 1942, 1945
Honorable Mention All Big Ten, 1942
Big Ten Scholar-Athlete, 1945

Education: Bachelor of Science
Doctor of Medicine
Post Graduate Study, 7 years

Career: General Surgery

Married: Lois – 15 years – Died of Cancer
Janet – 21 years
Four children & eleven grandchildren

Service: U.S. Army Medical Corps
Fitzsimons General Hospital

DON STEINBERG

There are few words that can aptly describe the advantages of being born the youngest child of a large family. The youngest child is endeared by his mother, protected and instructed by his older brothers, adored by his sisters, and, at times, when food might be scarce, he would still be well fed. Being well fed affords the probability of becoming larger and stronger than the other children in the family. But more than that, being the youngest gives one the opportunity to have a very advantageous and close look at the emotional relationships between the other members of the family. From this vantage point, I could easily discern that being agreeable and "doing what you were told" was far superior to being disagreeable. This background of being big, strong, and "agreeable", made me very "coachable".

It was the middle of the Great Depression. My older brother Morton, or Mutt as he was nicknamed, had already given up his boyhood dream of becoming a football coach. He had spent years studying the books written by the famous coaches of the time while he played football for Scott High School in Toledo and after graduation for the University of Toledo. Lastly, he became a "tramp athlete" when Arizona State University initiated its football program at Tempe, Arizona. The Depression was a hopeless time and seeing no future in his childhood ambition, Mutt returned to Toledo and became a common laborer in a junk yard for a dollar a day. He worked with the other unfortunate men for ten hours each day dismantling old automobiles and throwing the scrap metal on to huge piles of rusting steel.

From this ignominious experience, two ideals would emerge. He would spend his entire life caring for the needs of the poor in his chosen profession which he attained years later than most men. The other ideal fixed in his mind centered around the futures of his two younger brothers, my brother Ray and myself. He dedicated himself toward guaranteeing that we would never be relegated to this type of work which, in many respects, was almost servitude. He not only inspired us to be dedicated students, he demanded it. We happily acquiesced throughout our high school years—six nights a week throughout the school year. We did our studying together on a refurbished large oak table that Mutt had brought home covered with grease from the junk yard.

Mutt was never much of a student, but he had collected undergraduate college credits during his years in collegiate football. When he returned from the war, the President of Loyola University in Chicago permitted him to enter dental school at the age of 35. Never forgetting his junk yard experiences, he cared for the dental needs of the poor never inquiring as to their ability to pay for his services. He even got into trouble with the Internal Revenue Service for deducting the lab expenses that he could never hope to be paid for by these people. In summary, he had two dental offices, one for the poor and another for the poorer.

I would be his football player. When I was only 10 or 11 years old, he began to teach me the rudiments of contact football. We would frequently go over the fence to the neighbor's yard where grass was growing. (Very little grass grows in poor neighborhoods.) Here he instructed me in the stance of the linemen, various football blocks, and most important, tackling this full grown 200 pounds athlete as he carried the football across the yard using my brother, Ray, as his interference. Whenever I did not perform up to his expectations, he would use the term "cake eater" to motivate a better attitude or performance under pain.

While I was still in grade school, a group of us had organized a football team to play similar teams from the close-by schools. Our team would be going to Scott High School while the Cathedral Latin boys would be going to Central Catholic. We were not formally trained or coached, but I am sure the high school coaches were well aware of the competition. Many of these players would soon be the nucleus for their high school teams.

I followed Bill Vickroy into Scott High School when Scott was a center of academic excellence and had an athletic program that was well-respected throughout the state. Bill was not only an outstanding center on the football team but also a renowned catcher on the baseball team. But more than that, we were fine students. We would carry these attributes for the rest of our lives. One of the finest compliments I have ever received was the day that Mr. Demorest, our principal, took me out of class my senior year. He introduced me to the President of Depauw University, a small, highly regarded university in Indiana. It was in the spring, several months before graduation and after I had been named a first string tackle on the All City team and had placed eighth in the state among the boys in the Ohio State High School Scholastic Examination. The President of Depauw was a quiet, elderly, gray haired man who had come to Toledo to induce me to come to Depauw. He offered me a full scholarship and my books if I would accept. I had to refuse this wonderful offer for I had no money nor any prospect of going to any university at the time. I remember him saying, "Don, I know you want to be a doctor and we have a close relationship with the University of Louisville School of Medicine. We really would like to have you, even if you do not wish to play football." I answered by explaining that I had no money to pay for my board and room. It was clearly a wonderful opportunity for me, but my circumstances made going to Depauw impossible. Later that spring, I placed high on the list for an appointment to West Point, but the boy just ahead of me passed both the academic and physical exams for admission to West Point.

My coming to Ohio State was one of many wonderful and unexpected events in my life. One of our assistant coaches at Scott was a dentist by the name of Alex Klein. He was a practicing dentist who had been the Center on the Ohio State football team in 1925. He really wasn't an assistant coach but merely took time from his practice to assist the coaching staff. Dr. Klein had a brother in-law who was the president of the Zeta Beta Tau Fraternity at Ohio State. He convinced his brother-in-law, Irv, that the fraternity should have a football player, me, specifically, among its members to bring recognition to the chapter. Irv and his friend Herman Levitt, the current treasurer of the chapter, convinced the other members to offer me my board and room if I would pledge the fraternity. I had already received a two-year academic scholarship to Ohio State from my placement in the state Scholarship Examination which then filled all of my needs to enter college. I was recruited by Ernie Godfrey and entered Ohio State in the fall of 1940.

The fall of 1940 was a sad time at Ohio State as a darkening cloud was gathering over the football program. It was the end of Francis Schmidt's coaching career. Few Varsity players ever came to practice regularly and this breakdown was finally punctuated by the 40-0 loss to Michigan despite having a team whose personnel was equal to Michigan's. However, there was a silver lining to this cloud with the arrival of Paul Brown as Head Coach.

I recall our first meeting with Coach Brown in the conference area of the dressing room on the first day of spring practice in March of 1941. Many of the upperclassmen were well known All-Conference players with a sophisticated air about themselves. They would be the core of the team for the coming season in the Fall of 1941. However, they were openly doubtful about the high school coach who had come to Ohio State. There was Charlie Anderson, an All-Conference End at 225 and 6 ft. 3 in. and as fast as lightning. Charlie Magg was an equally large man at one tackle position and "Big" Jim Daniels, a giant All American at the other tackle. Jack Stevenson was also a veteran tackle and Captain for the coming year. Jack Graf, a fullback, was the epitome of a great athlete with an attitude and talent to fill any coach's dreams. Against this background of these "mature" seniors, Paul sat us down to watch a film of his Massillon High School team. The film illustrated Paul's concept of football. It demonstrated team work, speed, and execution of offensive plays as I had never experienced as a high school player.

Throughout the season, there was never any doubt of Paul's leadership. His demands for complete dedication and execution flowed with equal intensity to his coaching staff. There would be no deviation from his coaching methods or any compromise of a player's dedication. Given one's first opportunity, a player had to perform up to Paul's expectation for there would be no second chance. There was one event that completely stamped the 1941 team as a Paul Brown team—the departure of Charlie Anderson, his most valuable player, for infractions that if left unpenalized would have undermined Paul's self-imposed discipline.

The fall practices always started with the selection of eleven players as the basis for the future playing first team. Paul made it quickly apparent that there was no "pecking order" or other qualifications for a starting player than to be the best athlete in each particular position. The Captain of the 1941 team was Jack Stevenson, a right tackle. He was allowed to start the opening game of the season, but was soon replaced by Chuck Csuri, a sophomore. Another discipline, aside from the obvious ones such as punctuality and maintaining a good academic average, was that everyone practiced with the same intensity. Very frequently, two things would happen. If the opportunity to play presented itself, you would play without error and up to Paul's expectation. Secondly, there was a notable narrowing of the range of capabilities of all the players in the same position. This was particularly true of the 1942 team. The famous and talented backfield of Lynn, Horvath, Sarringhaus, and Fekete had little or no lowering of capability with the substitution of Tommy James, Bob Frye, George Slusser, Bill Durtschi, Cy Lipaj, Dick Palmer or Robin Priday. For whatever reason, when any of these backs were called into a game, the teamwork and play execution remained sharp and intact.

Playing third string in 1941, my playing time was confined to a few minutes at the end of the Southern California game, after winning was assured, and one play against Michigan. The score was 20-20 late in the fourth quarter against a Michigan team that was favored to win by a wide margin. Paul looked at me on the bench and sent me into the game to try to block the extra point after Michigan had tied the score. I ran on to the field to replace Bob Shaw without my helmet. I had to borrow his which was about five sizes too big so that it almost covered my eyes. The ball was snapped and I remember diving over the Michigan blocking back with my arm outstretched. The ball flew wide of the opposite upright of the goal post. The score remained 20-20, a great moral victory for Ohio State.

At the start of the 1942 season, I was still the third string End behind Dante Lavelli and John T. White. Dante would dominate the National Football League for ten or more years when he played for the Cleveland Browns, and John would later become the Captain of a Michigan National Championship team after the War. On the Tuesday before the first game against Ft. Knox, Paul walked up to me and merely said, "Steinberg, you are starting Saturday." Both Dante and John were injured and were unable to play. Another of Paul's axioms came into play—"Rise to the Occasion". As we were going on to the field to start the game, I recalled the advice given to me several years before coming to Ohio State by Jake "Canadian", a friend of my brother Mutt's. This, too, was his nickname as he had moved as a young man to Toledo from Canada. "The first play of the game is the most important. Never let the opposing player on offense or defense ever forget you. Let him know from the beginning of the game that he is going to have a long afternoon."

A defensive End's duties are mainly three. The first is to strip the ball carrier of his interference on an end run so your halfback can meet the ball carrier on the line of scrimmage and make the tackle. His second responsibility is to close the area between the tackle and end on an off tackle play. His third responsibility is to "stay in his own backyard". While the linebackers and tackles are required to roam and pursue, the End must stay put. He must not become adventurous until he is absolutely certain that a play is not developing to came around him as a naked reverse or Statue of Liberty play. As a defensive End, my love of contact football from my childhood, was made to order.

The offensive end is a basic pillar for running plays in addition to pass catching. In the days of the "single wing" formations, which was our basic offense, it was the End's responsibility to move the opposing tackle with the assistance of the wingback either inward on an off tackle play or outward on an inside tackle play. Here the basic law of Kinetic Energy comes into play. It matters little how big the opposing tackle may be if you can block him before he starts his charge. You will move him. In order to do this, Paul and his assistant coach, Fritz Mackey, taught me to start my block by springing from my stance without the delay of taking a step. As the season progressed, I became more and more proficient in this method of blocking. In spite being as slow as molasses and having the delicate hands of a future surgeon making catching passes an absolute failure, I remained an integral part of the starting team throughout the season except when I was injured.

After the 1942 season, I entered medical school at Ohio State. I received a letter from the medical school asking me to apply which was probably a first as I have never heard of it happening before or since. There was only one week between being drafted into the service and starting medical school. With my love for football, and having another year of eligibility, I declined taking my undergraduate degree. Paul had often remarked that, "One should play the string out to the end as good fortune often comes unexpectedly." By the university rules, I would be allowed to take both of my degrees at the end of my post graduate education. So I practiced with the football team in the spring of 1943 and 1944 although I was not allowed to play because of the Army regulations. The fall of 1945 found me not only a senior in medical school but an externe in the department of research surgery, doing my house obstetrics by going to the homes of women in labor to deliver their babies, making my daily classes and Army formations, going steady with a lovely girl, and playing Varsity football all at the same time. The war had ended and my Colonel allowed me to play with the only stipulation being that I was to wear civilian clothes on out of town trips to play other universities.

In 1945, the team was much different from a Paul Brown coached team. The season started with great expectations. Dick Fisher, and Thornton Dixon from the 1941 team and Paul Sarringhaus, Robin Priday and Jack Roe from the 1942 team were back from service. Paul Sarringhaus was featured on the cover of Life Magazine as the most outstanding player of the coming season having been the star power halfback of the 1942 National Championship team. Paul Bixler and Carol Widdoes were the coaches, having been Paul Brown's assistant coaches, but there were some things missing and some things very different. I personally was never worked hard enough to be in the same physical condition as in 42, and the preparations before each game were never as detailed. We lost two games which I do not believe would have happened had Paul Brown been the coach.

Following my graduation from medical school, I left Columbus for my internship in Detroit. Several months later, I was informed that I was selected as the outstanding scholar-athlete in the Big Ten from Ohio State. It was a secret hope of mine that was now fulfilled. This award is almost as satisfying as being named an All American.

For several months prior to graduation and leaving Columbus for my internship in Detroit, I was urged by Mel Stevens, the newly appointed coach of the Brooklyn Dodger Football Team, to come to New York to play professional football along with spending my internship in a hospital in New York. He made it very enticing as he offered a surgical residency along with the football contract. A general surgical residency at that time was the hallmark of post graduate medical training. I was now 22 years old and felt is was time to give up football for medicine and went on to Detroit.

After two years at Fitzsimons General Hospital in Denver where I completed my Army service, I spent six more years in general surgical residency at the Downstate Medical School in Brooklyn, New York. As an added footnote to the many fortunate occurrences in my life was the obtaining my surgical residency in general surgery. General surgical residencies were so difficult to obtain, that I had accepted a residency in pathology hoping to be accepted the following year in general surgery at Halloran General Hospital on Staten Island. When I obtained my acceptance to a residency at the Brooklyn Veterans Hospital, which was a satellite residency of Downstate Medical School, I had to cancel my signed contract at Halloran. The chief of Halloran General Hospital threatened to prevent my taking my boards in general surgery if I did not honor my contract in pathology. The night before the day I was waiting to appeal my case to the board of Halloran General, a directive had been received from Washington that the government was closing the Halloran Veteran's Hospital!

After being away from home for almost fifteen years, I returned to Toledo and the private practice of general surgery. My mother's dreams for her sons was fulfilled. Of her five boys, three became surgeons who practiced as partners for over fifteen years, and one son, my brother, Morton, practiced dentistry for the poor and his many friends. My eldest brother, Ted, and my sister, Ann, had made all of this possible.

The private practice of general surgery has been very gratifying as we made a practice of caring for anyone who requested our services with no monetary judgements to be considered. I have always maintained a continuing interest in the opportunities for clinical and laboratory investigations in medicine. I am sure it had much to due with our exposure to the creative genius of Paul Brown. I have had many articles published on my investigations in medicine ranging from surgical techniques to various areas in cancer detection and treatment. At the International College of Surgeons meeting in Paris in 1981, my report on the open treatment of peritonitis was deemed one of the outstanding contributions for that year from America. As the reports of other investigators are published, it appears that this approach to treat this frequently fatal complication is becoming the standard of treatment for generalized infections of the abdominal cavity.

I suppose that this biography appears to be one of only good fortune, but, of course, this is not the case. Our middle son, Jimmy, was born with a severe heart malformation and to our grief did not survive corrective surgery when he was five years old. My first wife, Lois, developed a tiny lump on her left breast at the age of 35, which proved to be a highly malignant cancer of the breast. She passed away after six years always facing her ordeal with unbending courage. It was her wish to live until our eldest son, Steven's Bar Mitzvah. She passed away a few months later. For the next three years, my home situation was an almost constant stress trying to properly raise two young sons of 13 and

9 years old, and maintain my busy surgical practice.

During my last year as a widower, many of my friends had urged me to meet Janet Ertis, a young lady who had two daughters and who had lost her husband a year before. I always kid my new mother-in-law that she made my second marriage, but it has been a wonderful relationship from the beginning and we became a whole family by adopting each other's children after our marriage. Of our sons, Steve is now a professor of surgery at Tulane University and Dan is a very successful insurance executive for Columbus Mutual here in Toledo. Of our daughters, Laurie is a nurse who is married to an anesthesiologist at Mt. Sinai Hospital in Cleveland and Stephanie is a rising star in the ladies ready-to-wear catalogue business in New York. She is married to a young man in the personnel division of the postal service. Janet and I now have eleven grandchildren and are expecting our twelfth in July of 1992. All of the grandchildren are eight years old or younger, and we might add that being grandparents is a totally happy experience.

THE DON STEINBERG FAMILY

Except for the number of children and grandchildren, all of our families are similar.

WILLIAM HACKETT, D.V.M.

Football: Ohio State, 1942, 1943, 1944
All American, 1944
Captain-elect for 1945

Education: Doctor of Veterinary Medicine
Distinguished Alumnus Award
Ohio State College of Agriculture

Career: Owner of Ohio Feed Lots Company
Inventor of process to convert animal wastes to fertilizer
and feed in a non-polluting environment.
Instrumental in bringing Paul Brown to Cincinnati Bengals.

Married: Mary – Four sons

Service: Army Student Training Program

BILL HACKETT, D.V.M.

The education of this future farmer began when I was five or six years old. I would ride with my dad in our old jalopy through the lanes between the fenced off fields. "Son," he would say, "Go over to that gate and open it so the cattle in that field can be driven through the gate to that yonder field where the grass is still high." While we were driving through the lanes and opening other gates to change the fields where the cattle would graze, he would tell me about our family in Ireland. They had raised cattle in Ireland and then came to America where they continued to raise cattle. Among the farmers who raised animals, there was an axiom that has come down through the centuries and is still true today. "The cattle are followed by the pigs, and the pigs are followed by the chickens." This may be a strange statement to a person who is not a farmer, but the droppings of the cattle help feed the pigs and the droppings from the pigs, in turn, fed the chickens. This axiom has helped feed mankind since the beginning of time. It is never forgotten by future farmers who are constantly seeking to improve the efficiency of farming and, consequently, the condition of mankind.

My father had this small cattle raising operation while I attended a small high school in the area. During the Great Depression, like many other farmers, we lost our farm. This must have been a deep blow after working so hard for so many years. Without any signs of anger or despair, Dad brought us to a small town near Columbus where he became a day laborer in a farm operation. Later, we moved to London, Ohio, where I attended my senior year in high school. My previous high school was tiny compared to London High School where we had a total of four hundred students, but we did have a football team. I played Guard for this team although I had no previous football experience and was named second team All Conference at the end of my senior year.

Being Catholic, I had already been recruited by Notre Dame before graduation in the spring. The University of Alabama had also offered me a full athletic scholarship. One evening, Paul Brown and Fritz Mackey, one of his assistant coaches from Ohio State, came to see me. They offered me nothing more than a part time job to work my way through school if I would come to Ohio State. During our conversation, I developed an indefinable affinity for Coach Brown that convinced me to go to college at Ohio State. In addition, the Ohio State University had one of the most prestigious agricultural colleges in the country where I would enroll as a pre-veterinarian student.

My freshman year I attended science and humanities courses which were similar to those taken by all the health science students and practiced with the Freshman football team. Trevor Rees was the freshman coach and we had little contact with Paul Brown throughout the fall. Towards the end of the season, the Varsity team played the freshman team in a full scrimmage. This was not the third or fourth string we would be playing but the first team. In spite of having some excellent players on the freshman team like Dante Lavelli, Bill Willis, Gene Fekete and Robin Priday, all of whom would figure prominently in the 1942 championship team, we were beaten unmercifully by the Varsity. I, in particular, had a very bad day. Paul Brown remarked to me that he doubted that I would ever be good enough to make the team. That remark really "stuck in my craw", and it would be years before I could redeem myself.

During the 1942 season, Wib Schneider and I played behind Lin Houston. In my opinion, Lin was one of the finest Guards who has ever played this position. Both of us learned a great deal from him as the Guards on every football team are the keys to the success of any running play. If he is not blocking the defensive man opposite him, he is pulling out of the line at the same instant the ball is snapped from the Center to the backfield man. It is critical, for by this maneuver, he will lead the interference for the ball carrier. The guard will then either open the hole for the ball carrier through the defensive line or he will block an oncoming defensive lineman away from the ball carrier just as he is about to tackle him. This play is called a "mouse trap" and is very common in all offenses

There were two things that deeply impressed me about the 1942 National Championship team. The first was that Paul Brown would play only the best athletes in each position. As long as this player was not injured, there would be no other reason for his starting. The second was the total lack of any animosity between the players in the same position. Lin Houston, Web, and I were always together and the best of friends. I am sure that Paul studied each player's temperament so that this would be true. Most of the games that I played in 1942 were games in which Paul would substitute entire teams after winning was assured. However, I did play in enough games to win my Letter, a heavy Scarlet wool sweater embossed with a large grey capital "O".

In 1943, after six months in the Army Veterinary Program, I was discharged in the fall as the Army had no need for more veterinarians. They allowed us to finish Veterinary College instead of sending us to other branches of the Army. I was the first string Guard on the "Baby Bucks" as we were called in 1943 as we had few experienced players and had to play against other university teams that had full compliments of collegiate and professional players in almost every position. This was a particularly bad year for Paul as he was very worried that someone would be badly injured because of the marked discrepancy in size and strength between the "Baby Bucks" and our opposings teams. Nevertheless, due to his remarkable coaching, we had developed a very fine line with a backfield that was thin at best. Following this season, Paul entered the service and became the Head Coach of the Great Lakes Training Center. Unheralded, this 1943 team was one of Paul Brown's finest coaching accomplishments. Paul had made "A silk purse out of a sow's ear".

There was a complete turn around in the football fortunes of Ohio State in 1944. Les Horvath and I had returned to the team along with three outstanding freshman backs, Bob Brunie, Jerry Krall and Ollie Kline. The line that Paul had trained and left for Carol Widdoes, Paul's previous assistant, had matured into one of the best in the country. I had grown to almost 200 pounds and the other linemen Bill Willis, Jack Dugger, Russ Thomas, Warren Amling, Dick Schnittker and Cy Souders gave the backfield ideal Paul Brown support. We were undefeated the entire season. One of our opponents was Great Lakes now coached by Paul. Although he had excellent personnel, he had not had time to mold them into a Paul Brown team and we defeated them. As Paul was leaving the field in his dapper Naval uniform, he was in deep thought as he was not one to take defeat without giving it serious thought. I followed him and called out several times. "Paul, Paul, Paul and if you don't turn around there will be 70,000 spectators see me tackle you!" Paul turned and then said, "You have really turned into a fine guard." My years of waiting for his approval were over. Ohio State placed second to Army as the best team in the country. Les Horvath was magnificent and was awarded the Heisman Trophy. Willis, Dugger, Amling and I were named to All American teams.

During the years, I had become very friendly with Jim Rhodes, the Governor of Ohio. He was always intensely interested in the fortunes and future of Ohio State. One evening in the early winter, Les Horvath and I had been invited to a banquet in the honor of Governor Rhodes. It was a snowy and slippery night and we were hit head-on by another automobile. I suffered an injury to my head which caused bleeding into my spinal fluid, as well as a possible intracranial injury. Although I was still having quite severe headaches, I was eager to play in the East-West game. I had weekly checkups at Ohio State and as nothing had developed to indicated brain injury, I decided to play against the stern advice of my neurosurgeon. After the game, Herman Hickman, our East coach, as well as the coach at Army, decided to change my plans of continuing in vet school at Ohio State and to draft me into West Point to play football for Army. This was the last thing I wanted to happen as I was near graduation as a Doctor of Veterinary Medicine. I called Paul Brown who contacted Senator Burton to put a stop to the plan to get me back in service to play for West Point. When I returned to Columbus, Dr. Lefevre, the neurosurgeon at Ohio State Medical School, was beside himself. He felt that I had jeopardized my future by playing in the East-West game. He convinced me that my athletic days were over.

After graduation from the College of Veterinary Medicine at Ohio State, my friendship with Governor Rhodes brought me many opportunities related to sports in Ohio. I became a racing commissioner for several years. At that time a movement was afoot to bring professional football to Cincinnati. In my mind, there was only one person for this job, Paul Brown. Paul had been out of football for almost four years after his separation from the Cleveland Browns. Through his wife, Katie, I knew that this forced retirement was the last thing that Paul wanted. As we gathered steam in bringing professional football to Cincinnati, I was working with Paul whose primary concern would be to have total control of the team both as to the selection of players and the coaching of the team. After his misunderstanding with Art Modell, he would have it no other way. A bond issue was passed to build a new stadium in Cincinnati through the good services of Governor Rhodes. The Cincinnati Bengals joined the National Football League. We had the finest coach in the history of football, and I was finally able to do something to express my personal appreciation to Paul.

While all of these events were taking place, I was the livestock director of the Sawyer-Oreton Farms, a national concern who prepared cattle for market in large feeding stations. With all of my activities as director of livestock, the age old formula for feeding pigs from the waste of the cattle and then feeding the chickens from the waste of the pigs sorely needed scientific re-evaluation. There were several issues that were involved in my analysis. First, it takes years for manure to be spread over a field before it can be converted by natural processes into fertilizer to be recycled into the vegetable economy. It would be a God-send to be able to shorten this period of time. Secondly, the raising of cattle in feeding stations to "fatten them up" was complicated by all kinds of illnesses that frequently would decimate a herd. I felt that the solution to the latter problem was the inability to remove the wastes generated by the cattle. The lack of proper ventilation, which allowed ammonia to fill the air, would injure the animals' respiratory systems. Lastly, there was a reason for cattle to regurgitate its food, "to chew its cud", in contrast to other animals. It had been scientifically shown that steers changed the bacterial flora of their intestinal tracts by this activity. Furthermore, animals are not 100% efficient in converting their food into energy or tissue. A goodly percentage of the protein in their feed was thus available to the pig and from the pig to the chicken. With these principles in mind, I decided to leave my position with Sawyer-Oreton and lease acreage from John Sawyer to further develop these ideas.

I decided to start the Ohio Feed Lots, a company designed to be a cattle motel to fatten cattle for market. My first objective was to build a facility completely under roof so that weather would not be a factor in our operations. Then the cattle were to be housed in long narrow buildings which were perpendicular to the prevailing winds. They would be partially open on their sides to allow animals clean air at all times. These buildings would be at least 500 feet apart to prevent the ammonia generated from the cattle urine from injuring the animals' respiratory systems. The under roof areas were divided into pens to house more than 1000 head of cattle in each building. Almost immediately we noted a marked drop in the frequency of respiratory diseases in these animals.

The pens in each building were bedded with sawdust that could be cleaned at regular intervals. Machinery was used to remove the soiled bedding material. Then clean sawdust, straw and other materials were used to replace the soiled bedding material. These two procedures of dividing the building into pens and regularly replacing the bedding material created an odorless and fly free environment. The old bedding material of sawdust filled with animal excrement was moved to a "bio-fermentation facility". I had conceived this process to reduce the natural time it took to convert the waste to fertilizer from years to days by an aerating process that stimulated the growth of aerobic bacteria and destroyed the anaerobic bacteria, spores, worm eggs, and viral disease particles that could cause diseases in animals. Spontaneously, this porous material became heated to 175 degrees Farenheit merely by this "fermentation" process. Thus it was essentially sterile for pathogenic germs and viruses. We had also solved the cattle-pig-chicken axiom. We noted that the product of the digester could be used to replace a large percentage of the feed mixtures that we used to fatten the cattle.

Our cattle consistently gained weight faster than cattle fed by traditional feeding mixtures. The product of the Digester could also be spread as natural fertilizer as the time of conversion of manure to useful fertilizer was shortened from years to days. Our success has been noted throughout the world. I honestly feel we have developed the solution to protecting the environment from further pollution in the area of food production and we will contribute significantly to solving the protein needs of an ever-growing world population. In 1984, I received the Distinguished Alumnus Award from the Ohio State University College of Agriculture for my research work and its application.

Our family has been blessed with four sons. William Jr. is manager of Ohio Resources. Robert is a general manager of Prudential Life Insurance Co. Keven is a Physician in Columbus, and James is vice president of Steel Case Co. in Grand Rapids, Michigan. Our trips to Columbus to watch the Buckeyes on Saturday and our trips to Cincinnati to watch the Bengals on Sunday renew, with pride, my memories and achievements from my education at Ohio State and football with Paul Brown.

FEEDLOT OPERATIONS

BOB McCORMICK

Football: Ohio State, 1942, 1946
            Ft. Bragg Bombardiers, 1945

Education: A.B. and Masters

Career: High School Teacher and Coach
            Industrial Packaging at Union Camp Corporation
            Eight U.S. Patents

Married: Martha
            Three sons & five grandchildren

Service: Captain and Tank Officer in Patton's Army
            Office of Strategic Services

BOB McCORMICK

It seems that intercollegiate football today has a completely different style from football during my years at Ohio State in the early 40's. I don't think it was so much the change to the two platoon system compared to a team whose players were expected to be able play the entire game. It was quite different from today's emphasis that is implied by coaches and the universities on athletes and athletics. We were just as talented athletes as we have today, but, aside from that, we were completely involved in the educational processes of the university. The university expected the same studious effort from us as the other students despite the time spent in training or on the football field.

While in high school I had participated in all of the team sports as well as being named to the National Honor Society. Following my graduation from Columbus South, I decided to explore several of the athletic scholarships that were offered to me, particularly, from southern universities. Their inducements were more financially oriented than the northern universities. All of the southern universities were athletically prominent but their academic goals for their student-athletes were uncomfortable to me. It seemed that your education would be secondary to football. I decided to go to Ohio State where the educational goals were not subverted by its athletics. There was a man in Columbus named Carlisle Dowling who contacted Ernie Godfrey at Ohio State in the summer of 1940. Several years later Mr. Dowling became the head referee for the Big Ten Conference. I joined the freshman football team in the fall prior to the appointment of Paul Brown as Head Coach.

My playing position on the 1941 and 1942 championship teams was a tackle behind Bill Willis, Chuck Csuri, and Don McCafferty. Jack Duggar, Jim Rees, Tom Taylor and I were the reserve tackles. I remember Paul telling me that the only difference between my ability and those of the starting tackles was being a step slower in the execution of my assignments. There was one remark that he always made to us that has always remained with me, for he was more than a coach. He had a sincere appreciation for the efforts of his players. Oftentimes, he would tell us that through our efforts in school and football, we would all be successful individuals after our college days were over. For every man on the squad, this came true.

Those were wonderful days of going to the university in the College of Education, playing Varsity football, and working part time in the Old State Office Building to pay our board and room. We developed friendships that would last throughout our lives. I and my wife were particularly friendly with Don McCafferty and his wife, Joan. But the war interrupted all of that. I entered the service at Ft. Knox where I was commissioned a 2nd. Lt. after Officer's Training School. I was attached to the 11th Armor Division. We entered the war in Europe shortly after D Day and fought our way across France into Germany. At the time of the Battle of the Bulge, we were attached to General Patton's Army and spearheaded the drive north to cut off the neck of the bulge that relieved the divisions in Bastogne. During the course of my training as an officer, I had volunteered for hazardous duty not knowing exactly what it meant at the time. While overseas I was transferred to the Office of Strategic Services, the forerunner of the Central Intelligence Agency. I finished my service as a Captain and was fortunate to have fought through the war without serious injury.

Returning from overseas duty in 1945, I was stationed at Ft. Bragg, North Carolina. I was appointed the head football coach of the "Bombardiers", our service displaced Buckeyes. We had Don McCafferty and Carmen Naples still playing with me as player-coach. The team had taken over the remaining football schedule of the North Carolina Pre-flight School team. We beat many of the service teams as well as Duke University that year. This was the end of my active playing career. However, I did try to play after returning to Ohio State but some of the injuries that I had sustained in service made any return to active Big Ten football impossible.

Following my discharge, I returned to Ohio State to go on to graduate school and receive my master's degree in Education. As a graduate assistant, I was appointed the coach of the Junior Varsity, a group of players who intended to become athletic coaches after college on the high school level. After leaving Ohio State, I became a teacher and coach at Columbus North High School. I later coached at Wopekoneta High School. Here, I became friends with the Neal Armstrong family. The next year I moved on to Wittenburg College, a small Ohio School, where Ernie Godfrey started his career in coaching. However, after five years in teaching and coaching, it became apparent that one could not raise a family with this income. I decided to enter business.

At the age of 36, I started a new career in the packaging division of the Westinghouse Corporation. Shortly after, I rose to production coordinator of the entire division. The next year I left Westinghouse to join the Union Camp Corporation, the world's largest packaging company. Here, I would spend the rest of my working years. My work carried me to many cities and states across the country. Martha and I moved repeatedly from Columbus, to the Detroit area, to Florida, to Cleveland and then back to Columbus. All this time we were raising our family. My work with Union Camp was particularly interesting to me. I was involved in the designing of a variety of containers. During this period I was awarded eight U.S. Patents for my designs. One of the most interesting products we developed was at the request of the Defense Department. They asked us to develop a collapsible light weight stretcher to assist in moving wounded soldiers. I developed the stretcher which was enthusiastically received by the military. Hundreds of these stretchers could be quickly and easily transported wherever they would be needed. I believe they are still in use today.

After twenty-four years with Union Camp Corp., Martha and I have retired to Palm Harbor, Florida to enjoy the fruits of our labor. We have been blessed with three sons and five grandchildren. One of our sons has followed my career in the packaging business following his graduation from Florida University. Another is a fishing boat Captain here in Florida. Our third son graduated from Annapolis and spent many years in the nuclear submarine service. He is now the head of one of the nuclear energy plants in the Tennessee Valley Authority. Between traveling, golfing, and the other enjoyments of retirement, I look back with sincere fondness to my life tempered by the remembrances of Ohio State University, Paul Brown and the contributions that football made in my life. Paul was very right in his prophetic assessment of happy successful lives for all of us.

DON McCAFFERTY

Football: Ohio State, 1940, 1941, 1942
Ft. Bragg Bombardiers
New York Giants, 2 years

Education: B.A. and Masters in Education

Career: Kent State Football Coach, 10 years
Baltimore Colts Football Coach, 12 years
Baltimore Colts Head Coach, 3 years
Detroit Lions Head Coach, 2 years

Married: Joan – Four children

Service: Artillery Instructor at Ft. Bragg

Don Passed Away in 1978

DON McCAFFERTY

D on McCafferty, the Head Coach of the Detroit Lions, died unexpectedly of a heart attack in January, 1973. He had come to Detroit after many years with the Baltimore Colts as an assistant coach to Weeb Eubank and Don Shula. When Don Shula left for the head coaching job at Miami, Don McCafferty was named the Head Coach of the Baltimore Colts. In his first year, the Baltimore Colts won the National Football League Super Bowl. It was the first time that a first year coach had won a Super Bowl.

Don's football life began at Rhodes High School in Cleveland with Les Horvath, our Heisman Trophy winner in 1944. He was recruited from high school to play for Ohio State and was one of the four seniors on the 1942 team. Bill Willis, Chuck Csuri, and Don were the mainstays of the Tackle position with the team. The backup tackles were Jack Dugger, Jim Rees, Bob McCormick and Tom Taylor. During the 1942 season, Don played behind Bill Willis. Tackles are usually envisioned as big blustering men but none of them displayed any of these characteristics. Don was the tallest but none weighed over 210 pounds. To quote Jim Rees, "They played like giants". Instead of threatening personalities, all of the tackles were quiet and introspective. Don was the quietest and most introspective.

Of all of our players who were looked upon as personal friends, none had so many friends as Don McCafferty. His closest friend was Les Horvath and this friendship lasted his entire life. They came together to Ohio State and were pledged to the Delta Tau Delta Fraternity. To help make expenses so they could go to school and play football, they worked part time in the kitchen of the frat house. One day, an inspiration was born between the potato peels. Don said to Les, "I have a great idea to make a little more money. Let's send letters to people whose names appear in the newspapers. We'll write that we have noticed their names in the paper and for twenty-five cents in cash or stamps, we will send them a copy of the newspaper article." Things worked well with this collegiate scheme until the inspector of the post office got wind of their activities and paid them a visit. Without much ado, he made it very clear to Les and Don that they would be in plenty of hot water if they did not live up to their arrangements in the letters. Bill Geil, the Rhodes Center, who had come to Ohio State with Les and Don was anxious to get in on this great deal. After the Postal Inspector's visit, they let Geil join them if he would keep the records and files in return for the stamps they received. The scheme worked well with Geil doing most of the work until Geil left school to enlist in the service their freshman year. It takes "talent" to be so enterprising.

Among his other close friends from the 1942 team were Dick Palmer and Bob McCormick. Dick arranged a job for Don at Peninsular Steel in Cleveland the summer of 1942, and Bob developed a close friendship with Don and his wife, Joan, while in service at Ft. Bragg. In Dick's biography are some of his thoughts about their friendship. Lin Houston and Don formed the Ft. Bragg "Bombardiers" as the player-coaches of the team. In the last analysis, Don's quiet friendliness exemplified the friendships that the entire team had for one another. Several of them had gone back to their high school days.

Don stayed on at Ft. Bragg along with Carmen Naples as part of the camp cadre training incoming troops in artillery. After three years in service, he was discharged. Don signed a pro contract with the New York Giants and stayed with the squad for two years. He felt he had no future with the Giants and decided to return to the university to complete his degree and work towards a master's degree in education. With the experience that he obtained while assisting Lin Houston with the Bombardiers, coaching was the profession he chose to pursue.

The number of players who had turned to coaching after playing under Paul Brown and the number of coaches who assisted Paul at Ohio State, Great Lakes and the Browns were almost as impressive as the number of great athletes who had played for him. Trevor Rees, our former Freshman coach in 1942, was now the Head Coach at Kent State University. After graduation, Don joined Trevor as an assistant coach. He remained at Kent State for ten years. Then Don joined Weeb Eubank as an assistant coach with the Baltimore Colts. Johnny Unitas, the Colt's Quarterback, was at the height of his career. Weeb had been an assistant coach to Paul Brown at Great Lakes during the War. Don Shula, who had been with the Browns as a player, replaced Weeb as the Head Coach and McCafferty stayed on as his assistant. When Schula left for the Miami Dolphins, Don McCafferty was named the Head Coach of the Baltimore Colts. His first year as Head Coach, the Colts beat the Dallas Cowboys in the Super Bowl. His second year in pro coaching was almost as successful, just losing the conference championship. During his third year with the Colts, the General Manager Thomas decided to revamp the Colts's coaching staff and the roster of players who had been with the team for many years. Johnny Unitas was nearing the end of his career being 36 years old. With the best record in professional football, Don was replaced by John Sandusky. John Sandusky, who had played for years with the Browns, was hired the year before by Don as the defensive coordinator.

After the resignation of Joe Schmidt as Head Coach of the Detroit Lions, Russ Thomas, the general manager of the Lions, lost no time in hiring Mccafferty as the Head Coach of the Lions. Russ had been a starting tackle with Ohio State in 1943, 1944 and 1945 and later with the Lions. Don's rookie year with the Lions was not the success he experienced with the Colts and the Lions placed second in their conference. Before he could start his second year with the Lions, Don did not survive a heart attack he suffered while working around his home.

Don and his wife, Joan, had four children. He kept a close relationship with many of his teammates at Ohio State, especially Les Horvath. Whenever the Colts or Lions would play in Los Angeles, Don and Joan and Les and Shirley would spent the evening together. Don McCafferty had reached the pinnacle of success in his chosen profession.

CAPTAIN GEORGE LYNN

Football: Ohio State, 1940, 1941, 1942
            Captain, 1942
Education: B.A. and Masters in Commerce

Career: College Level Coaching
            Kent State, Oklahoma and Stanford
            Insurance Agency

Married: Doris – 46 years
            Three children

Service: Naval Commander of Personnel Landing Craft

GEORGE LYNN

Of the many events in my life, being the Captain of the Ohio State University National Championship football team in 1942 is among my fondest memories. Until Paul Brown came to Ohio State in 1941, I had almost given up hope of ever playing football for Francis Schmidt, the Head Coach at the time. For two years, I had never been given the opportunity to play in a game, and I began to feel that I had no future in football. Fritz Mackey, one of Paul's assistant coaches, convinced me to stay with the squad now that Paul had taken over the coaching reins. In 1941, I alternated with John Halliburton, the first string quarterback. Paul would be calling all of the plays during each game that year. We were the alternating messengers to bring in each play. Having lost only to Northwestern and tying Michigan during the 1941 season, Paul picked me to be Captain for the next year. This was a singular honor. I hope that I fulfilled Paul's expectations as to the type of team leader he wanted for his team. During the year, we would have frequent meetings together as he depended on me to call all of the plays during the 1942 season. It was necessary for me to understand what type of play he wanted called in each situation that we found ourselves. There were many reasons for calling a particular play and it was an education in football which proved very valuable in my future coaching career. As I recall, this responsibility was the foremost factor in choosing coaching as my career. Paul's football squad was far different from Schmidt's as we were a team of only 40-45 players in contrast to over 150 members of the squad under Schmidt. During the last years of Schmidt's coaching career at Ohio State, many of the players would only suit up for the game and never come to practice during the week. Schmidt had many talented football players on his squad, but he had lost the ability to weld them into a team.

I had come to Ohio State from Niles, Ohio, a small river town near Youngstown in the Ohio River valley. Football, my senior year in high school, was not a great success by any standards. We played Massillon and were clobbered 56-7. I contributed the 7, but we were nowhere near the caliber of Paul's Massillon Tigers. In high school I had been the president of the junior class and Captain of the football team. I was recruited by Ernie Godfrey to come to college at Ohio State. My freshman year, with something less than adequate financial means, I became a member of the Tower Club. This was a dormitory built under the stadium for poor boys to live while they attended the university. Enrolled in the College of Commerce, I was able to attend college for only $45.00 a quarter for board and room. The university provided the lodging and meals for $15.00 a month! This was only half of what the other boys in the Tower Club paid as I worked in the kitchen of the club. I was also provided with a part time job to supplement my income by working two hours a day in the men's gym for 35 cents an hour. This would pay my expenses during my freshman year.

Except for our loss to Wisconsin in 1942, the season was an overwhelming success. As the future would prove, this team had been molded out of athletes with superior skills. Paul's ability to achieve a sustained level of excellent performance made us the National Champions. Paul had one characteristic that has always impressed me. It was one that I would frequently use during my coaching years at Kent State, Oklahoma, and Stanford. If my performance in a particular game was below his expectations, he would never criticize me, but, in the same vein, if I had played well, there was always a comment about my performance which would bring me back "out of the sky". All things considered, Paul made me play much better than I thought I was capable of playing. This was true in the thoughts of many of the other players on the team. We "rose to the occasion" to accomplish our goals.

My service in the Navy in World War II was much different from the fighting experiences of our other players. I was the commander of a landing ship that carried our troops on to the beaches during the invasion of Europe. This was a ship that carried about 200 soldiers and their personal equipment. The ship had a flat bottom with a six foot draft that we had to sail from the United States to England. Bringing a flat bottom ship across the North Atlantic was filled with frightening experiences until we reached land in England. We landed on Utah Beach nine hours after the invasion had started and the Germans were straddling the shore line with a merciless bombardment. It was the duty of the crew to carry the anchor line on to the beach and secure it in the sand so the soldiers could disembark with their equipment in the six foot water and pull themselves to shore. Many of the men lost their grips on the line and were probably lost as well as the other soldiers who were hit by enemy fire. After all of the troops disembarked, we headed back to England for another contingent. After the invasion, we were ordered to sail into the Mediterranean Sea near Naples Italy, to prepare for a possible invasion into southern France.

After my discharge, I received a contract from the New York Giants Professional Football Team with a bonus of $5000.00 just to sign my contract. During the pre-season practices, I played in several games but this was as far as I would go in pro ball. I returned to Ohio State in 1946 to complete my master's degree in education. My coach and friend, Trevor Rees, was now the Head Coach at Kent State University. He hired me to be his backfield coach. Coaching became my profession. After several years with Trevor at Kent State, I joined Bud Wilkinson at Oklahoma. Our teams played two undefeated seasons and two Sugar Bowl games after winning the Southwestern Conference. After Oklahoma, I accepted the backfield coaching position at Stanford. We went to the Rose Bowl in 1951. I had interviewed for the head coaching position at both Iowa State and Harvard while I was at Stanford. The recruiting objectives that were presented to me at Iowa State were not to my liking. I was the last of two men considered to be the Head Coach at Harvard, but the position was given to the other man. Like Gene Fekete, I felt that it was time for me to change my career as my children would need more financial support than football coaching was able to pay. Since leaving coaching, Doris and I have reared three children, all of whom were college graduates. Incidentally, my wife, Doris, is the daughter of Bill Vickroy and Don Steinberg's chemistry teacher in Toledo. My son, Tom, attended Stanford and was the punter and a defensive back. Cathy attended San Diego State and is a teacher. Barbara graduated from the University of California at Davis and specializes is physiotherapy.

Our travels frequently bring us back to Ohio. We visit Niles and Toledo to see our relatives, and we drive to Columbus to renew the wonderful life long opportunities that Ohio State University and Ohio State football afforded me.

BILL VICKROY

Football: Ohio State, 1940, 1941, 1942
All Conference, 1942

Education: B.A. and Masters in Education

Career: Coach and Athletic Director at the
University of Wisconsin at LaCross
President of N.A.I.A.
N.A.I.A. and University of Wisconsin Halls of Fame

Married: Marge – 49 years
Three children & seven grandchildren

Service: Artillery in South Pacific
Six Island Invasions
Purple Heart and Bronze Medal of Honor

BILL VICKORY

Having spent my life in the education and training of young people, I can make a very strong argument that one always should live honestly and never be distracted from what is good and true. What is good and true comes not by chance for it is molded into a person by his respect for his parents, by his friends who are also dedicated to learning and extracurricular activities, and by the guidance from men like Paul Brown.

Our family in Toledo, Ohio, was of limited means. My father was a machinist whose work days were often irregular because of the Great Depression and my mother was a Nurse. They both stressed the importance of scholarship and athletics as the basis for a healthy and happy future. In the latter years of the 1930's, I attended Scott High School in Toledo where I was born. Scott High was a beehive of scholarship and high level high school athletics. Scott boys and girls were prepared for professional college-oriented careers and Scott athletes could compete at major university levels. By the time of my graduation, I was a member of the National Honor Society, and the All City Center in football with All Ohio recognition.

Despite being recruited by many universities who offered numerous amenities, I chose to attend Ohio State as I had a strong affinity for my city and state. I was convinced that the scholarship and athletic programs at Ohio State were perfectly suited to my ambitions. The total amenities from the university were a summer job and a part time job during the school year. My major course of study would be in the College of Education with emphasis on health and physical education. At that time, Conference rules excluded freshmen from intercollegiate varsity participation. I had ample time to study as well as being able to participate in freshman football and in baseball as the catcher.

During my sophomore year, I had very limited playing time as the second string Center to Claude White. This was Francis Schmidt's last year at Ohio State being replaced by Paul Brown in 1941. For both the 1941 and 1942 seasons, I remained the first string Center. In contrast to the current heavyweight football lines, in those years, the lines averaged

only about 195 pounds per man. In 1942, there were only four first
string players who weighed over 200 pounds. Having to play both on
offense and defense demanded players who were proficient in all aspects
of football fundamentals coupled with mental alertness, speed and
agility. A player with restricted abilities was only useful in special
situations. Blocking, tackling, and finely-tuned coordinated action were
essential to basic football. Paul often stressed the need for perfect
physical conditioning and an overall appreciation of the duties of each
player during the execution of a play. Each player could then visualize
the contribution of his assignment in the successful completion of the
play. I am convinced that these were the essential elements in achieving
National Championship recognition for the 1942 team. We were a
squad of very intelligent players who were trained to think during
practice and so developed correct spontaneous conditioned reflexes
during the games on Saturday.

My memories of the 1942 National Championship team are those
of all young men who have had the opportunity to have similar
experiences. At home games we spent our Friday nights at the
prestigious Columbus Country Club away from the helter skelter of
fraternity and campus life the night before a game. So very memorable
were the superb sirloin steak dinners, the pre-released movie after
dinner to mentally relax the team and the overall camaraderie of our
players who really enjoyed one another. The morning of the game we
were served orange juice and toast in bed as Paul wanted to keep us off
our feet as much as possible. For brunch we were served a small filet
mignon, a small baked potato and a wedge of lettuce before boarding
the bus for the trip to the stadium. Our police escort with sirens roaring
served to heighten our excitement as we traveled west on Broad St. and
then northward to the Ohio State stadium. The stadium was always
packed with our supporters whose roaring approval further added to the
excitement. We were a far different team than Ohio State fans had ever
seen before. First, we were a team in every sense of the word. The
passing years have more than proven the players' athletic talents that
were so finely sharpened and guided by Paul Brown. Paul's opinion of
me in his book is an enduring compliment, "Bill Vickroy had
tremendous quickness which counted more than speed at his position."
Perhaps other teams have had outstanding players, but we were a team
in the strongest sense of the word—43 men always attired in sports

jackets, dedicated, smart and fast. When the season ended we were declared the National Champions and I was chosen as the All Conference Center.

While in college, I spent four years in the Reserve Officer's Training Corps. or ROTC as it is commonly known. Being a "land grant" college, it was a requirement to spent at least a year as a Freshman in ROTC. Having completed four years with the ROTC, I reached the level of Reserve Colonel in our Field Artillery Corps. I entered the service as a Lt. assigned to the Field Artillery. While serving in the South Pacific, I received word that I had been awarded the Big Ten outstanding athlete-scholar medal for 1943. I served as a forward observer for the artillery as we advanced island by island against the Japanese. As my length of service progressed, I became a staff officer. I had participated in six island invasions and had been awarded the Purple Heart, the Bronze Medal of Honor, and multiple service ribbons depicting our various battle actions. Following the war I remained in the active reserve until my retirement as a Lt. Colonel in 1969.

After my discharge from the service, I returned to Ohio State to complete my master's degree in graduate school in 1948. My graduate student training from 1946-48 was spent at Oberlin College teaching and coaching a variety of sports. I accepted a offer from LaCross Teacher's College in LaCross, Wisconsin where I would spent my professional life as well as raise my family with my lovely wife, Marge. During our stay in LaCross, this tiny teacher's college of 300 students would progressively grow into university status with almost 11, 000 students. Like Paul Brown, during his years at Massillon where he was a history teacher as well as basketball and football coach, I was Head Coach in baseball for 20 years, Head Coach in swimming for 14 years and Head Coach in football for 16 years. From 1952 through 1954, our small college football team was undefeated and participated each year in the Cigar Bowl in Tampa, Florida. With the rapid expansion of our men's and women's intramural and intercollegiate sports programs in 1969, I gave up my coaching duties to become the Athletic Director of 11 men's and 10 women's athletic programs. We had a nationally recognized athletic program that offered no athletic scholarships to its students. During the course of my athletic directorship, I served as President of the N.A.I.A. Having spent my career in the pursuit of athletic excellence in small colleges, I was recently inducted into the

N.A.I.A. Hall of Fame as well as the University of Wisconsin at LaCross Hall of Fame. Thus all of my athletic life from high school through my playing days at Ohio State and my long coaching career at LaCross has been a personally gratifying one and filled with happy memories.

Just before my graduation from Ohio State in 1943, Marge, my high school sweetheart, and I were married. The life of a coach's wife is not an easy one. Coaching requires long hours, and often days, away from home with no respite during the years. In our early married years, she would frequently participate in needs of our team, as football coaches wives frequently do. So often their work goes unrecognized and unrewarded except by their appreciative husbands. While we were raising our family, Marge and I, were always a part of the civic community and our church activities. Living in a small town makes people in our position an integral part of the community. It has always been a welcome activity and one would naturally join in. We were blessed with three wonderful children and seven grandchildren. All of our children have received their college degrees, and, like their parents and grandparents, have continued to participate in teaching young people both in the classrooms and the playing fields. We have always stressed community contribution to our children and each of then has made us very proud. 1992 will be a very special year for us. It will be the year of our 50th reunion of our 1942 Ohio State team and the year of our 50th wedding anniversary.

JACK DUGGER

Football: Ohio State, 1942, 1943, 1944
All American, 1944
Big Ten Scholar-Athlete, 1944
Pro Football, 4 years
Lions, Bears and Bills

Education: B.A. in Education

Career: Motor Freight Industry

Married: Helen

Jack Passed Away in 1989

JACK DUGGER

My brother, Jack passed away last year after a brilliant athletic career in high school, college and professional football. In high school, both at Mansfied High School and Canton McKinley High School, he was their most valuable player in both football and basketball. At Ohio State he was acclaimed an All American tackle, and he spent four years in professional football after one year of coaching at Lancaster High School, in Lancaster, Ohio.

Jack was the eldest of three sons in our family. We grew up in Northeastern Ohio, in Mansfield and Canton, where my father was employed as a salesman. Just before his senior year at Mansfield High School, our family moved to Canton, Ohio, where my father gained "unexpected" employment and Jack was enrolled in Canton McKinley High School. High school "recruiting" was still extant in this hot bed of high school football in the early 1940's, although absolute proof of its association with our moving to Canton was not definite.

I was ten years younger than Jack and he became my role model. I began to admire Jack while he was still in high school. I was so proud to have a brother that was the most outstanding athlete in the school. I am sure this had much to do with my becoming an All American End at Ohio State ten years after Jack's All American designation.

Jack was recruited for Ohio State by Ernie Godfrey and spent four years at Ohio State. After his freshman year, he was a second string tackle to Bill Willis and Chuck Csuri on the 1942 National Championship team. He was drafted into service in 1943, but was declared 4-F due to his long history of bronchial asthma. Bill Willis, Bill Hackett, Jack, Gordon Appleby, and Cecil Souders were the only members of the 1942 team that were able to return for the 1943 season and were the only experienced linemen. Bill was 4-F due to his severe varicose veins, Jack for his asthma, and Gordon for a chronic ear perforation. Cecil Souders was drafted after the Wisconsin game and was sent to the Great Lakes Training Center where he played against Wisconsin, again, the next week. I suppose the Wisconsin defensive tackle is still wondering about all of this as he seemed to recognize Cy from the week before. With only Bill Willis, from the first team of the

1942 squad returning in 1943, and the entire team except for Jack, Cecil and Gordon in the service, the Ohio State Buckeyes were re-nicknamed the "Baby Bucks". They were scheduled to play against other universities loaded with either experienced collegians or professional football players attached to service programs at those universities. They played their schedule against these overwhelming odds. With Paul's genius for coaching, by the second half of the year, they had improved so much, that for the first half of the Michigan game, the score remained very close in spite of a Michigan team that was declared the best team in the country that year.

The 1944 football season was another highly acclaimed year for Ohio State. Led by Les Horvath, Bill Willis, Bill Hackett and Jack, the team went undefeated. Les and Bill Hackett had been discharged from their respective ASTP programs at Ohio State, as the Army had no need for more dentists and doctors of Veterinary Medicine. They were free to return to the squad. Led by Les Horvath, the team went undefeated the entire season and was rated as the second best team in the nation behind the Army team with Davis and Blanchard. Les Horvath won the Heisman Trophy, and Les, Bill Willis, Bill Hackett, Warren Amling and Jack were named to All American teams.

Jack's major in college was physical education. He was the fourth of the players on the 1942 team to be awarded the outstanding Scholar-Athlete Award in the Big Ten. Following his graduation, he accepted a position as Head Coach at Lancaster High School. His coaching career lasted only one year as he signed with the Lions in Detroit to play professional football. Jack played for four years with the Lions, Bears, and Buffalo and then entered business. He had joined with several other men to develop a trucking line but this venture failed after several years. He spent may years working under Cecil Souders at Suburban Motor Freight.

Jack and Helen had many happy years together. They had no children. As I look back to Jack's and my own career in football, they were unforgettable experiences for a young boy admiring his older brother and a major reason for my own personal success in sports.

Dean Dugger

J. T. WHITE (JOHN THOMAS)

Football:	Ohio State, 1942
	Ft. Bragg Bombardiers, 1943
	University of Michigan, 1946, 1947
	National Champions, 1947
	Drafted by Lions and Dodgers
Education:	B.A. in Education
Career:	Football Coach
	Michigan and Penn State, 20 years
Married:	Verna – 45 years
	One son
Service:	Sports Director of Ft. Hood and Army Corps

J. T. WHITE (JOHN THOMAS)

One phrase Paul Brown often used, "No matter the circumstances, play the string out to the end" aptly describes my boyhood and teenage years. Our many family problems could well have discouraged anyone. I could have easily give up the hope of an education and a bright future. Poverty, The Great Depression, and the early death of my father were circumstances which had to be overcome during these years. I was the elder boy of three children born to my parents who were sharecroppers in Wadley, Georgia. We raised cotton and watermelons on the farm. When I was six years old, my dad decided to move to River Rouge, Michigan, where he worked in a mill. My father passed away when I was a senior in high school. In order to support our family, I dropped out of high school my senior year to go to work for two years in the Great Lakes steel mill. During much of this time, I attended night school so that I would have enough credits to graduate to go on to college. All of the honors and awards that I had received in high school could not be wasted. My younger brother, Paul, was an outstanding athlete. He went on to the University of Michigan the year before I was able to attend Ohio State.

My years at River Rouge High School were filled with sports activities. I was named the All State Center in football. I was captain of the basketball team, pitched in baseball and was the high school boxing champion. Having been out of high school for two years could easily have been the end of my education except for my desire to gain enough credits to graduate and the intervention of a woman in our city who contacted Hugh McGranahan, Paul Brown's assistant coach at Ohio State.

I began my freshman year at Ohio State fully aware of the omnipresent intense and unforgettable stare of Paul Brown. When he often stated that your purpose in college was to get an education, he really meant it. During my freshman year, I had to present him with a written report of my academic progress from each of my instructors or professors. This report was required every week. He also made it very plain that he did not wish all of the football players to be concentrated in one or two fraternities. This was the state of affairs during the

Schmidt coaching years. My sophomore year, I joined the Alpha Tau Omega Fraternity and roomed with Gene Fekete for the remainder of my stay at Ohio State. The 1942 season was very special to me as I am sure it was to all of the other players on the squad. The intense friendships we have kept through all these years is a fine testament of our feeling for one another. The Ohio State–Michigan game was one I will always remember as my brother, Paul, was the first string halfback for Michigan and I was one of the Ends for Ohio State. I played a good portion of that game and I still cherish the pair of gold pants we received for beating Michigan. This two inch medal is a tradition at Ohio State that was started under Frances Schmidt. It relates to a remark made by Coach Schmidt that no matter how outstanding the players on the Michigan team may appear, they still put their pants on one leg at a time like everyone else.

In the spring of 1943, I entered the military service with most of our 1942 team. My first station was Ft. Bragg where our football team was known as the Ft. Bragg "Bombardiers". We were in reality the 1942 Ohio State National Champions with Lin Houston, Don McCafferty, Hal Dean, Dante Lavelli, Jim Rees, Carmen Naples and myself. I remember that our most important game was against another Army camp whose players were from Auburn University. I remained stateside for the remainder of the war. I was transferred to Camp Hood where I was the sports director of the entire Army Corps. Basketball was probably my favorite sport and, prior to my discharge from service, I played for the National Service team who won second place in the AAU Basketball Tournament.

Following my discharge from service, I took advantage of the G.I. Bill and entered the University of Michigan to complete my college education. I was again caught up in football fever except now it was with Michigan. I played for two more seasons but now as a Center. In 1947, we won the National Championship. I am sure no other player has ever played for two universities who were National Champions. During these years, my brother, Paul, was playing pro ball for the Pittsburgh Steelers after being the Michigan Captain in 1946.

Following my graduation, I was invited to join the Michigan coaching staff as an assistant line coach. I had been drafted by the Detroit Lions and Brooklyn Dodgers but felt that I should pursue my coaching profession as I was now 28 years old. My wife, Verna, was soon to present me with our son, Brian. My long term goals were uppermost in my mind. After two years with Michigan, I moved on to my permanent career with Rip Engels and later Joe Paterno at Penn State University. As part of the Penn State staff, I was either defensive End coach or coach of the line. We participated in post season bowl games almost every year. After 30 years in coaching at Penn State, I retired in 1982. My playing career in service or collegiate teams covered six years. During this entire time as a player or a coach, I had never been associated with a losing team. Working with all of these outstanding players and coaches has made all of these years one very happy experience.

Verna and I spend a great deal of time traveling about the world and visiting our son's family and children. We are celebrating our 46th year of married life and continue to live near the campus of Penn State University.

WILBUR (WIB) SCHNEIDER

Football:	Ohio State, 1941, 1942, 1946
Education:	B.S. in Agricultural Sciences and Education
Career:	Wib Schneider Insurance Agency
Married:	Helen
	Three children
Service:	Transport Pilot in Africa and European Command

Wib Passed Away in 1986

WILBUR (WIB) SCHNEIDER

Wib passed away about five years ago. He was a dear friend to all of the players on the 1942 team. As a reserve Guard, his build resembled a fire hydrant being short and extremely muscular. Even in childhood, his strength was almost legendary. The information about Wib's life came from his wife, Helen. Her descriptions of Wib, from his childhood onward, are filled with the same affections expressed by the wives and children of the other players. Wib, Gene Fekete, and Robin Priday have planned and developed each of our five year reunions which have done so much to renew our memories.

Wib was born and raised on a farm near Gahanna, Ohio, just east of Columbus. Both his father and mother's families had migrated from Germany in the 1840's. They came to Gahanna in the 1850's where they owned a shoemaker's shop. Wib grew up on the farm tough, strong and stocky. Oftentimes, his parents related the stories of his childhood about driving a team of horses when he was but six years old, or lifting bales of hay twice his weight, or thrashing wheat with the "big boys". Wib entered high school in 1936. He had a natural love for sports, especially football. However, the full crunch of the Depression hit his family and there was no money to hire outside help on the farm. Wib was needed on the farm for many of the chores that could not be neglected. Wib had to help with the milking of the cows in the early morning and after school, there were duties to keep their small dairy business going. Nevertheless, in spite of his father's orders, he continued to play football. That meant rising at dawn to milk the cows, catching the bus for high school, attending classes and practicing football after school, and walking four miles back to the farm to finish the farm work that was waiting for him.

High school football brought Wib a number of honors as a halfback and fullback. In 1939, he received the high school's most outstanding athlete award. As short as he was, he set the record in the county track meet for the low hurdles. He played four years of basketball and was the All County halfback his senior year. Since he was so short, his athletic advisors recommended a small college after graduation. Wib was determined to go to Ohio State. The fact that he had no money only made life more of a challenge to Wib. He worked every job available, borrowed, studied somehow, and played football.

No one recruited Wib for Ohio State football. He was a "walk on" who succeeded in making the Varsity his sophomore year. It was one of the highlights of his memories to be selected to make the traveling squad to play Southern California in Los Angeles in 1941. Wib was the second string guard to Lin Houston in 1942. It was a wonderful year for Wib—to be the Big Ten Champions and National Champions—the mountain top!

The Army called and he left school in the Spring of 1943. Wib applied to the Air Force and served as a pilot for the Air Transport Command in North Africa and Europe. In 1946, he returned to Ohio State and the 1946 team now coach by Paul Bixler who had been an assistant to Paul Brown. There were several returning members of the 42 team, but things were far different in 1946. It was not a memorable year for Wib or Ohio State. Wib graduated in 1947 and stayed on the next year as an assistant coach under Wes Fesler. Helen and Wib were married in 1948 and they moved back to Gahanna to the friends and relatives who meant so much to him.

Wib went into the insurance business and rose to be the managing agent for Equitable Life. Some years later he started his own independent insurance agency, The Wib Schneider Insurance Agency. Wib was involved in about every athletic and civic activity in Gahanna and Columbus. He loved Gahanna and nurtured its growth from a small village to a small city. He was on the school board, the church board, the Boosters Club of Gahanna, and started the Gahanna Athletic Hall of Fame into which he was inducted in 1986. In 1969, Ernie Godfrey induced Wib to be a charter member of the Central Ohio Intercollegiate Hall of Fame chapter. This chapter later was named in Ernie's memory and soon became the largest of any of the country's chapters. Each chapter of the organization honors outstanding high school football scholar-athletes throughout the country.

Wib loved Ohio State and Ohio State football. Helen and Wib have three children. Two sons run the insurance agency since Wib passed away and they continue Wib's involvement in the civic and church activities of Gahanna. Their daughter is a teacher and has worked many years with disturbed children. Wib lived such a full life and he is deeply missed by his teammates, his wife and his family.

PHILLIP DRAKE

Football: Ohio State, 1942

Education: B.A. from Ohio State

Career: Senior Vice President
             McDonald and Company Securities

Married: Marilyn
             Three children

Service: World War II – Fighter Pilot

PHILLIP DRAKE

For the past year or so, I have had the time to reflect on those circumstances in my life that I have considered most noteworthy and most cherished. Among the most noteworthy has been largely one of attitude. I truly believe that success in life is gained through attainable "goal seeking". These goals are often made easier to reach when you have a man to look back on who nurtured this concept in your mind. In my life, this man is Paul Brown. The most cherished memories are, of course, the growth of our family. My wife, Marilyn, and I have been married for over 41 years and have three children. All of the children are well educated and have embarked on successful careers. As for myself, I had retained my position in the securities industry for many, many years and have finally retired as a senior vice president of McDonald and Co. During these many years, there was an education, participation in Big Ten athletics, a family and a service career. All of them must be considered for they have brought me to this stage of my life.

I was born in Columbus, Ohio where my father was an administrator for the board of education. My mother's family had come from Norway and Germany before she was born. My father had come to America with his family in the steerage of a ship from England. His family settled in Akron, Ohio, and by the time he was twelve years old, he was put to work with only an eighth grade education. How much a twelve year old boy can contribute to the relief of poverty has always puzzled me. I am sure my father's parents could never appreciate the wonderful opportunities that education offers. They had come from Europe where an education was almost impossible to obtain if you were an average citizen. After a few years, he decided to go to night school to study accounting. By the time I was ready for college, my dad had worked his way up the ladder at the board of education in Columbus to the position of treasurer. It was his responsibility to write the bond issues for the building of new schools in this ever growing city.

My senior year in high school, I was an All State halfback. Along with this honor came scholarship offers from Notre Dame, Cornell and Florida. The University of Florida made the most intense recruiting effort of the three. My father had other ideas. He wanted me to go to Princeton and induced them to offer me a pre-college scholarship at Hun School, the prep school for Princeton. As luck would have it, just before I was to leave for school, Hun school closed due to financial difficulties. Soon after, I had my first meeting with Paul Brown. My mind was made up. I would go to Ohio State and join the Buckeyes in football.

My freshman year at Ohio State, I enrolled in biological sciences hoping some day to become a physician or, if not, some type of health professional. There were three boys on the football team with whom I became fast friends, Bob Frye, Don McCafferty, and George Slusser. These are friendships that one cherishes all of his life. Sadly, my friendship with George was short lived as he was killed in a dog fight in the Far East at the end of World War II.

Although I was a reserve halfback, I did get to play in almost all of the games in 1942. One of my most vivid recollections of 1942 was that of Paul Brown. It is difficult to describe the intensity of his desire to mold us into a great football team. There were many facets to his personality and his approach to achieving his goals. The one that stands out most memorably was his absolute leadership.

In the spring of 1943, I enlisted in the Air Force as an aviation cadet. I received my wings in April of 1944. I was transferred to the B-26 Bomber School and later joined the instructor staff at Randolph Field in San Antonio, Texas. Shortly after arriving at Randolph Field, I received new orders to report to the Air Base at Coffeyville, Kansas for training as a P-51 fighter pilot. After several months, I was sent to the European theater of operations as an F-5 pilot which was a photo reconnaissance version of the P-38. The war was drawing to a close and our unit was assigned to map the border of Germany and Switzerland from the air. I was honorably discharged as a Captain in Oct. 1946.

I returned to Ohio State after service. Marilyn and I were married shortly afterward. My career interests had now changed from the health fields to economics. I was particularly interested in the financial aspects of business. After graduation with my A.B. degree, I entered the securities business with McDonald and Co. where I have spent most of my years. I had found my "niche" dealing with stock transactions, bond sales, and innumerable other financially related activities. After 34 years, my health has recently began to fail in a rather unusual way. It has forced my retirement as a Senior Vice President of McDonald and Co. No one is quite sure of the cause of my disability which has markedly affected my equilibrium.

Marilyn and I have three children of whom we are very proud. One son has followed my career in the securities business. Our other son is in the management level of a large restaurant chain. Our daughter is now attending Duke University. I really believe that Paul Brown introduced me to the concept of "goal climbing". When one has achieved one goal, the next idea was a new goal to work towards.

TOM ANTENUCCI

Football:	Ohio State, 1942
	Iowa Pre-Flight, 1943
Education:	Engineering
Career:	Antenucci Inc.
	Mechanical Contractors
Married:	Betty
	Eight children
Service:	Air Force Bomber Pilot
	Distinguished Flying Cross

TOM ANTENUCCI

I have little information about my parents both of whom passed away while I was a young child. They had immigrated from Italy into northeastern Ohio. I had two older brothers, a sister and an aunt. It seemed that I lived with all of them from time to time. The first three years in high school were spent in Niles, Ohio and my senior year in Troy with my brother, Joe. My closest association with Ohio State prior to enrolling was my brother, Frank. He played for Ohio State in 1935 in their famous game against Notre Dame. He intercepted a pass and lateraled the ball to a Back who scored for a touchdown. It appeared that Ohio State would win the game until Notre Dame came to life in the last quarter to win on a long pass from Bill Shakespeare to Wayne Milner.

I was a "walk on" for the freshman team in 1941. This was Paul Brown's first recruiting year. Although I had no high school football background, I felt that I had worked very hard. I was invited to join the Varsity for spring practice and was a substitute on the 1942 championship team. I found Coach Brown to be very tough but very fair. There was great talent among the players on the first two teams, but Paul as a leader, and Paul as a coach were the primary reasons for their great success. I don't think there were any incidents during the entire year that detracted from the goals that Paul had set for this team.

In 1943, I enlisted in the Naval V-5 Program. There followed a series of moves from one training center to another reminiscent of my youth. We were supposed to go to Iowa pre-flight school but there were no available billets for our group. We were sent first to Highland Junior College outside of Detroit to begin our training. After two months we transferred to the Iowa Pre-flight School. I played on the Seahawk team with Dick Fischer and Jim Langhurst who were stars on previous Ohio State teams. The next step was to Kansas for primary fight training and then on to Corpus Christie, Texas where I received my wings and my Ensign commission. After a short stay in Melbourne, Florida, Bombardier School, we were joined into a squadron in San Diego for our flight to the Far East. We had four refueling stops on our way to Iwo Jima. For the remainder of the War, I flew four-engine bombers out of

Iwo Jima. I received many citations as well as the Distinguished Flying Cross. I was always under the impression that our commander was "medal happy" as he arranged our flight plans.

Following the war, I intended to return to finish my education at Ohio State. However, I joined my brother, Joe, in the construction business as well as "joining up" with my wife, Betty, to raise our family. We moved to Warren, Ohio, and started the Antenucci Inc. Mechanical Contractors whose profits were invested in the education of our eight children. Tom is a lawyer and a graduate of Harvard and Boston University. Jody attended Harvard and Ohio State and is now completing his Ph.D. at Virginia Tech. Betsy is the Assistant Director of Nursing at the Cleveland Clinic in Pediatrics. Her university training was at Case and St. John's University. Our son, Bill, attended Kenyon College and is the Vice President of Antenucci Inc. Jack was educated at Miami, Ohio U. and Ohio State. He is an anesthesiologist at Mt. Carmel Hospital in Columbus. Bob attended Western Reserve in Cleveland and received his Master's in Business Administration at the University of Chicago. Peggy is teaching English in Washington D.C. after receiving her Master's Degree at Ohio State. Finally, Chris has his B.A. from Ohio State. As I list the accomplishments of all of our children, I don't believe I can really express my true joy in the development of our sons and daughters. Educating all of these children has interrupted my full retirement, but we do get away to Florida each winter. The miracles of modern medicine have given me a new hip and left knee to enable me to keep going to the office.

BILL DURTSCHI

Football: Ohio State, 1942

Education: B.A. in Education

Career: Secondary Education
Coaching
Athletic Director
Galion High School Hall of Fame

Married: Betty – 45 years
Three sons

Service: Medical Discharge – Injury

BILL DURTSCHI

My grandfather had left Oberheffen, Switzerland to come to America leaving his family behind. This was the usual arrangement for destitute families in Europe. He had to find work and save enough money to send for my grandmother and my father. He was twelve years old when he came to the United States. There were three occupations open to immigrants with limited educations; the coal mines, the steel mills and the railroads. Dad worked for the New York Central Railroad and, after forty years, retired as an engineer. I was the youngest child in our family of nine children and was born in Galion.

Like so many small cities in Ohio, Galion High School was often a football powerhouse in this area of the state. During my high school years, I joined numerous clubs and participated on most of the team sports, but football was my game. Our team was the league champions both my sophomore and junior years. In 1938, my junior year, I received All State recognition as a halfback. Our team played against several players from other high schools who would later join me on the 1942 Ohio State Championship team, namely Cy Souders and Bob Frye. After graduation, I was recruited by Eddie Blickles who was then an assistant coach under Frances Schmidt. This was a decision I have never regretted.

I enrolled in the College of Education on entering Ohio State in 1940 and played freshman football that fall. There is one special feeling I have had all of my life about Ohio State. The members of this 1942 team are the epitome of what this country is all about. The 1942 team is a perfect example of how a combination of all the nationalities and religious creeds were molded into a winning combination. They played as a team and never put individuality or self above the team. It was never important that one would be on the starting team for we all made contributions to the success of our team. I played as a halfback on both offense and defense and frequently had the job of punting the ball.

I entered military service in the spring of 1943. While I was still in basic training, I again injured my knee on the obstacle course. Both Dante Lavelli and I had sustained knee injuries in our game against

Southern California in 1942. For 78 of the 99 days I would be in service, I was confined to the hospital. When my leg did not respond to treatment, I was given a Medical Discharge. For the next three years, I alternated between working and going to Ohio State to complete my education. After I finally graduated, I accepted a teaching position at Newcomerstown, Ohio, the early home of Woody Hayes.

I met my wife, Betty, in 1942 and we became engaged in 1944 after my discharge from service. We celebrated the occasion that night by attending the Galion-Bucyrus football game. The Galion team soundly defeated Cy Souder's alma mater 84-0. We were married two years later, and this year we will be celebrating our forty-fifth wedding anniversary. In these times, it must seem unusual to find that almost every member of the team has had lasting marriages. Our sons and daughters, of whom we are intensely proud, have college degrees and successful livelihoods. I am sure these are indications of the soundness of the players and their attitudes that continued unchanged after our exposure to the ethics and coaching of Paul Brown.

I remained in teaching and coaching at Newcomerstown for four years. I became the Head Coach in football in 1949. For the first time in twenty years, the team was undefeated and the League Champion. The following year, we moved on to Cuyahoga Falls where I remained the backfield coach for the next four years. The next year, we climbed the high school ladder moving on to Mansfield, Ohio, one of the leading high school teams in the state. While I was at Mansfield we had two young men who were named as All-Ohio Backs. My coaching and teaching career finally completed its orbit in 1957. I was hired as the Head Coach in football at Galion High, my alma mater. The team had fallen on bad times the previous year as they lost every game. For the next two years, we completely reversed the fortunes of the team. We were undefeated in every game for an eighteen game winning streak and two League Championships. One of our team members was named first string All Ohio and another was named to the All American High School team. I added to my agenda the position of Athletic Director of Galion High School. In 1973, I was honored by the people of Galion by being installed in the Galion High School Hall of Fame. In 1982, I completed my years of teaching after 34 years. We retired to spend part of the year at Put-In-Bay and part of the year in Leesburg, Florida.

Betty and I have had 45 years of happy married life together. We have three sons all living in Ohio. Two of our sons live in Galion and the youngest has just completed his master's degree in business administration. I know it may seem to be repetitious, but after several decades spent in the education and training of our youth, I truly believe there are no role models as impressive to young people as Paul Brown and the players on the 1942 Ohio State National Champions.

CARMEN NAPLES

Football: Ohio State, 1942
            Ft. Bragg Bombardiers, 1943, 1944

Education: Chemistry
            Unable to complete education due to father's death.

Career: Owner of Golden Dawn Restaurant
            Youngstown, Ohio

Married: Pat – 49 years
            Seven children & twenty-six grandchildren

Service: Instructor in Field Artillery

CARMEN NAPLES

My father, mother and older brother landed on Ellis Island and were immediately Americanized by the custom's agent. They had come from a small town in southern Italy as the Napolizian family. Through the haste of processing hundreds of immigrants coming to America, they suddenly were the Naples. Like so many other families who had stood in these long lines, we remained the Naples. Dad intended only to visit America and then return to his home in Italy. That was until he attended a Yankee baseball game. His enthusiasm for all sports, reinforced by the screaming fans in the stadium, convinced him that America should be his home. Dad had a younger brother already living in Youngstown, Ohio. When word reached him that his brother was seriously ill, he brought his family to Youngstown. This was at the time of the devastating flu epidemic that was sweeping America.

His first job in America was working in a steel mill. This lasted until the Great Depression when there was no longer any work available. Mom and Dad started a small restaurant they called the"Golden Dawn" and the "Golden Dawn" it is called today some 57 years later. There aren't many restaurants today that are managed by two brothers, one a chemical engineer and the other with a degree in education. This has been our livelihood from which my wife and I have raised and educated seven children and who have been blessed with 26 grandchildren.

I was the fourth child of seven children of a father who loved sports and it seemed that sports came naturally to me. I was playing basketball on an intramural team in high school when the varsity coach must have noticed something that impressed him. He offered me a position on the varsity team. This led to my participation both in basketball and football where I lettered in each sport for three years. I was selected on the All City football team my senior year. An Ohio State alumnus, Dr. Myron Steinberg, must have been impressed by my play in football as he arranged for an interview with Head Coach Schmidt and his assistant coach Fritz Mackey at Ohio State. That summer, before enrolling at Ohio State I was given a job with the State

Highway Dept. cutting grass that would provide the money I would need for school in the fall. At Ohio State, I reached the highlight of my sports career by playing varsity football. I have always felt it was a privilege to be a member of the 1942 team that was so talented.

I enlisted in the service and was stationed for the entire war at Ft. Bragg, North Carolina. As an instructor in field artillery and chemical warfare, I played football with the Ohio State 1942 players who were stationed at Ft. Bragg while they were in training. At one time our starting lineup for the "Bombardiers" were largely players from our 1942 team. For a short time I bunked next to Bob Shaw who was passing through to another assignment. I was discharged from service in 1946 and returned to Ohio State to complete my education. I stayed only for two quarters but was unable to finish. My father passed away suddenly and I was needed at home to manage the restaurant. I married Pat, my high school sweetheart, in June of 1942. Pat and I have seven children and 26 grandchildren. Our restaurant is the center of activity for the workers who live near the mills. One year, during a strike, we were featured on nationwide television as the gathering place for all levels of employees from the plant manager to the janitorial service people.

All of our children have had college educations. One son is the head of the chemical division for B.F. Goodrich Co. Chemistry has been the educational goal for three members of our family beginning with my elder brother who came to America at the age of fifteen not being able to speak English. By the time he was 21, he had his doctorate in Organic chemistry and physics. Another son is a federal employee in the personnel division of the post office and another son is a physician.

Being a member of the Ohio State 1942 Championship Football team has provided some wonderful memories and if you are ever in Youngstown come and see us at the "Golden Dawn".

DICK PALMER

Football:	Ohio State, 1942, 1946
Education:	B.A. from Ohio State
Career:	Regional Manager Peninsular Steel Corporation
	Life long involvement in civic activities in Dayton, Ohio.
Married:	Kay Two children & two grandchildren
Service:	Air Force Flight Instructor
	Dick Passed Away in 1990

DICK PALMER

My husband, Dick, passed away this past year. I think the best way to convey his character and his affection for the 1942 Ohio State players is to recall a paragraph he wrote on the sudden death of Don McCafferty shortly after he assumed the position of Head Coach of the Detroit Lions. "The sudden death of Don McCafferty was a hard blow to me as, I am sure, it was to many others. Don and I had become great friends over the years and kept in close contact. I had just seen Don in Dayton a short time before his untimely death. I can remember getting Don a summer job with me at Peninsular Steel in Cleveland during a summer vacation while we attended Ohio State. We used to unload steel from trucks and make up bundles of steel to ship to different Peninsular warehouses. I recall a narrow escape from a mishap we had one day. We were standing on each side of a scale putting a bundle of steel together. As the bundle started down, the crane came off its track and fell unto the scale, smashing it, and just missing both of us. He will be missed by many people for we lost a great member of our 1942 team."

Dick was an outstanding athlete, but, more than that, he was a "people person." He spent his life being involved with people as individuals, people as members of organizations, and people as members of his community. He was born in Cleveland and attended Shaw High School. This wonderful attribute of involving himself with people was evident throughout his high school years. He lettered in and was Captain of the football and basketball teams as well as being the president of the senior class, Hi-Y and Varsity "S" Club.

During the summer, after graduation from high school, he worked in the warehouse of Peninsular Steel Co. until Ohio State football practice began in the fall. This association with Peninsular Steel would last until his retirement a few years ago. One might say it was the only job he ever had. For the next two years, while he played varsity football, he was a member of the Student Senate at Ohio State, The Council of Men's Organizations, YMCA, and president of the Varsity "O". During the 1942 season, Dick and Cy Lipaj played behind Gene Fekete at Fullback. His college studies were interrupted when he was called into the Army Air Cadet Program.

May of 1944 was an eventful month for both of us. Dick had just graduated and received his wings after completing his training as an Air Force pilot. During his leave following graduation, we were married at my home in Toledo, Ohio. My husband was now Lt. Dick Palmer. Getting his commission required transferring to four different air force installations. Dick served as a flight instructor at Stockton (Calif.) Air Force Base. He was later transferred to flight engineering school. The rest of our time in the Air Force is kind of a blur, and then the war was over.

After his discharge from the Air Force, we returned to normal living. We returned to Ohio State so Dick could complete his education. In addition to playing football with the 1946 team, he worked part time in sales for Peninsular Steel in Columbus. The camaraderie, the dedication, and the intensity of attitude he felt during the 1942 season was largely lacking in 1946. Dick received his degree upon graduation in the spring of 1947.

From the sales office in Columbus, Dick was transferred to Dayton as the assistant manager of the Peninsular Steel warehouse. He and his superior formed a wonderful sales force that lasted for seventeen years. During this time they increased their steel business as they grew from last in sales to the second best among the ten national warehouse locations of the company. Only the Detroit home office did more business with four times the sales force. The increase in business required two expansions of warehouse space. Dick became the district manager in 1975 following the retirement of his superior.

The extracurricular involvement that Dick had started in high school and college continued in Dayton. It was a very important part of his life. He was a member of numerous organizations in Dayton which included the Dayton Chamber of Commerce, the Masons, the Dayton Agonis Club, organizations related to his work, and, of course, the Dayton Ohio State Alumni Association where he headed the Athletic Committee.

We have one son, Christopher, and one daughter, Pamela. Chris is employed at General Motors while his wife is working toward her master's degree at Wright State University here in Dayton. Pamela has two children and lives in a small town of Centerville, nearby Dayton. Dick's fondest memories were involved with the 1942 team. He always looked forward the five year reunions when old memories were recalled and vividly described to bring back those wonderful months in the fall of 1942. I really felt this team was his extended family. "This was a great group of guys, a team's team where every player worked toward a common goal—to be the best team in the country. And we were."

BILL SEDOR

Football:	Ohio State, 1942
Education:	B.A. and Masters in Education
Career:	Secondary Education
	High School Industrial Arts
Married:	Marie – Died from Cancer
	Two children
	Shirley – One son
Service:	Army in North Africa

BILL SEDOR

Shadyside, Ohio, is a small town about nine miles south of Wheeling, West Virginia. Here I was born and raised by my mother who had come to America from Poland. Unfortunately, my Father had died when I was only four years old. My mother was left to raise five children, my sister, my three brothers and myself. These dire circumstances seems to have similar parallels with several members of our 1942 Ohio State football team.

I was a tall somewhat ungainly boy in high school where I played Center on the basketball team and End on the football team. By my senior year, I was regarded as one of the outstanding Ends in our Ohio Valley Conference. There was a local judge in Shadyside who recruited athletes for Ohio State University. It was his avocation to help young boys in our town. When I graduated from high school, he had a very good year as he was influential in sending Joe Storer, Bill Cherokee, and myself to Ohio State. Joe would become an outstanding Wrestler for State and Bill Cherokee was part of the playing team for the 1941 Buckeyes in football. I am sure he would have been an integral part of the 1942 team, but he decided to enlist in the service instead of continuing his education. After the war, Bill Cherokee did play a short time with the Cleveland Browns professional football team. I am quite sure he was one of the pioneers in using isometric exercises and weight lifting to further develop his muscle strength.

Our 1942 football team at Ohio State was rather unusual in that there was a total dedication on the part of every player as well as a close camaraderie among the players at the same position which lasted throughout the entire season. I am sure it is an important reason our five year reunions are almost always attended by every player and his wife. Our Right End position was played successively by Don Steinberg, Dante Lavelli, John T. White and myself. It was an absolute necessity for each of us to be prepared the assume the starting end position as injuries were so common among us. Don had injured his shoulder against Indiana and was unable to play for several weeks. Dante was lost for the season as he severely injured his knee against Southern Cal when he caught a pass on the goal line and was hit by the defensive back. Against Northwestern, John White was also injured so I had to play the entire game. The next week against Wisconsin, I injured my knee while backing up the line on one of our defenses. I thought that I would be able to play and return to the game. On one of Wisconsin's sweeps around my end, my knee buckled beneath me and ended my football career. The remaining four games were played by Don Steinberg and J.T. White. I have always wondered why we had so many serious injuries, which my have been coincidental, but we only averaged between 185 to 190 pounds. The defensive end position had to strip the ball carrier of his interference who were often two or three men as large or larger than any of us.

I tried to enlist in the Navy but was turned down because of my knee injury. I was drafted into the Army in 1943 and was sent to Ft.Devon for basic training. Our division was part of the invasion into North Africa where I spent three months. I contracted malaria and was sent stateside for treatment. After I had recovered, I was assigned to the military police at several of the Army camps. After my discharge I was back to Ohio State in a record breaking twelve days.

I was still an undergraduate, and I felt that I would like continue my education in the College of Industrial Arts. Part of my work in the college required student teaching and I would be unable to continue to play football. There was really no choice as I really wanted to be a teacher above all else. I remained in secondary education on the high school level throughout my teaching career. I furthered my education by returning to Ohio State in 1972 to complete my Master's degree in Education. Teaching and working with young people has always given me a feeling of wonderful satisfaction. In 1964, in the publication, "Machine and Tool Blue Book", we described an adaptation in the use of an Arbor Press to bend sheet metal. It is one of the satisfaction a teacher receives when he sees the pride that his students had in publishing their work. My teaching career ended with my retirement in 1982. It has been so fulfilling that if I had the opportunity to repeat these years, I most certainly would return to the high school classroom.

After returning from service, Margaret and I were married. We had two children but unfortunately we lost one of our sons to viral myocarditis at the age of twelve. Margaret passed away in 1953 from cancer. I remarried Shirley Voit who is also a nurse in 1981. We have one son who graduated from Ohio State in horticulture. Every five years at our reunions, the occasion recalls again the great pride I have in knowing that I was part of this wonderful football team.

KEN EICHWALD

Football: Ohio State, 1942

Education: B.A. in Business Administration

Career: Sales
Farm Machinery and Industrial Coatings

Married: Lois
Three children

Service: Air Force in North Africa

Ken Passed Away in 1985

KEN EICHWALD

A year after my husband, Ken, had passed away, he was selected posthumously to the Lakewood High School Hall of Fame. This selection is particularly important. As a former athlete in the community, only a few men are individually recognized for their athletic contributions from among hundreds of other players of varsity sports at Lakewood. Some forty-seven years had passed since his graduation from high school, and Ken was selected the first year that Lakewood High had initiated its Hall of Fame. We had started our loving relationship in junior high school which has given me a broad view of the wonderful qualities of my husband besides his outstanding ability in basketball and football.

Ken was born in Cleveland, Ohio, in 1923, to parents whose families had migrated from Germany. When Ken was only ten years old, his father passed away. His mother was left alone to raise her family in the midst of the Great Depression. She started a small beauty parlor to support her children. Ken would help doing small chores and doing odd jobs. When he was old enough, he received a small wage from the city for umpiring sandlot baseball games. We attended junior high together and then went on to Lakewood High where Ken became a star athlete, lettering in basketball, football and baseball. During his senior year, he was selected as the All State Forward in basketball. One of his feats has been fondly remembered. On the occasion of the state basketball tournament against Martin's Ferry High School, in the closing seconds of the fourth quarter of the game, Ken was lying on his back holding the basketball. While still laying on the floor, he threw the ball through the hoop to win the game! This "miraculous" shot was only one of the memorable events in the life of this fun-loving, spirited man who had this wonderful gift of enjoying life.

After Ken graduated from Lakewood High, he was pursued by the University of Southern California to accept an athletic scholarship. Nevertheless, he chose Ohio State who offered only a part time job to help financially. He often said in later years, that this decision to attend Ohio State was one of the best he had ever made. Ken was only a sophomore at Ohio State and a reserve End on the 1942 Championship team.

Shortly after the end of the football season, Ken enlisted in the Air Force. After his training in a number of Air Force installations, he was sent to North Africa where he spent the duration of the war. After the end of the war, Ken returned to Ohio State and graduated with a bachelor's degree in business administration. He was a member of the Delta Upsilon Fraternity and served as their treasurer. Many of the friends we made during these years in school have remained so throughout our lives.

In 1951, we were married, tying the knot to a loving relationship that had started many years before in junior high school. We were blessed with three children, two daughters and one son. Ken had a very successful sales career in industrial coatings, conveyor belting and grain machinery. In 1985, he was honored by his peers for his distinguished service and dedication for the betterment of the grain industry.

Our children have carried on their parents' wishes for them in higher education. Our son, Ken, Jr. is a vice president in an international banking firm. Carole Lee has two children and has her degree in special education. Barbara Lynn is a supervisor for Traveler's Insurance. Ken was deeply loved by his family and is missed by his many friends and relatives. The world was made a brighter, happier place because he was here.

LORAN STAKER

Football: Ohio State, 1942

Education: Engineering

            College of Engineer and Architecture

Career: Architect
            President of Columbus Architecture Society

Married: Marilyn
            Two children & six grandchildren

Service: U.S. Army Engineers

Loren Passed Away in 1981

LORAN STAKER

I t isn't often that a woman of 90 has the opportunity to relate the highlights in the life of one of her sons who passed away almost ten years ago. Loran was a very special person, not only to me but to his community, his church, his university and his college. His athletic ability during high school was outstanding as a halfback for Columbus East High School. He continued his interest in sports throughout his years in swimming, golf and skiing.

` Our family was native to southern Ohio immigrating largely from German stock. The families engaged in farming large tracts of land. They had to be blessed with a prodigious number of children who would provide much of the labor necessary to work the farms. Our family moved to Columbus to enable my husband to complete his medical studies at Ohio State. After graduation, he established his practice near the university. Our five children were born in Columbus, four boys and one girl of whom Loran was the middle child. It was our intention to educate our children at Ohio State and except for our daughter who completed her degree in interior design in Fullerton, California, we accomplished our mission – one physician, two engineers, and one colonel in the Army mechanized forces.

Our son, Loran, attended East High School in Columbus where he was not only a fine student but an outstanding athlete. It is a pleasant memory to recall the many articles in the newspapers about his exploits as the star halfback. On one occasion he was featured on the sports page by a large composite sketch of Loran for his athletic excellence. Following his graduation, he received a scholarship to Baylor School in Tennessee, an Episcopal Seminary. He later enrolled in the College of Engineering at Ohio State, majoring in architecture. He often related with intense pride in being a member of the 1942 football team while he was in the engineering college. Following his Army service he returned to Ohio State to complete his studies and receive his degree. After his graduation, he remained on the faculty of the engineering college for several years. Later he entered private practice in architectural design in Columbus.

Loran's professional career was filled with accolades. He designed hospitals, shopping centers, and homes. His design for small homes was awarded a prize among the community architects. The small home design featured an opportunity for people of moderate means to live in a home whose rooms could be altered to suit the needs of each particular family that would be living in the house. His achievements were further recognized as he was selected to be the president of the Columbus Architectural Society. Many of the newspaper clippings of his accomplishments remain with me as cherished evidence of his outstanding qualities.

Much of Loran's time was spent in church activities. He and his wife, Marilyn, were the parents of two children and six grandchildren. In his later years, Loran moved to Jensen Beach, Florida, where he designed and built a beautiful new home for himself and his wife. He knew he was already ill with leukemia, but he continued to be the positive cheerful man we always loved. Loran passed away in Jensen Beach, and it was very fitting that his close friend and classmate at Baylor School would perform his last services.

It has been my fortune to have outlived all but two of my children. My fond memories and having much of my family nearby continue to bring me much warmth and happiness.

TOM TAYLOR

Football: Ohio State, 1942
Notre Dame and San Francisco Air Base
Furman University

Education: B.A. from Furman University

Career: Owner
Top Cat Redimix Concrete Company

Married: Barbara
Two children

Service: Pilot Training
Underseas Demolition

Tom Passed Away in 1984

TOM TAYLOR

Tom Taylor was the gentle giant of our 1942 team. Beneath his cherubic countenance was a very independent, fun-loving man whose penchant for comedy and "horseplay" persisted throughout his entire life. Although he was a fine athlete who loved playing football, I don't think he could ever quite comprehend Paul Brown's intense drive toward winning and perfection. He played football for three years in high school, during his years at Ohio State, during his years in service, and, after discharge, at Furman University.

Tom's father moved from Slippery Rock, Pennsylvania, to Lancaster, Ohio shortly after the First World War. He had left his engineering profession to enter the readimix concrete business in partnership with another man. There were two sons in the Taylor family, one son who attended Dennison University and Tom. During the years that Tom played football for Lancaster High School, they had outstanding football teams. After three years of varsity football, Tom was recruited by Ohio State. During the 1942 season, Tom was a reserve tackle along with Jim Rees, and Jack Dugger.

Tom had a constantly changing career in the service. He started out in pre-flight school in 1943 as a fighter pilot. His instructors soon discovered that the airplane could accommodate Tom or his parachute, but not both. Having thus been eliminated from this arm of service, they discovered that Tom was a non-conformist. This reputation as a "non-conformist" led to an assignment to the Underwater Demolition School in San Francisco. His wife seemed to feel that this was the branch of the service where all the bad boys were sent. He had two years of service football. One was at Notre Dame where he was sent for specialized training with the Underwater Service and the other while he was on the West coast. He seemed to follow the "training tables" which were set up to feed the soldier-athletes. When football season was over, he turned to basketball in his continuing quest for the service "training tables".

After stateside training was completed, the time came to ship out for overseas duty. The troops were lined up at dockside to embark on the troop transport ship. Suddenly, without prior notice, orders were changed for Tom and three other soldiers. Tom remained stateside and how this happened no one knows.

After his discharge, Tom returned to civilian life and enrolled at Furman University. He had to abandon his education and football to return home. His father had had a heart attack and he was needed to run the family business. Tom married his wife, Barbara, in 1947. They had two children, Amy and Tom, both of whom graduated from Ohio State. After several years with the partnership, Tom decided to start a new company in Lancaster, the Top Cat Ready Mix Co. I think that the company name reflected Tom's personality as he had a continuing love for life. Besides his business, Tom had many and varied avocations which included boating on Lake Erie, playing the horses, and visits to Las Vegas. Tom passed away in 1984. He was a quality person.

PROFESSOR CHARLES DIESEM

Football:	Ohio State Student Manager
Education:	Doctor of Veterinary Medicine
Career:	Emeritus Professor of Anatomy Ohio State University
Married:	Janet – 46 years Three children
Service:	U.S. Army Veterinary Corps

PROFESSOR CHARLES DIESEM, D.V.M.

Athletic Manager 1942 O.S.U. Football

Throughout this narration, we have repeatedly emphasized the importance of a college education coupled with participation in intercollegiate athletics. High school graduates from every walk of life who participate in a "team experience" and seek a university education, no matter their financial situation, will find these two aspects of maturing to be the motivating forces to a happy and successful life. No high school graduate has ever had any premonition that he will rise to the levels of always admired accomplishment. Charlie was too slow afoot for Ohio State football and became our student manager, pursued a career in veterinary medicine, climbed the academic ladder to become the Professor of Anatomy of the Ohio State College of Veterinary Medicine, and was the recipient of their annual Distinguished Alumni Award.

The majority of the fathers of the members of the 1942 squad were either coal miners, steel mill workers, or laborers with the railroad systems. Charlie's father worked as a machinist on the New York Central Railroad in Bellefontaine, Ohio, a small town in central Ohio. He passed away during Charlie's junior year in high school leaving a destitute family and a son whose only access to a higher education was the Tower Club at Ohio State costing only thirty dollars a month for board and room. He arrived at OSU in the Fall of 1939.

The Tower Club was a dormitory built in the underside of the football stadium. Here hundreds of boys would be able to receive a higher education with the only criteria being a good scholastic average. One day a notice was placed on the bulletin board seeking freshman managers in football. 1940 was Frances Schmidt's last year at Ohio State and the year Charlie volunteered for a manager's position. Charlie was introduced to the unique personality of Coach Schmidt and watched his sad demise as Head Coach precipitated by the 40-0 loss to Michigan.

When Paul Brown arrived at Ohio State, he chose Charlie to be his student manager in 1941. Among his many duties was to be the "water boy". Being the "water boy" has always been the butt of athletic jokes but Charlie was assigned to care for the large milk cans of water we took with us on our train trip to play Southern California in 1941. These cans of water had to be trucked to the train station in Columbus and loaded on the train for Chicago where they were transferred to the magnificent Santa Fe Super Chief for our trip to Los Angeles. Paul was aware that changes in water often caused a gastroenteritis and he did not want this to happen on our week long trip to Los Angeles. In 1942, almost the entire team was afflicted with dysentery when we failed to take our own water to Madison, Wisconsin, and was a major factor in our only loss of the season.

After his graduation from vet school, Charlie was drafted into military service where he had many positions varying from food procurement and inspection to caring for the Army mules that were to be sent to Europe during and after the war. He remained in the Active Army reserve until his retirement as a Lt. Colonel in the U.S. Army Reserve.

Charlie returned to Ohio State University to pursue an academic career in veterinary medicine. He progressed to be named the Professor of Anatomy at the veterinary college. In addition to his many posts as a teacher, he has had numerous research projects and over 25 published articles on a variety of subjects related to his research work and various aspects of the anatomy of animals.

Like the rest of our team, Dr. Drisem has been married since 1945 and he and his wife Janet have three children. His two daughters were teachers and his son also became a Veterinarian.

I think that every reader will be impressed by a man who was the son of a railroad laborer and received his Doctor of Veterinary Medicine degree in 1943, his master's degree in science in 1949 and his Ph.D. in 1956.

PAUL BROWN

WHAT MAKES PEOPLE SPECIAL

In any group of people there are individuals who stand out from all the others. What makes these individuals special are qualities that can be debated endlessly without coming to any common conclusions. However, when you explore the lives of an entire group of people who have led exemplary lives, one can identify common threads that can characterize each of them.

This particular team who became the proclaimed National Collegiate Football Champions in 1942 could well form a "template" for the "Right Stuff." As we look deeply into their lives, their willingness to work as a team is of singular importance. Their willingness to be imbued with the abstract idea that winning has great rewards in the future seems to be a basic tenet for success and happiness. Success and happiness go hand in hand. No matter the goal that one is seeking, there should be only one consideration. You will be the winner or you will be the one who is chosen. The achievement of any goal, like many a sports contest, is often decided in the closing seconds. As Paul Brown would frequently remark, "Play the string out to the end."

I don't believe that any of us could have been content always being a spectator. To be a player on any team in any sport requires an understanding that any achievement requires "pain and exhaustion." Even from childhood, anything that comes easily is a threat to one's future success in life. A great athlete is often emotionally overwhelmed by his natural ability. The same can be said for any professional or businessman. His success may influence him to neglect other very important aspects of living. Even easily acquired sociability as a teenager can interfere with one's need to study and to become a multi-faceted person. To be a good student does not require greater intelligence than other students. One must merely "open the clam shell" through a persistent unswerving effort to learn. To look back upon my own life, there were much "smarter" boys and girls in classes than I. However, I did realize very early that the students who learned easily, forgot more easily than the students who had to put more effort into learning. Many of one's college or high school courses will have little to do with your professions or businesses in the future but they are very necessary building blocks to the next stage of learning. This is the pathway to one's successful future.

One cannot divorce himself from the events that make up one's life. There will be disappointments, delays, and frustrations that everyone must overcome. A college degree does not guarantee a successful future, but a college degree associated with many years of team participation will very often do so. You may never "get off the bench," or you may be confronted by the unwarranted biased opinions of other people. Nevertheless, you must stay a part of the "team." Be able to look back with pride toward those people who motivated you, as we look back on our coach, Paul Brown.

All team athletics from high school through college and even into professional sports contribute to this concept of "team." One's coach becomes a very special person who you respect and admire for your entire life. He or she is more than a teacher and perhaps more than a motivator. As he molds his squad into a team, he has inserted a part of himself into each of his players. This is the "winning edge," if properly nurtured while one pursues his education. This "winning edge" makes a different person of each of the members of the team. Very often this different person becomes very special. Bill Vickroy, who spent his life in the education of young people said very succinctly, "I can make a strong argument that one should always live honestly and never be distracted from what is good and true." Here, again, Paul Brown's "honesty."

One must be a part of any group before he can interpret the value or purpose for the group's existence. Drawing conclusions as to value without you yourself becoming directly involved is very hazardous. Books or articles in the press that criticize intercollegiate sports, because the expense appears greater than the reward, do not appreciate the effects of participation on every member of an intercollegiate or high school team. In later years there will be remarkable contributions to society by an unusual number of these men. These contributions will be decidedly more frequent and more important than those made only by students who have never dedicated any effort toward team involvement. Each contribution will sustain and perpetuate a dynamic society in America.

These men of the 1942 Ohio State football team were excellent high school football players but they were molded into great college athletes and professional athletes. None of the players who reached national acclaim had "two left feet." Bill Willis has often been proclaimed as the greatest Nose Guard in all of the history of the National Football League. The same could be said of the careers of Dante Lavelli and Bob Shaw. They had no equals as offensive receivers during the years of their careers in professional football. Lou Groza, Lin Houston and his brothers, Tommy James, and Les Horvath will never be forgotten when one recalls the great players of the past. Had athletic injury not intervened, I am sure Gene Fekete and Paul Sarringhaus would have reached the pinnacles of recognition in professional sports.

A college education, never to be forgotten motivators, willingness to put forth your best efforts both physically and mentally, and being a member of the team – these were our common threads.

Paul Brown has recently passed away. More than any other coach he molded football into a scientific strategy rather than ragtag assembly of able players. All of the phases in the preparation and playing football that Paul Brown insisted upon have been incorporated by all coaches into their coaching methods. He had an unwavering attitude toward the play of the game. His concepts, his preparations, his demands for total dedication were coupled to his unerring perception. He made football a sport of unequalled quality. For players who had the good fortune to be selected for one of his many teams, one can never forget the look in his eyes that carried that subliminal message that he knew what you were capable of doing and he expected you to know it as well.

Paul Brown was a great man and he will truly be missed.